Fearon's
World History

Joanne Suter

Fearon Education
Belmont, California

Pacemaker Curriculum Advisor: Stephen C. Larsen

Stephen C. Larsen holds a B.S. and an M.S. in Speech Pathology from the University of Nebraska at Omaha, and an Ed.D. in Learning Disabilities from the University of Kansas. In the course of his career, Dr. Larsen has worked in the Teacher Corps on a Nebraska Indian Reservation, as a Fulbright senior lecturer in Portugal and Spain, and as a speech pathologist in the public schools. A full professor at the University of Texas at Austin, he has nearly twenty years' experience as a teacher trainer on the university level. He is the author of sixty journal articles, three textbooks, and six widely used standardized tests including the Test of Written Learning (TOWL) and the Test of Adolescent Language (TOAL).

Subject Area Consultant: Jan Grodeon

Jan Grodeon, M.A., San Jose State University, has been teaching U.S. and World History for twenty years. She was Santa Clara County Teacher of the Year in 1989 and has been a District Mentor Teacher for several years in the Campbell (California) Union School District.

Editor: Stephen Feinstein
Text Designer: Dianne Platner
Cover Design: Dianne Platner
Production Manager: Teresa A. Holden
Production Editor: Mary Dickinson
Graphics Coordinator: Joe C. Shines
Illustrator: Duane Bibby
Cartographers: Jean Ann Carroll, Sharon Johnson
Cover photo: The Photo File, Ed Young

Photos and illustrations: The BETTMANN ARCHIVE, except those by Duane Bibby on pp. 31, 33 (bottom), 56, 73, 94, 134

ISBN 0–8224–0805–8

Printed in the United States of America
1. 9 8 7 6 5 4 3 2 1

Contents

A Note from the Publisher
to the Student

What do you think? Do events of hundreds or thousands of years ago have anything to do with our lives today? How about 100 or even 50 years ago? Would our lives be different if certain people hadn't lived or certain things hadn't been invented? And what about other places? Does it matter to us which side wins a war—as long as that war is fought halfway around the world?

The study of world history helps us answer questions like these. It shows us the connections between past, present, and future events. It shows us how all nations are related to one another. And it reminds us that history is still being written.

Sometimes history seems like nothing more than a long list of wars. But the history of the world is much more than that. It is also a record of discovery: better ways of farming, new machines, and new ideas. Mostly it is the story of people. The study of history tells us how the people of different times and places lived through hardships. It tells us how they taught their children, and how they created beauty in their art and music. It tells us about the efforts they made to improve their lives. It tells about their gains and their losses, their mistakes and their successes.

By the time you finish this book you will have some idea of how the world came to be the way it is today. Chapter by chapter you will learn about the rise and fall of many nations, the ideas of the great thinkers, and the incredible richness of many cultures. You will be able to name important people in history and the times in which they lived. You will learn how geography has affected the history of nations and how scientific discovery has affected the history of the whole world.

Further study of history can prepare you for an interesting career. Perhaps you would like to help dig up the ruins of ancient civilizations. Maybe you would like to work for a newspaper or magazine and be involved in historic events as they unfold. Perhaps writing or teaching would be a good job for you. These are just a few of the careers that require a solid grasp of history.

Look for the notes in the margins of the pages. These friendly notes are there to make you stop and think. Sometimes they comment on the material you are learning. Sometimes they give examples. Sometimes they remind you of something you already know.

You will also find several study aids in the book. At the beginning of every chapter, you'll find **Learning Objectives**. Take a moment to study these goals. They will help you focus on the important points covered in the chapter. **Words to Know** will give you a preview of any unusual or difficult terms you'll find in your reading. And at the end of each chapter, a **summary** will give you a quick review of what you've just learned.

We hope you enjoy reading about the history of the world and its people. Everyone who put this book together worked hard to make it interesting as well as useful. The rest is up to you. We wish you well in your studies. Our success is in your accomplishment.

Carol Hegarty
Publisher

Looking at the World's History

Chapter 1

What Is History?

The Temple of Karnac in Egypt is more than 3,000 years old. Try to imagine what it would have looked like before it fell into ruins.

Chapter Learning Objectives

- Describe how historians learn about the past.
- Describe how archeologists learn about the people of ancient times.
- Explain why life in ancient times was just as exciting as life today.
- Explain why people needed to make maps in the past, and why we still need maps today.
- Use a time line to compare the dates of historical events and periods.

Words to Know

A.D. (Anno Domini)   dating from the year Jesus Christ was born

agriculture   the use of land for growing crops and raising animals; farming

archeologist   a scientist who studies cultures of the past by digging up and examining the remains of ancient towns and cities

artifact   a simple handmade object, such as a tool or weapon

B.C. (Before Christ)   dating from before the year Jesus Christ was born

civilization   the society and culture of a particular people, place, or period

culture   the way of life—religion, ideas, arts, tools—of a certain people in a certain time

historian   someone who writes about the past; an expert in history

revolution   a complete change, especially in a way of life or a government

History Is All About Change

World History is the story of how the people of different times and places lived. It tells of good times as well as bad. It is the record of discoveries such as better ways of farming and new machines. It is also the story of the building of cities and nations, and the creation of beautiful art and music.

History is all about change—changing times and changing ideas. This book tells of many changes. Long ago, for example, slavery was an accepted part of everyday life. The ancient Egyptians made slaves of their prisoners. So did the Greeks, the Romans, the Aztecs, and many others. But today, people all over the world know that slavery is wrong.

The invention of television in our own century changed the way many people lived. Can you think of any other invention of recent years that has changed the way *you* live?

About 500 years ago, there was a big change in the way people pictured their world. People came to understand the true shape of our planet. They realized that the Earth is round, not flat. Explorers set out from Europe on long ocean voyages. They discovered a huge body of land where they had thought there was only ocean. North and South America took their role in the story of the world.

Another word for change is **revolution**. Ideas of freedom, democracy, and independence swept across the world. This led people in many countries to revolt. In both the Old World and the New World, people rose up and demanded freedom.

Revolutions in industry and in **agriculture** changed the way people lived. Discoveries and inventions often helped people lead better lives. But sometimes changes made life harder. For example, the development of industry in England made life better for many people. But life became harder for the people who had to work in the factories.

Columbus arriving in the West Indies, October 12, 1492

Out of the age of exploration grew an age of imperialism. Imperialism is the quest for more land and more power. Large nations set out to rule smaller ones. Weaker lands were forced to accept foreign **cultures** and ideas. A strong Europe tried to set up colonies all over the globe.

Many countries tried to fight this. People wanted to control their own lands and lives. The spirit of nationalism led people to unite under their own flags.

As histories must, this book talks about wars. Down through the ages there have always been wars. Tribe fought against tribe, city fought against city, and nation fought against nation. World Wars I and II in our own century were the worst wars of all time. Sometimes history seems like nothing but a long list of wars. This book tells how wars happened and how they changed nations. Some nations became weaker; others found new power.

And what about today's world? We are still in the process of revolution. Day after day there are changes in science, in technology, and in relations between countries. And there are still many difficult problems that need to be solved.

To us, ancient times may seem very simple and uncomplicated. But were they? Five thousand years ago the Sumerians in the city of Ur were kept very busy. They worried about feeding their people and making barren lands yield crops. They struggled to defend themselves against their enemies. And they also had to face the dangers of nature, like floods. They invented new ways to get from one place to another faster. They set up governments and made laws. They tried to explain their own existence through religion. And they educated their children. They celebrated life through art and writing.

The ancient Sumerians invented new ways to get from place to place more quickly. Five thousand years later, we are also inventing ways to travel faster.

Are we really so different today? People go into space. They use the great power of the tiny atom. But were the events of ancient days any less exciting to the people who lived then? What about the day a human being first put his ideas down in writing? Was the first wheel any less exciting than the first rocket engine? People in ancient times must have found discovery and changes to be just as exciting as we do today.

The cultures of the past are our best clues to history. By looking at yesterday's people, we can better understand the world as it is today . . . and as it might be tomorrow.

History Practice

Write answers to the following questions on a separate sheet of paper.

1. History is all about change in the world. What change has taken place over the years in the way people feel about slavery?

2. At one time people used to think the Earth was flat. Then about 500 years ago people began to hold a new idea about the shape of the Earth. What was this new idea, and what discovery did it lead to?

3. History is also about war. During which periods of history did wars occur? Are any wars going on in the world today? Where are they being fought?

How Historians Learn About the Past

We find out about the people of the past by looking at the things they left behind.

The easiest way we can look into the past is by reading papers and books of days gone by. **Historians** look at old maps that tell how the borders and names of countries have changed. They study all kinds of written records that have come down to us. Then they write books about what they have learned.

But what about **civilizations** from long, long ago? There were times when no one wrote books or drew maps. How do we know so much about the ancient days? People called **archeologists** go digging in the ruins of ancient civilizations. They find **artifacts** that have long been underground. They study each artifact they find. They piece bits of information together. And they come up with a picture of the past.

Scientists have many ways of deciding how old things are. A piece of cloth, an iron tool, a painting on a wall, may all be pieces of the puzzle. And as the pieces come together, bit by bit the story is told!

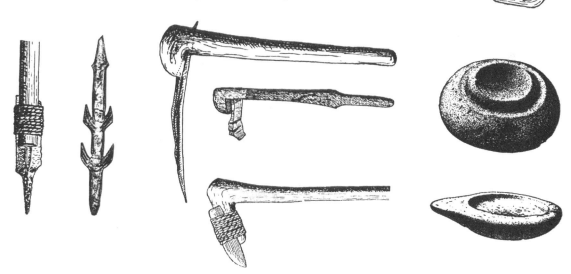

Ancient artifacts

LEARN MORE ABOUT IT: The Trojan War

Thousands of years ago, the Greek poet Homer wrote about a mighty city called Troy. According to the legends, Paris, son of the king of Troy, was visiting Sparta in Greece. There he fell in love with Helen, the wife of King Menelaus. Paris took Helen home with him to Troy. The Greeks swore revenge. A huge army set sail for Troy. For ten years the Greeks fought the Trojans, but they were unable to capture the city. Then, they built a gigantic wooden horse. The Greek soldiers hid inside it. The Trojans were curious about the horse and dragged it inside the city walls. The Greeks climbed out and killed most of the Trojans, including Paris. Then they looted and burned the city. And Helen returned to Menelaus in Sparta.

But did all of this really happen? Was there ever a city called Troy? A German archeologist named Heinrich Schliemann believed there *was* such a place. In 1870 he traveled to Turkey with a team of assistants. There they began digging in a mound that seemed to fit the location described in Homer's *Iliad*. Sure enough, they uncovered the ruins of several cities piled on top of each other. At least one of the cities had massive stone walls. Schliemann had discovered Troy!

Maps Show the Way

This book has many maps. These maps show how countries have changed, and how groups of people moved. They show that cities were built along rivers and on seacoasts. They show how those waterways made it possible for different people to come together.

People have been making maps for a long time. They drew maps to try to understand their world. And they used maps to find their way from one place to another. Since ancient times, the art of mapmaking has come a long way. Now there are maps to show landforms, maps to show weather, and maps that picture continents, countries, and cities.

But mapmakers have more work ahead. Think about the maps of the future. Will maps be needed to help people find their way among the stars?

The World

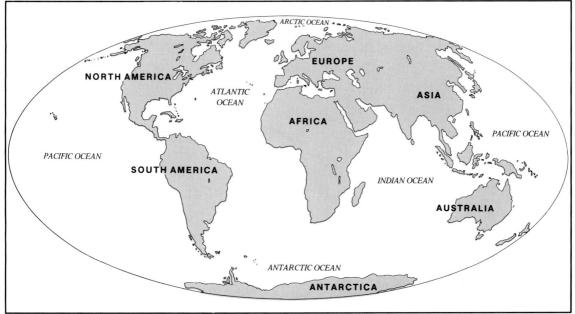

Map Skills
How many oceans can you find on the map on this page? How many continents? Name the oceans and continents.

History Practice

Write answers to the following questions on a separate sheet of paper.

1. Name two ways that historians find out what happened in the past.

2. Describe the work of an archeologist.

3. Name two reasons that people first started making maps.

Time Lines

The history of the people of the world is a long and exciting story. The time lines in each chapter will help you keep events clear and in order. Look at the time line on page 11. It gives some idea of just how long the story is. The chart lists some of the time periods and some of the people you will hear about as the story unfolds. If you look closely at it, you should be able to find just where you fit on the time line of history.

It may seem as if some of the civilizations in this book came and went very quickly. But the time line shows that the Roman civilization lasted for about 1,200 years (from about 700 B.C. to A.D. 500). The Sumerian civilization lasted 2,000 years (from about 4000 B.C. to 2000 B.C.). And the time line shows that the "modern times" section is only about 500 years old. How does the period in history that we call *ancient times* compare in length with medieval and modern times?

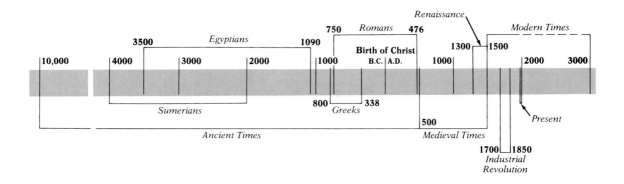

WHICH CAME FIRST?

Use the time line to choose the date that came first.
Write your answer on a separate sheet of paper.

1. 4000 B.C. *or* A.D. 1300?

2. 3500 B.C. *or* 4000 B.C.?

3. 1000 B.C. *or* A.D. 1000?

4. A.D. 1500 *or* 2000 B.C.?

5. 750 B.C. *or* A.D. 476?

Chapter Review

Chapter Summary

- World history tells us not only what happened, but why it happened, what people thought, how they lived, and how they changed.

- The things that happened long ago help explain the world as it is today.

- People in ancient times were real people with many of the same worries that we have today.

- Historians learn about the past by studying the written records that have come down to us.

- Archeologists learn about the past by studying artifacts that have long been underground.

- People draw maps to help find their way from one place to another.

- Time lines are useful in comparing the dates of historical events and periods of time.

Chapter Quiz

A. Checking Your Facts

wars	records	inventions	archeologists	slavery

Complete each sentence below. Use the correct word from the box. Rewrite the sentences on a separate sheet of paper.

1. People called _____ study artifacts.

2. Historians study all kinds of written _____ .

3. At one time, _____ was an accepted part of life.

4. New _____ often helped people lead better lives.

5. Sometimes history seems like a long list of _____ .

B. Think About It!

Write answers to the following questions on a separate sheet of paper.

1. The time line on page 11 shows that ancient times lasted for a much longer period than medieval and modern times. Why do you think we know so much more about medieval and modern times?

2. Give two examples of how life today is almost the same as it was in ancient times. Give two examples of how life today is very different.

3. Do you think that maps are just as important today as they were a long time ago? Give two reasons for your answer.

Chapter 2

Early Humans: The Story Begins

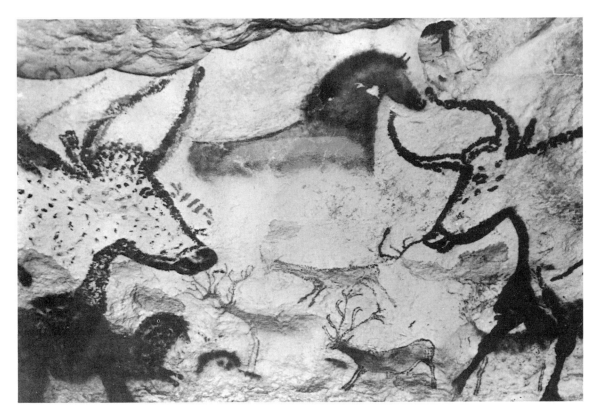

This cave painting at Lascaux, France, is thousands of years old. Why do you think people painted animals on the walls of caves?

Chapter Learning Objectives

- Describe what people learned when the Ice Age ended.
- Explain how the development of agriculture changed the world.
- Name the kinds of jobs people had in the new settlements.
- Locate the Fertile Crescent on a map.
- Explain how the people of ancient Jericho tried to protect their town.

Words to Know

craft a trade or art that takes special skill with the hands

crescent something shaped like a quarter moon

fertile able to produce large crops, as in rich soil

glaciers large, slow-moving masses of ice and snow

settlement a small group of homes in an area that hasn't been populated

specialize to work in, and know a lot about, one job or field

The Hunters

Our story of the world's history begins more than one million years ago. It was a time called the Ice Age. Most of the world was frozen then. It was covered with thick sheets of ice called **glaciers**. These glaciers had formed in the north.

In the northern parts of Europe, Asia, and North America, ice piled up about 10,000 feet thick. The weight of all that ice caused the glaciers to spread out. As they moved, the glaciers pushed soil and rocks out of their way. Many valleys and lakes were formed. Slowly the glaciers moved farther and farther south.

In the southern parts of the three continents, the ice melted some during the short summers. Little groups of people lived there, scattered about. They were the hunters. They had learned to make spears and other simple weapons and tools. They used wooden sticks, bones, and stones. They had not yet learned how to use metal. So historians call these people and their way of life a *stone age* culture.

YOU ARE THERE:
A Cave in Southern Europe, 15,000 B.C.

Firelight glows inside the cave. It is winter, and the weather is very cold. The ground outside the cave is frozen. But you and the others inside the cave are warm. You are wearing animal skins. One of you has started the fire by striking flint against a rock.

The corners of the cave are dark. But the fire lights one wall. Pictures cover that wall. In the flickering light, the pictures seem to move. One picture shows a man chasing a reindeer. In a second picture the reindeer lies on its side. A spear is sticking out of its body. The people in the cave have painted the pictures for an important reason. They believe it will bring you good luck in the hunt. As soon as the snow melts, you and the other hunters will be going out again.

Such was life on Earth for tens of thousands of years. The hunters left their caves in the summer to move around. They could not settle down for good. They had to follow the herds of wild animals. They also gathered some food from shrubs and trees, such as nuts, berries, and fruits. But they mainly counted on animals for food and clothing. Hunting was the most important thing in their lives. Without a good hunt they would die. Just staying alive was a constant struggle for people during the Ice Age.

The Farmers

The Ice Age ended about 10,000 B.C. The glaciers began melting. The land was no longer frozen. People now learned how to grow food. They no longer had to chase wild animals across the lands. Once they learned to raise their own food, they could settle down. That change, from hunting to farming, made civilization possible.

The people of long ago watched the winds blow seeds across the ground. They noticed that new plants grew where the seeds landed. This is how the people learned. They tried planting seeds themselves. They broke up the ground to make it soft. They chose the best seeds, and they grew plants. Next, they made tools to use in farming. They used flint sickles to cut grain and wooden plows to help them dig up the ground.

Once the glaciers were gone, life became easier for people. Now they could count on a ready food supply. Often they grew more than they could eat in one winter. They could store food for the future. They would not have to move away from their homes to search for food. People began to live in **settlements.**

They also learned to tame animals. Some say the dog was the first animal tamed. Next came cows, goats, sheep, and pigs. With their own herds, people had a steady supply of meat, milk, and wool. They now had animals that could live side by side with them. The animals could carry loads and help people with their work.

History Practice

Write answers to the following questions on a separate sheet of paper.

1. Why do you think people lived in caves during the Ice Age? What would happen to a group of people that had bad luck in their hunting?

2. When the Ice Age ended, people learned how to raise their own food. Do you think this was good? Why?

3. If you had lived around 10,000 years ago, would you rather have been a hunter or a farmer? Why?

For thousands of years people have used animals to carry loads and help with work.

The Agricultural Revolution

When people began to farm, their lives changed. The change brought about by agriculture was very great. For this reason it is often called a revolution, the Agricultural Revolution. Now people could settle in large groups, in one place. They chose areas with plenty of water and good soil. They built houses out of whatever materials were nearby. Often the houses were built of mud.

Now the people could plan on how much food to plant each year. They could decide on how many animals to raise in the herds. Now they had more control of their own lives.

Having a large enough food supply and staying in one place gave people spare time. Not everyone in the group was needed to raise food or care for the animals. People began to **specialize.** Some people farmed. Others took care of the animals. And now there were chances to do things they had never done before. People had time to work on their **crafts.** Weavers wove grass into fine baskets. Others made pottery for mud and clay and baked it in ovens. With wool from the sheep, some people learned to spin thread and to weave cloth.

People today still work on crafts. Name some of these crafts.

As different jobs developed, so did trading. A weaver might trade his cloth for food from the farmer. A goat might be traded for an ax from the toolmaker. First, trading was carried on within the village. Later people traded from one village to the next.

With the Agricultural Revolution, people's most important needs of food, shelter, and clothing were easier to meet. But now people owned things. The potter had his jars and bowls. The herdsman had his animals. Now there were things to protect! And so people made laws. Most likely a group of the oldest, wisest people in the village would meet. They would decide on rules for the rest of the people.

People started to worry when their villages grew rich. Someone might attack them and try to steal some of their riches! And so people formed armies to protect their villages.

As time went on, villages grew into cities. Later, cities joined together to form small kingdoms. Agriculture is what made this development possible.

The Fertile Crescent

The earliest known farming took place along the great rivers of the Middle East. These lands include what are now the countries of Jordan, Syria, Iraq, Iran, and Turkey. This area is called the **Fertile Crescent.** The Tigris and Euphrates rivers provided plenty of water for the land. The soil was rich. The land between the Tigris and Euphrates was called Mesopotamia. That name means *land between two rivers.*

Within the Fertile Crescent was the town of Jericho. It is one of the earliest known towns. By about 8000 B.C. Jericho was probably a farming village. Its people built rounded houses of mud and bricks. Archeologists have found remains showing that the people of Jericho buried their dead right under their houses.

The land around Jericho was very fertile. The people grew many crops and became rich. The town grew. Jericho now had to protect itself. The people built a stone wall around their town.

But the wall was not enough. Around 7000 B.C. archeologists say Jericho was probably captured. The houses built after that time were no longer round, but had square corners. This clue suggests that a new group of people must have taken over and settled there.

The Middle East: Then

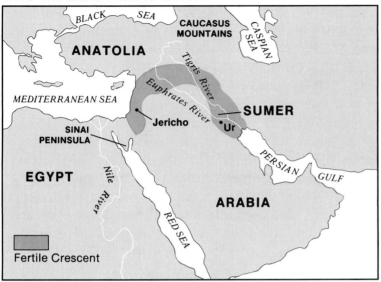

The Middle East: Now

Map Skills

Compare the two maps. Notice that some of the names from the ancient Middle East show up on the map of today's Middle East. Which names are they?

More is known about the early farming villages of the Fertile Crescent than anywhere else. But farming was developing in other parts of the world, too. By 6000 B.C. farming had spread to Europe. By 4000 B.C. a culture of rice farmers had grown up in China. Between 5000 B.C. and 2000 B.C. agriculture spread across northern Africa.

People began to settle wherever there was good soil and plenty of water. Now they had food and clothing. They had time to learn. Certain cities began to grow into great civilizations.

Walls of Jericho coming down

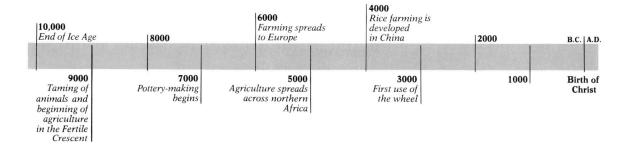

10,000
End of Ice Age

8000

6000
*Farming spreads
to Europe*

4000
*Rice farming is
developed
in China*

2000

B.C. | **A.D.**

9000
*Taming of
animals and
beginning of
agriculture
in the Fertile
Crescent*

7000
*Pottery-making
begins*

5000
*Agriculture spreads
across northern
Africa*

3000
*First use of
the wheel*

1000

**Birth of
Christ**

WHICH CAME FIRST?

Use the time line to choose the event or period of time that came first. Write your answers on a separate sheet of paper.

1. First use of the wheel *or* Farming spreads to Europe?

2. Agriculture spreads across northern Africa *or* Pottery-making begins?

3. Birth of Christ *or* Rice farming is developed in China?

4. End of Ice Age *or* First use of the wheel?

5. Taming of animals and beginning of agriculture in the Fertile Crescent *or* End of Ice Age?

Chapter Review

Chapter Summary

- During the Ice Age people lived in caves all winter. They hunted for food during the short summers.

- Hunters could not form long-term settlements. They had to follow the animals.

- With the coming of the Agricultural Revolution, people learned to farm land and tame animals.

- Farming meant that people could control their own food supply. They could build houses and settle in one place.

- In the new settlements people had different jobs. New crafts developed.

- Thanks to agriculture, rich cities grew up and trading began.

- One of the earliest areas of farming was in the Middle East, along the shores of two great rivers. It is called the Fertile Crescent.

Chapter Quiz

A. Checking Your Facts

Choose the correct word or words to make each of the sentences below a true statement. Rewrite the sentences on a separate sheet of paper.

1. During the Ice Age, the people who lived in caves were (hunters / farmers).

2. The change from (farming to hunting / hunting to farming) made civilization possible.

3. Once the (wild animals / glaciers) were gone, life became easier for people.

4. During the (Agricultural / Fertile) Revolution, people began to specialize.

5. The earliest farming took place along the great (highways / rivers) of the Middle East.

B. Think About It!

Write answers to the following questions on a separate sheet of paper.

1. Life was hard during the Ice Age. Give two reasons why you agree or disagree with this statement.

2. Why were people able to invent new things and perfect their crafts after the Agricultural Revolution?

3. Look at the map of the ancient Middle East on page 21. Why do you think the area of the earliest known farming is called the "Fertile Crescent"?

Unit One Review

Write answers to the following questions on a separate sheet of paper.

1. What do historians do?

2. What do archeologists do?

3. What are artifacts? Give two examples.

4. Who was the archeologist who discovered the ancient city of Troy?

5. What can you learn by looking at a time line?

6. Do you think it is important to learn about the past? Give two reasons for your answer.

7. What is a "stone age" culture?

8. Thousands of years ago people lived in caves. Why did they paint pictures of animals on the walls of their caves?

9. Why did the people of Jericho build a stone wall around their city?

10. Why do archeologists think that Jericho may have been captured?

11. Why didn't early hunters settle down in one place?

12. When did the Ice Age end?

13. When did agriculture spread across Northern Africa?

Ancient Civilizations

Chapter 3

The Sumerians:
The First Great Civilization

This mosaic from ancient Sumer shows us one of the greatest inventions of the ancient world. Can you name it?

Chapter Learning Objectives

- Describe what daily life was like in a Sumerian city-state.
- Locate the land of Sumer on a map.
- Name the most important Sumerian inventions.
- Explain why Sumer grew weak.
- Describe the Sumerian method of farming.

Words to Know

canal   a man-made waterway

chariot   an open two-wheeled cart, pulled by horses

city-state   an independent city and the surrounding land it controls

contract   a legal written agreement between two or more people

cuneiform   a wedge-shaped form of writing used in ancient Sumer

dike   a wall built along a river or sea to hold back the water from low land

irrigate   to bring water to dry land by means of canals

merchant   a person who buys and sells goods for profit; a trader

scribe   a person whose job it was to write out copies of contracts and other manuscripts. People worked as scribes before the invention of printing.

swamp   an area of low, wet land

tablet   a small, flat piece of clay used for writing

temple   a building for the worship of a god or gods

ziggurat   a huge, towerlike temple

The Land Between Two Rivers

The land that would one day be called Mesopotamia lay between two rivers. The rivers were the Tigris and the Euphrates. Sometimes the rivers flooded and washed rich bottom-soil up on the land. This made the land good for farming. People settled on this rich land. They grew their crops and raised animals. In the south, in a land called Sumer, a great civilization grew.

The people of Sumer are called Sumerians. Although the land they settled was fertile, it was not a perfect place to live. The weather was very hot in the summer. In spring there was always the danger of the rivers flooding. Sometimes whole villages would be washed away. Many people would die.

Part of Sumer was **swamp** land. Other parts were very dry. Land that was flooded in the spring dried hard under the late summer sun. It was necessary to make the land ready for crops. The Sumerian farmers had to get water from the rivers to their fields.

Sumer

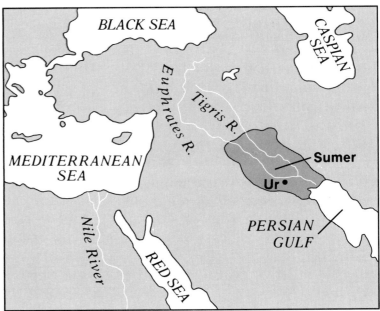

Map Skills
Name the large bodies of water on this map. Now find the rivers and name them.

Sumerian Farmers

The farmers found a way to **irrigate** their fields. They made cuts in the river banks and dug **canals**. The canals carried the river water out to the crops. The Sumerians also built **dikes** to hold back the flood waters.

A Sumerian farmer worked hard from early morning until late at night. His oxen were his treasure. They pulled the farmer's plow and carried the crops in from the field.

Sumer was a wealthy land, and its wealth lay in farming.

Trading

The people of Sumer had different jobs. While some were farmers, others were **merchants**. Sumer had no metal, stone, or timber of its own. Sumerians depended on trading to get these things. They sent their fine crops to other lands. In return, they brought back the goods they needed at home.

A Sumerian trading ship

Boats carried the goods to and from Sumer. The Sumerian boats were among the first ever used. There were two kinds of boats. River boats were small. They moved along under the power of long oars or poles. Trading ships were much longer, and they were narrow. They had big sails. The trading boats brought home treasures of gold, silver, pearls, and copper from other lands.

A Sumerian river boat

Villages Grow into City-States

The earliest Sumerians lived in houses made from reeds. The reeds, or tall grasses, grew in the swamps. Later, the people learned to make bricks from mud. They dried the bricks in the sun and built houses from them. The brick houses stayed cool inside during the hot summers.

What are houses built of today? What is your own house built of? Does it stay cool inside during the summer?

Each Sumerian village was built around a **temple.** The people believed a god or goddess lived in the temple and protected the village. The farmers took part of their crops to the temple to offer to the god. The priests of the temple became very wealthy and powerful.

Over the years, the villages grew. They became **city-states**, each one with its own government. A temple still stood at the center of each city-state. There was farmland all around the edge of the city. The city-states often fought among themselves. So the Sumerians built walls around their cities.

One of the greatest city-states of Sumer was called Ur. A gigantic temple called a **ziggurat** was built in Ur. This tall temple-tower was built to honor the god who watched over the city. The people of Ur came in great numbers to bring gifts to the temple. They believed that if their god was happy, the city would be wealthy.

Ur-Namme, King of Ur, about 2300 B.C.

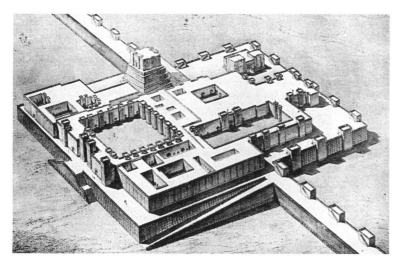

Ziggurat (tall tower near top)

The Invention of Writing

The Sumerians' inventions were their gifts to the world. All the civilizations that followed used inventions of the Sumerians. There are still things in the world today that date back to Sumer.

The greatest gift the Sumerians gave to the world was the invention of writing. The Sumerians were a wealthy people. So they needed some way to keep track of what they owned. They began by drawing pictures. They used a reed as a pen. They drew on soft pieces of clay. The soft clay was then dried in the sun. And the **tablet** became a permanent record.

Later, the Sumerian drawings changed. They began to look less like the real objects they represented. Instead, they became simple symbols that were easier to draw. Because of the shape of the reed, the symbols were wedge-shaped. This kind of writing is called **cuneiform.** By putting symbols together, the Sumerians could write whole sentences.

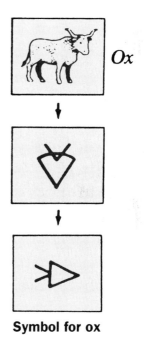

Symbol for ox

Not all Sumerians knew how to write. Specially trained people called **scribes** learned how to write. They drew up business **contracts** for the farmers and merchants. The scribes were paid very well for their special skill. They were among the richest of the Sumerians.

We know a great deal about this earliest of civilizations. This is because Sumerian scribes wrote down their ideas and kept records.

Other Gifts from the Sumerians

The Sumerian farmers had to pay a tax on their property. And so the Sumerians invented a way of measuring land. Fields were divided into even squares. Then the squares were counted up to decide how much tax a farmer owed. Since the Sumerians used silver as money, payments were made in silver. The value of the silver was measured by its weight.

The Sumerians also learned to measure time. The 60-second minute and the 60-minute hour come from the Sumerian way of counting time.

What if the wheel had never been invented? What would the world be like today? How would people travel?

Historians believe that the wheel was first used in Sumer. Sumerian armies rode in wheeled **chariots.** There were no horses in all of Sumer. So wild donkeys were taught to pull the chariots.

Irrigation canals came to us from the Sumerian farmer. And sailboats came from the traders.

Although there was no metal in Sumer itself, the Sumerians traded for metal. They became skilled metalworkers. They learned to make fine jewelry of copper, silver, and gold.

Sumerian ideas and Sumerian inventions brought about changes that would affect life for ages to come.

History Practice

Write answers to the following questions on a separate sheet of paper.

1. Why did the Sumerians trade with other lands?

2. Why did the Sumerians have to invent a way to measure land? What else did they learn to measure?

3. What was the greatest gift the Sumerians gave to the world?

Life in Sumer

A Sumerian boy might awaken to a hot, dry summer day in the city of Ur. If his father were a farmer, the boy would go with him to work in the fields. They would leave their small house with the earliest rays of the sun. Perhaps that day the father and son would clean the irrigation canals. Even if the day were very hot, the boy would work hard. Those canals were important to the farm. Without them, nothing would grow. The boy might work alongside other farmers. They would have help from the slaves from one of the larger farms.

Boys from wealthy families could go to school. If a boy learned well, he might become a scribe. A scribe could work in the king's palace or in the great temple itself.

The king ran the city of Ur. He ruled in the name of the city's god. Priests, scribes, and nobles helped him rule. These people were very rich. They lived a fine life. They were members of the highest classes in the Sumerian culture.

YOU ARE THERE:
A Schoolroom in Ur, 2500 B.C.

It is late afternoon on a summer day in ancient Ur. The farm boys are hard at work out in the fields. But you and the other sons of wealthy merchants and scribes are at school. There are no girls in your class—school is only for boys. And school is not a place for fun. You've been sitting on your bench since sunup. And you have to stay there a few more hours until sundown.

In the basket at your feet are reed pens and wet clay for your tablets. You've been working on your reading and writing. Now you're doing your arithmetic lesson. The rules here are strict. Nobody is allowed to stop working. You feel very hot and tired. Your mind wanders and you begin to daydream. Suddenly you snap out of it! Oh, no! The teacher is coming toward you! There is no way out. Now you are going to get a beating.

The people of Ur believed that when they died, they went to another world. Archeologists have discovered graves filled with fine gold jewelry. Some graves of the noblemen hold many skeletons. It may be that other people killed themselves, or were killed, when the noblemen died. This way they could follow the dead noblemen to that other world.

Attack on Ur

The Sumerian city-states fought with each other. So after a while Sumer grew weak. Around 2000 B.C. Sumerian cities came under attack. The Sumerian armies, even with their wheeled chariots, were not strong enough to save Sumer. Ur was destroyed.

The city's wealth was stolen. Men and women were killed. Children were taken as slaves.

Soon other Sumerian cities fell, too. The invaders, called the Babylonians, built new cities. Later, some of those cities died away, too. Dust and dirt covered them over. Today archeologists dig into great mounds that still stand in the Middle East. Under the mounds of dirt lay all that is left of these ancient civilizations.

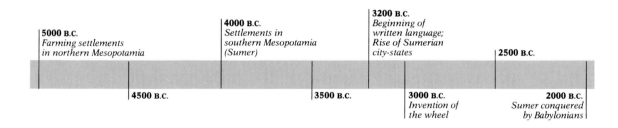

5000 B.C.
Farming settlements in northern Mesopotamia

4000 B.C.
Settlements in southern Mesopotamia (Sumer)

3200 B.C.
Beginning of written language; Rise of Sumerian city-states

2500 B.C.

4500 B.C.

3500 B.C.

3000 B.C.
Invention of the wheel

2000 B.C.
Sumer conquered by Babylonians

WHICH CAME FIRST?

Use the time line to choose the event, year, or period of time that came first. Write your answers on a separate sheet of paper.

1. Invention of the wheel *or* Farming settlements in northern Mesopotamia?

2. Beginning of written language *or* Invention of the wheel?

3. Sumer conquered by Babylonians *or* Rise of Sumerian city-states?

4. Farming settlements in northern Mesopotamia *or* Settlements in southern Mesopotamia (Sumer)?

5. 3500 B.C. *or* 3200 B.C.?

Chapter Review

Chapter Summary

- The first great civilization grew up between the Tigris and Euphrates rivers in the land of Sumer.

- The Sumerian civilization was based on farming.

- The Sumerians had to irrigate their land.

- The Sumerians traded with other lands for goods they needed.

- Sumerians lived in city-states. Each city-state had its own government.

- The Sumerians invented writing.

- The Sumerians invented the wheel, the sailboat, irrigation, and a way of measuring.

- The Sumerians were conquered, but their ideas lived on.

Chapter Quiz

A. Checking Your Facts

| irrigate | scribe | cuneiform | chariots | ziggurat |

Complete each sentence below. Use the correct word from the box. Rewrite the sentences on a separate sheet of paper.

1. A large temple called a _____ was built in Ur.

2. The Sumerian system of writing based on wedge-shaped symbols was called _____.

3. A _____ was a person who was trained to write.

4. Sumerian farmers found a way to _____ their fields.

5. Sumerians used wild donkeys to pull their _____ .

B. Think About It!

Write answers to the following questions on a separate sheet of paper.

1. The Sumerian civilization is a very old one. Give one reason why we know so much about it.

2. How did the Sumerian civilization come to its end? How do you think the Sumerians might have been able to prevent the destruction of their cities?

3. Do you think you would have been able to get a good education in a Sumerian school? Why or why not? Name two ways in which a Sumerian school was different from your own school.

Chapter 4

Ancient Egypt: Land of the Pharaohs

The Egyptians built these great stone pyramids thousands of years ago. Why do you think they built them?

Chapter Learning Objectives

- Explain why people settled along the Nile River.
- Describe what happened to the Nile River Valley every July.
- Explain why the pharaohs had their people build the pyramids.
- Tell what archeologists found inside Egyptian tombs.
- Name some important Egyptian inventions.

Words to Know

desert   dry, sandy land with little or no plant life

hieroglyphics   a system of writing using pictures or symbols to represent objects, ideas, or sounds

mummy   a dead body kept from rotting by being treated with chemicals and wrapped in cloth

papyrus   a writing paper the Egyptians made from water plants of the same name

pharaoh   a king of ancient Egypt

pyramid   a huge stone structure with a square base and four triangular sides that meet in a point at the top. Egyptian rulers were buried in the *pyramids*.

tax   money paid to support a government

tomb   a grave, usually one that is enclosed in stone or cement

upstream   in the direction against the flow of the river; at the upper part of a river

Along the Nile

At one time the area now called the Sahara was a green plain. People lived there. There was water and wildlife. But the weather changed. The Sahara dried up and became a **desert**. The people living there went looking for water. Some of them went to a land called Egypt.

A great river called the Nile ran through Egypt. The Nile River Valley was a swampland. It was a dark jungle filled with dangerous animals. But the people needed water badly. So they cleared the land. They built their villages along the river where the jungle used to be.

Like the Sumerians, the people of Egypt built a civilization along a river. They were able to do this because the land along the Nile had what they needed. The Egyptians learned to farm, to tame animals, to make pottery, and to weave. They learned to make tools from metal.

The weather in Egypt was hot. But each year, in July, the Nile River spilled over its banks in a great flood. Land that stood dry all year was suddenly under water for several weeks. The floods left the land very fertile.

Farmers learned to use the floods to help them. They learned to save up some of the flood waters. Then they could water their crops during the rest of the year. Like the Sumerians, they learned to dig canals to irrigate their fields.

Each July the farmers moved to higher ground, taking their animals with them. They knew that the floods would be over in a few weeks. They waited until the Nile once again flowed peacefully within its banks. Then they planted their seeds in the rich, soft ground.

Lower Egypt and Upper Egypt Become One

The civilization along the Nile did well. Villages joined together to form larger settlements. There came a time, around 3200 B.C., when two kings ruled all of Egypt. One king ruled Lower Egypt, in the north. Another king ruled Upper Egypt, in the south. A look at the map shows each of these areas. A person in Lower Egypt who followed the Nile River **upstream** would come to Upper Egypt.

Upper and Lower Egypt

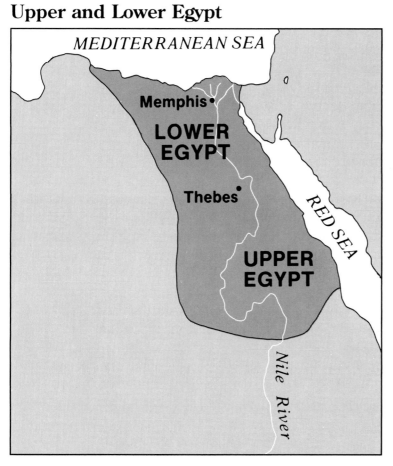

Map Skills

Name two ancient Egyptian cities. Which part of Egypt, Upper or Lower, bordered on the Mediterranean Sea?

The king of Lower Egypt wore a red crown. The king of Upper Egypt wore a white crown. The two kings ended up fighting to control all of Egypt. Around 3100 B.C. King Menes, of Upper Egypt, conquered Lower Egypt. Now Menes wore a "double" crown. he ruled all of Egypt.

King Menes became the first great **pharaoh** of Egypt. The Egyptians called their ruler *pharaoh,* meaning *The Great House*.

People today still have to pay taxes. Name two ways the government spends tax money.

The pharaohs were powerful rulers. Each year they collected **taxes**—huge taxes—from all the people. Farmers had to give the pharaoh a large part of their crops as a tax.

The pharaoh had many men to help him carry out his orders and collect the taxes. The pharaohs lived rich, splendid lives.

The Pyramids

The Egyptian pharaohs wanted people to remember just how rich and how powerful they were. Some had huge statues of themselves made. And they had their people build great **tombs** for them. When the pharaohs died, their bodies were placed in the tombs. Jewelry, food, clothing—all the pharaoh's favorite things—went into the tomb with him. The Egyptians believed that a person would need those things in the next world.

These great, towering Egyptian tombs are called **pyramids.** The pharaohs of Egypt, from about 2650 B.C. until 1637 B.C., were buried within those huge pyramids. There are many pyramids still standing in Egypt today. They are considered one of the wonders of the world.

The most famous pyramid is the Great Pyramid near Cairo. It covers an area larger than ten football fields. It contains more than two million stone blocks, each weighing about 2 1/2 tons. Somehow, the stones had to be cut into shape and then transported to the building site. Then the stones were raised into place. They were laid so that they fit together exactly. From a distance the pyramid looks as if it were cut out of a single white stone. The Egyptians of 4,500 years ago had no machinery or iron tools. So how did they do it? We don't know for certain. In fact, we don't know if *we* would be able to build pyramids today, even with our modern building methods.

The ancient Egyptians did use copper chisels. And they probably hauled the stones on some sort of wooden sled. Most likely they built a system of ramps and wooden planks to haul the stones into place. But mostly they had to rely on human muscle power. The ancient Greek historian Herodotus wrote about the pyramids. He said that 400,000 men worked each year for 20 years to build the Great Pyramid. Archeologists doubt these numbers. But we'll never know for sure.

Tombs within the pyramids have served as a wonderful record of the Egyptian civilization. Some tombs were broken into by robbers, and the artifacts inside were stolen. But archeologists have discovered some tombs still filled with goods from daily Egyptian life. The walls of the tombs are covered with picture-writing. The pictures tell the story of the ancient Egyptian world.

History Practice

Write answers to the following questions on a separate sheet of paper.

1. Why do you think people settled along the Nile River?

2. Why did the Egyptian pharaohs have their people build the pyramids?

3. Why did the pharaohs want all of their favorite things to be buried with them?

Egyptian Mummies

Archeologists found more than bowls, pictures, jewelry, and pottery within the tombs. They found the pharaohs themselves! The Egyptians used certain chemicals to keep the dead body from rotting away. Of course, only the rich Egyptians could afford this special treatment.

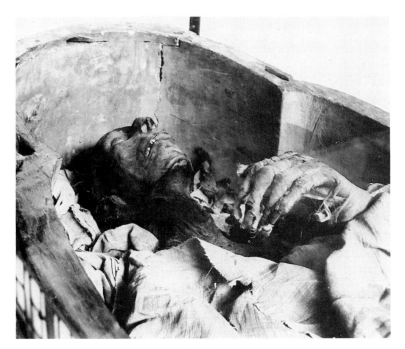

Mummy of Ramses II (1304–1237 B.C.)

Burying people this way was not a simple matter in ancient Egypt. First the brain and organs had to be removed from the body. Then the body was treated with a special chemical. It was then wrapped around and around in cloth bandages. A body wrapped like this is called a **mummy.** Many mummies were found deep within the Egyptian tombs. Egyptian mummies and artifacts have been taken from these tombs. They are on display today in museums around the world.

Egyptian Life and Religion

The Egyptian pharaohs and their nobles lived rich lives. But all the rest of the people led very simple lives. The farmers worked hard in their fields. There was usually plenty of food. So Egypt's craftsmen had more time to work on their skills.

The Egyptians were concerned about the way they looked. Drawings and statues show Egyptian women with long, dark hair worn in many braids and ringlets.

Both men and women wore makeup. They painted their lips red. They drew around their eyes with a dark green or gray paste called *kohl.* And the Egyptians liked perfume. Both the men and the women rubbed sweet-smelling oils into their skins.

The ancient Egyptians believed in many gods. Just as in the land of Sumer, each city had its own special god. All Egyptians believed in Osiris, the powerful god of death.

The river played an important part in Egyptians' lives. It also played a part in their belief about death. They believed that the dead were ferried across a great river to meet Osiris in the next world.

Egyptian Inventions

The Egyptians learned to write. They invented a system of picture-writing called **hieroglyphics.** They learned to make paper from river reed, called **papyrus.** Our word *paper* comes from the word *papyrus.*

The Egyptians learned to chart the stars. And they decided that there were 365 days in a year.

The Egyptians made jewelry of gold and precious stones. They used metals for tools and weapons. The Egyptians made music, too. Archeologists have found ancient Egyptian instruments and the words to songs. The Egyptians built ships. They traded with other people.

But most of all the ancient Egyptians are remembered as the builders of the pyramids. The Egyptian builders have left us possibly the most amazing works of any civilization. And many of their secrets still lie buried within the pyramids.

The Egyptian calendar was based on the sun. There were three seasons of 120 days, and a five-day celebration at the end of the year.

Hieroglyphics carved in stone, Temple of Hathor, Abu Simbel, Egypt

WORDS FROM THE PAST: The Rosetta Stone

Hieroglyphics can still be seen in many places in Egypt. But for many hundreds of years, nobody could read them. The meaning of these ancient Egyptian symbols had been lost sometime in the distant past. But in 1799, a French engineer in Egypt discovered a large stone. It was half buried near the mouth of the Nile River.

The Rosetta Stone, as it came to be called, was completely covered with writing. Carved into the stone were three languages: hieroglyphics, a second

Egyptian language, and Greek. A French historian named Champollion translated the Greek portion first. Then he carefully compared this to the other languages. He was finally able to learn the meaning of the hieroglyphics. In 1822 he published the results of his work. And today many historians can read ancient Egyptian writing.

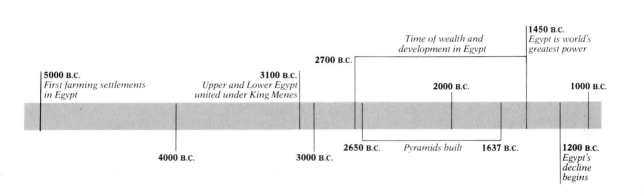

WHICH CAME FIRST?

Use the time line to choose the event, year, or period of time that came first. Write your answers on a separate sheet of paper.

1. Upper and Lower Egypt united under King Menes *or* Pyramids built?

2. Egypt's decline begins *or* Time of wealth and development in Egypt?

3. 2650 B.C. *or* 2700 B.C.?

4. Egypt is world's greatest power *or* Time of wealth and development in Egypt?

5. 1637 B.C. *or* 1200 B.C.?

Chapter Review

Chapter Summary

- When the Sahara became a desert, people went to live along the Nile River.

- The river flooded each year, leaving the land around it fertile.

- Lower Egypt and Upper Egypt were united under King Menes.

- Egyptian rulers, called pharaohs, were very powerful.

- The pharaohs' tombs were in giant pyramids.

- Ancient Egyptians believed in life after death. And many of the things they owned were buried with them.

- We know a lot about the Egyptians from the artifacts found in their tombs.

- The Egyptians made paper from a reed called papyrus.

Chapter Quiz

A. Checking Your Facts

Choose the correct word or words to make each of the sentences below a true statement. Rewrite the sentences on a separate sheet of paper.

1. At one time the Sahara was a (large swamp / green plain).

2. A person who followed the Nile River upstream would come to (Lower / Upper) Egypt.

3. King (Menes / Menelaus) became the first pharaoh of Egypt.

4. The Egyptian word *pharaoh* means (great mouse / great house).

5. A French historian named (Champlain / Champollion) learned the meaning of Egyptian hieroglyphics.

B. Think About It!

Write answers to the following questions on a separate sheet of paper.

1. How did the yearly floods help the people who settled along the Nile River?

2. What kind of rulers were the Egyptian pharaohs? Do you think this kind of ruler would be good for the United States today? Why or why not?

3. People say that the Egyptian pyramids are one of the "wonders of the world." Give two reasons why you agree or disagree with this.

Chapter 5

Mediterranean Kingdoms

Phoenician explorers were the first people who could sail beyond the sight of land. How do you think they were able to do this?

Chapter Learning Objectives
- Locate Phoenician trading routes on a map.
- Name two important Phoenician inventions.
- Explain how the religion of the Hebrews was different from that of other Mediterranean people.
- Describe the system of laws known as the Code of Hammurabi.
- Tell what the Assyrians did when they captured a city.

Words to Know

capital a city or town where the government of a nation or state is located

colonies groups of people who settle in a far-off land but are still under the rule of the land they came from

commandment a law or order, most often a religious law, as in the Ten Commandments in the Bible

conquer to get control by using force, as in a war

empire a group of lands all ruled by the same government or ruler

navigate to plan the course of a ship; to sail or steer

nomads people who move from place to place looking for food for their animal herds

siege the surrounding of a city by soldiers who are trying to capture it so that food, water, and other supplies cannot get in or out

treaty an agreement, usually having to do with peace or trade

tribe a group of people living together under a leader

tribute a payment or gift demanded by rulers of ancient kingdoms

---

Many groups of people settled along the eastern shore of the Mediterranean Sea. Others settled the lands farther east. They farmed the fertile valley between the Tigris and Euphrates rivers. New civilizations began to grow. These groups traded with each other. They also made war with each other. They fought for control over the Mediterranean lands. Strong kingdoms took over smaller city-states. Powerful kings ruled **empires.**

One of these civilizations was the Hittites. They learned how to make tools and weapons out of iron. Other Mediterranean civilizations left their mark on world history in other ways. The Hebrews gave us the Jewish religion. And the Phoenicians invented an alphabet. It was very similar to our modern alphabet.

The Phoenicians: Traders on the Seas

The Phoenician civilization grew up along the eastern shores of the Mediterranean. It was unlike most of the other Mediterranean civilizations. The Phoenicians were not farmers. They built their cities on rocky shores. The Phoenicians were people of the sea. They were sailors and traders.

Few farm crops grew in Phoenicia. But there were plenty of trees. The people cut down the trees to use as wood for sailing ships.

The Phoenicians were the best sailors in the ancient world. They learned to use the stars to **navigate**. This made it possible for them to sail beyond the sight of land. The Phoenicians sailed where no other people dared to go. Their ships went to every corner of the Mediterranean. They reached the coast of Spain. They even sailed out into the Atlantic Ocean, beyond Gibraltar. They sailed along the west coast of Africa. Then they went all the way around the whole continent of Africa!

Wherever they traveled, the Phoenicians set up **colonies**. Their people settled in places all around the Mediterranean Sea. The Phoenician colonies became trading centers. One of the largest Phoenician colonies was Carthage. It was on the north coast of Africa. The people of Carthage traded their African gold, ivory, and ebony for Phoenician pottery, glass, and beads.

The colonies paid taxes to the Phoenician homeland. Great Phoenician cities, like Tyre, Sidon, and Byblos, grew rich and strong.

The Phoenicians were traders and sailors, not warriors. They paid soldiers from other lands to protect their cities. They built high, stone walls to protect themselves from attack.

Phoenician trading routes

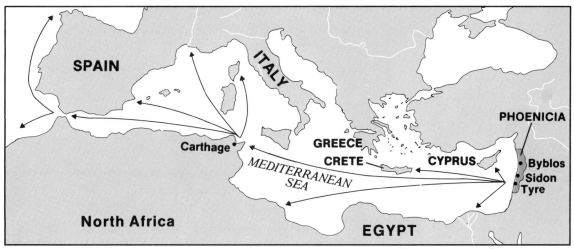

Map Skills

Name at least five places on the map the Phoenicians sailed to. Which large body of water did they explore beyond the Mediterranean?

Phoenician Inventions

The Phoenician ships were powered by oars and sails. They sailed all about the ancient world. And as the Phoenicians traded goods, they also traded ideas.

One of the most important ideas the Phoenicians spread was the alphabet. They turned pictures into letters. In fact, our own alphabet comes from the letters the Phoenicians invented.

The Phoenicians became famous for another invention, too. It was a secret dye used to color cloth. The dye was made from snails that lived along the coast. The Phoenicians boiled thousands of snails to make just a tiny bit of dye. The dye was very costly. Named after the city of Tyre, it was called *Tyrian purple*.

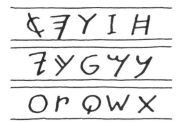

Some Phoenician
letters. Which letters
look like those in our
alphabet?

The Phoenicians traded the purple cloth. Only very rich people could buy it. Royalty throughout the Mediterranean world decorated their palaces with the purple cloth. They wore robes of Tryian purple. The color purple came to stand for power and wealth. It became a royal color.

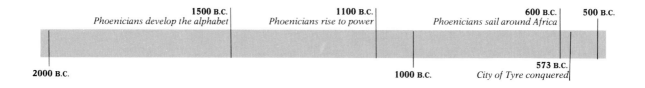

2000 B.C.

1500 B.C.
Phoenicians develop the alphabet

1100 B.C.
Phoenicians rise to power

1000 B.C.

600 B.C.
Phoenicians sail around Africa

573 B.C.
City of Tyre conquered

500 B.C.

The Hebrews: Under One God

The Hebrews lived along the east coast of the Mediterranean Sea. Their civilization grew up just south of Phoenicia.

The Hebrews wanted their own land. They wanted a place where they could worship their god. In the Mediterranean world most people believed in many gods. There were gods of death and gods of the sun and rain. But the Hebrews believed in only one god.

The Bible says that a man named Abraham was the father of the Hebrew people. Abraham lived near the Sumerian city of Ur. One day he left with his family to become a **nomad**. Abraham and his people followed their herds into a land called Canaan. When they found themselves short of food, they went on to Egypt.

Abraham's people, the Hebrews, were treated as slaves in Egypt. The Egyptian pharaoh was cruel. A man named Moses became the Hebrews' leader. He led them out of Egypt. He led them into the desert, away from the cruel pharaoh.

Name another group of people who left home in search of a land where they could worship as they pleased. (Hint: Think about the people who came to America.)

WORDS FROM THE PAST:
The Ten Commandments

The Hebrews did not find their land of freedom right away. They wandered, searching, for many years. The Bible says that during that time, Moses was given the Ten **Commandments**. It says that the commandments came directly from God. The commandments are laws to live by. They became laws for the Hebrews' religion, Judaism. The first commandment says that people must believe in only one god. "The Lord is One," the Bible reads. The Jewish religion was the first religion to teach belief in one God.

The Ten Commandments also tell how people should act toward each other. It is wrong to steal, the commandments say. It is wrong to kill. The Hebrews were the first to look upon hurting others as a sin.

Moses bringing the Ten Commandments

The Promised Land

The Hebrews finally reached Canaan. They called it the "Promised Land." They believed it was the land that God had promised them. They settled there. They built towns. They followed their religion.

Holding onto the Promised Land was not always easy. A warlike people, the Philistines, lived nearby. The Philistines fought the Hebrews for their land.

There were 12 **tribes** of Hebrews. At first, the Philistines were able to **conquer** some of the tribes. Divided, the Hebrews were weak. But then, the tribes joined together under one king to fight the Philistines.

There is a famous story of a Hebrew shepherd boy named David. He fought a Philistine giant called Goliath. David killed Goliath with a rock from a slingshot. The Hebrews then won the war against the more powerful Philistines.

David later became king of the Hebrews. The town of Jerusalem became his **capital** city. Jerusalem was a religious center and a trading center.

When David died, his son, Solomon, became king. Solomon built a beautiful temple in Jerusalem. He built a fleet of fine sailing ships. King Solomon was known to be good and to be very, very wise. Under his rule, Jerusalem became a mighty city.

Israel and Judah

When King Solomon died, the Hebrew kingdom split. The tribes in the north made their own kingdom. They called it Israel. The people of Israel were the Israelites.

The tribes in the south formed the kingdom of Judah. Jerusalem was in Judah. The name of the Jewish religion came from the word Judah. And the people were called Jews.

The two kingdoms were in danger! For the next 200 years they fought. They fought each other. And they fought the powerful kingdoms that were all around them. These were the Egyptians, the Hittites, the Assyrians, the Babylonians, and the Persians. They all wanted control of the lands around Jerusalem.

At last the fierce neighbors were too strong. In 722 B.C. the Assyrians took over Israel. The Israelites were moved out or taken as slaves. About 150 years later, Judah fell to a Babylonian people known as Chaldeans. The Babylonian king destroyed Solomon's fine temple in Jerusalem.

And so it went. One power after another fought for the city that everyone wanted to control. Jerusalem was right in the middle of things. It came under many different rules. Today it is more than 2,500 years since the Babylonians destroyed the temple. Very little has changed. Different groups of people are still arguing over who should control Jerusalem.

The two main groups who are arguing over Jerusalem today are Israelis and Arabs. You will read more about this in Chapter 31.

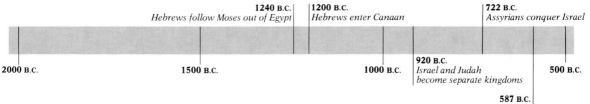

	1240 B.C. *Hebrews follow Moses out of Egypt*	**1200 B.C.** *Hebrews enter Canaan*			**722 B.C.** *Assyrians conquer Israel*	

2000 B.C.   1500 B.C.   1000 B.C.

920 B.C. *Israel and Judah become separate kingdoms*

587 B.C. *Babylonians take Jerusalem*

500 B.C.

Babylon

The Babylonians: The Rule of Law

Babylon was the capital city of the Babylonians. It stood on the banks of the Euphrates River. Little remains of it today. There are a few ruins in the middle of some dirt mounds. Archeologists have been digging through the ruins. They have learned that Babylon was one of the greatest cities of the ancient world. It contained some of the most beautiful temples and palaces to be found anywhere. They were decorated with blue glazed bricks and pictures of mythical beasts. People entered and left the city through huge bronze gates. Near the center of the city stood the great Tower of Babel. This tower is mentioned in the Bible. Not far from the tower were the Hanging Gardens of Babylon. The gardens were one of the wonders of the ancient world. They were built by a Babylonian king for his wife. She had been homesick for the beauty of her homeland in the mountains.

Name the "wonder of the world" in Egypt that you learned about in Chapter 4.

Babylon became an important city about 2000 B.C. This was nearly the same time that the Babylonians were destroying the Sumerian civilization. The Babylonians went on to build a large empire in what had been the land of the Sumerians.

GREAT NAMES IN HISTORY: Hammurabi

Hammurabi was one of the greatest kings of Babylonia. He ruled from about 1792 B.C. to 1750 B.C. Hammurabi created a system of laws. It was called the Code of Hammurabi. For the first time anywhere, there were laws to deal with almost every aspect of life. There were nearly 300 laws. They dealt with marriage and divorce, property and business, taxes, wages, loans, military service, and so forth. The Code also listed punishments for anyone who broke a law. People no longer had to depend on an "eye for an eye" when seeking justice. The Code was created to protect the rights of the individual citizen.

Today, we, too, follow a system of laws instead of an "eye for an eye." Which do you think is better? Why?

In time, the Babylonians were conquered by another people, the Assyrians. But some of the Babylonians' ideas about laws and justice have come down through the ages. They are included in our own laws today.

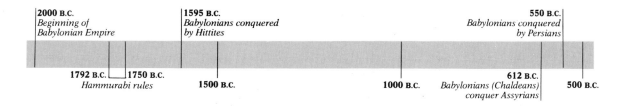

2000 B.C.
Beginning of Babylonian Empire

1792 B.C.   1750 B.C.
Hammurabi rules

1595 B.C.
Babylonians conquered by Hittites

1500 B.C.

1000 B.C.

612 B.C.
Babylonians (Chaldeans) conquer Assyrians

550 B.C.
Babylonians conquered by Persians

500 B.C.

History Practice

Write answers to the following questions on a separate sheet of paper.

1. Name two important Phoenician inventions.

2. What happened to Solomon's temple in Jerusalem in 587 B.C.?

3. Who was Hammurabi? What was the "Code of Hammurabi"?

The Hittites

The Hittites were warriors. The Hittites came to the eastern Mediterranean around 2000 B.C. No one knows for sure where they came from but they quickly swept through the lands called Anatolia. They found city-states already there. They conquered one after another. By 1650 B.C. the Hittites ruled all of these lands. Today this area is called Turkey.

The Hittites were mighty fighters. They used their might to create an empire. After they conquered Anatolia, they began attacking neighboring lands.

The Secret

The Hittites had a secret that gave them their great power. For hundreds of years, they were the only people who knew how to make iron. Iron was strong. It made better weapons. No other people could beat the Hittite warriors and their iron spears.

The Egyptians looked upon the Hittites with great respect. They thought of the Hittites as the only other great power around the Mediterranean. In 1283 B.C., after years of fighting with each other, the Hittites and the Egyptians made peace. To help keep the peace, a Hittite princess married an Egyptian pharaoh.

The Hittites and the Egyptians signed an agreement to keep the peace. It became the first recorded peace **treaty.**

In time other people learned the secret of making iron. The Hittites were no longer the strongest. Around 1200 B.C. new people came and attacked the Hittites. They were called the *Sea People.* They came from islands in the Mediterranean. They brought about the end of the Hittite empire.

The Assyrians

The Assyrians were another warrior civilization. At first Assyria was a small kingdom. But when the Hittite civilization ended, the Assyrians began to look toward an empire of their own.

The Assyrians built up a great army. It was the best trained army of the ancient world. The Assyrians sent their army to attack the neighboring kingdoms. As more and more cities were captured, the Assyrian empire grew.

The Assyrians built their capital city on the banks of the Tigris River. The city was named Ashur, after one of the Assyrians' many fierce gods.

Assyrian kings were hard rulers. They made their people pay heavy taxes. Assyrians lived under strict laws. Anyone who broke a law could be cruelly punished. Many law breakers were beaten. Some even had their ears cut off!

Assyrian King

The Assyrian Army

The Assyrian civilization was a military one. All Assyrian boys knew what their future held. All men had to go into the army. The Assyrians needed soldiers in order to keep their power. And the Assyrians were builders as well as fighters. They built military equipment to help them conquer cities. They beat down city walls and gates with their huge machines called siege engines. A city under **siege** from fierce Assyrians stood little chance.

The Assyrians were not kind to the cities that they took. Sometimes they burned the city and killed the people who lived there. Often they took the people as slaves.

Sometimes, after they captured a city, the Assyrians acted as its new rulers. The people from the city had to pay **tribute** to the Assyrian king. If they did not pay the high price, they were punished.

Assyrian Developments

The Assyrian civilization did leave some things behind besides a successful military record. They built fine buildings and statues. They invented siege machines. But they also built machines to help lift water from the river into canals.

The Assyrians were among the first people to have a library. The library stored clay tablets with writings from the ancient world.

Even the fierce Assyrians were defeated at last. By 670 B.C. the empire was so big that it was hard to control. It began to break up. In 612 B.C. the Assyrian city of Nineveh was under siege itself. The Assyrian empire came to an end. The Assyrians had been conquered by a new Babylonian people—the Chaldeans.

2000 B.C.
Hittites arrive in Anatolia

1200 B.C.
*Hittites conquered by Sea People;
Beginning of Assyrian Empire*

670 B.C.
*Assyrian Empire
begins to break up*

1650 B.C.
Beginning of Hittite Empire

1500 B.C.

1283 B.C.
*Hittite peace treaty
with Egypt*

1000 B.C.

612 B.C.
End of Assyrian Empire

500 B.C.

Chapter Review

Chapter Summary

- There were many kingdoms around the eastern Mediterranean Sea.

- The Phoenicians were sailors and traders.

- The Phoenicians developed an alphabet much like ours.

- The Hebrews started the Jewish religion and were the first to believe in one god.

- The Hebrews left slavery in Egypt to follow Moses to the Promised Land.

- The Hebrews lived by rules called the Ten Commandments.

- The Babylonian king Hammurabi created one of the earliest systems of laws.

- The Hittites and the Assyrians were both warlike civilizations.

- First the Hittites, and then the Assyrians, controlled the eastern Mediterranean world.

Chapter Quiz

A. Checking Your Facts

nomads	navigate	tribute	conquer	siege

Complete each sentence below. Use the correct word from the box. Rewrite the sentences on a separate sheet of paper.

1. Stronger tribes were able to _____ weaker ones.

2. _____ are people who wander from place to place.

3. The Phoenicians used the stars to _____ .

4. The Assyrians attacked cities with huge _____ engines.

5. The people of the city had to pay _____ to the king.

B. Think About It!

Write answers to the following questions on a separate sheet of paper.

1. Why did the Hebrews call Canaan the "Promised Land"?

2. How was the Hebrew religion different from others in the ancient world? Can you think of any other religion today that has something in common with Judaism? Name that religion. What is similar about it?

3. The Hittites had a secret weapon that helped them become a great military power. Not so long ago, the United States had a secret, the atomic bomb. This weapon helped it become the world's greatest military power. Do you think it is good for a country to have secret weapons? Why or why not?

Chapter 6

Early Civilizations of India, China, and the Americas

The Great Wall of China is about 4,000 miles long. Why do you think the Chinese built this wall?

Chapter Learning Objectives

- Name the social classes of the Indian caste system.
- Explain why the Chinese empire remained separated from the rest of the world.
- Tell why it was possible for large Chinese families to live together happily.
- Name two early civilizations in the Americas.
- Name three new crops grown in the Americas.

Words to Know

ancestors   people from whom one is descended
castes   the social classes into which the people of India are divided
classes   groupings of people according to social rank
dynasty   a series of rulers who belong to the same family
isolated   set apart from others; alone
maize   Indian corn
shrine   a place of worship believed to be sacred or holy

Ancient India: The Indus River Valley

One of the world's earliest civilizations grew up around the Indus River. These lands are now known as India and Pakistan. The people, like so many others, settled near the river. They learned to irrigate their fields and to grow crops.

The people along the Indus made pottery, jewelry, and statues. They traded goods and ideas with the civilizations of the Fertile Crescent.

One of the main cities in the Indus River Valley was Mohenjo-daro. It was a fine, beautiful city. But it met a very sad end. Mohenjo-daro was a neat, well-planned city. It had long, straight main streets. Covered drainage systems ran under the streets. The people built brick houses. They even built apartment houses.

Life was good in Mohenjo-daro. The streets were clean. There were public swimming pools and bath houses. People could cool off on hot Indus Valley days. Brick courtyards circled shaded wells so that people and animals could drink in comfort. Many houses in Mohenjo-daro had their own indoor wells and tile-lined baths. Wheat and date palms grew on farms outside the city.

Mohenjo-daro stood peacefully for close to 1,000 years. Then, around 1500 B.C., the city was attacked. People from the north, the Aryans, swooped down on Mohenjo-daro. The Aryans showed no mercy. They ran through the streets of Mohenjo-daro killing most of the people.

The Aryans believed that they were born to conquer and control. The word *Aryan* meant *nobleman* or *owner of land*. The Aryans soon controlled all of the Indus River Valley.

The Aryans were fierce conquerors. But they also brought new ideas. They became known for making beautiful cloth decorated with gold and silver. And they also became known for their skilled doctors and mathematicians.

The Indus River Valley

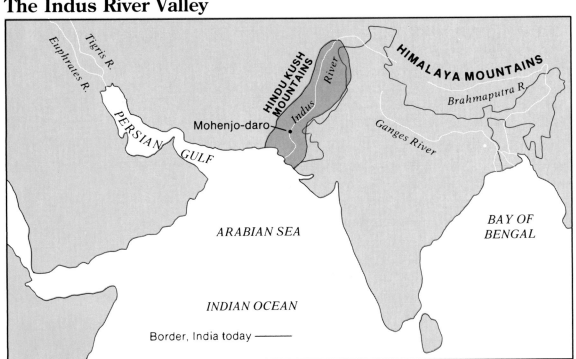

Map Skills

The Indus River flows between which two mountain ranges?

India's Caste System

The Aryans believed that they were better than the people they conquered. Their religion was based on the idea that some people are born "better" than others. Their religion developed into the Hindu religion. It divided all people into social **classes**, or **castes.** The Aryans divided people into four castes ranging from higher to lower.

1. priests and scholars
2. rulers and warriors
3. crafts workers, merchants, and farmers
4. unskilled workers

The Aryans called the people they conquered *outcastes* or *untouchables.* The outcastes had no place in society. Any Aryan who married one of the conquered people would also become an outcaste.

Caste laws were strict. A person born into a certain caste would always stay there. No one could ever in his or her life rise to a higher caste. If somebody were good and obeyed all the rules, that person would be born into a higher caste in his or her "next life." If a Hindu led a bad life, he or she could be born again as an outcaste.

The Aryans conquered the Indus Valley first. Then some of their tribes moved on to the east and to the south. They conquered one kingdom after another. The people who had been living there were forced to flee farther south. The Aryan tribes settled down in the lands that they conquered. They formed a number of city-states. Each one was ruled by a *raja* or prince. The rajas lived in fine palaces. Each raja had a highly trained army to protect his lands.

Do you believe it is ever right to *cast out* anybody from society? Why or why not?

China: The Yellow River Valley

They called themselves the *Black-haired People*. They lived in the valley of the Huang Ho, or Yellow River, in China. Their civilization grew up apart from the rest of the world. Steep mountains, wide deserts, and deep seas circled their lands. Northern China and the people of the Yellow River Valley were cut off from other civilizations.

Most of the people in the Yellow River Valley were farmers. They fought floods that were so terrible the Yellow River became known as "China's Sorrow."

The Shang Dynasty, Yellow River Valley, China

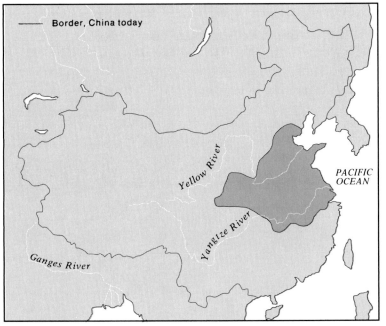

Map Skills

Name two large rivers in China. Into which ocean do these rivers flow?

They dug pitlike houses in the ground and wove roofs of grass. Their kings lived in palaces made of wood and mud.

These early Chinese learned to write. They cut letters, or characters, into animal bones. They kept a record of their own history. It is one of the world's oldest written histories.

The people of the Yellow River Valley made fine cloth. They raised silkworms. They carefully unwound the long, thin threads that the silkworms spun. They wove the threads into silk cloth.

The Chinese had a special feeling for their **ancestors**. They also showed honor toward their homes, their families, and their land. There were many rules of courtesy in the Chinese culture. Those rules made it possible for large families to live together happily.

The Chinese culture did not change for many thousands of years. This is because people honored the ways of their ancestors. Also, the land was cut off from the rest of the world.

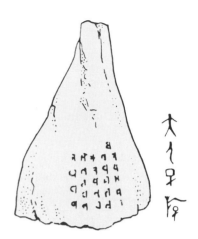

Chinese characters carved on bone

Chinese Dynasties

A period of rule in China is called a **dynasty**. For about 500 years *Shang* kings ruled the Yellow River Valley. This period is called the Shang dynasty.

Around 1028 B.C. a more warlike people, the *Chou*, came to power. The Chou leaders developed systems of irrigation and flood control. And they extended their rule southward. Chinese civilization now reached from the Yellow River to the Chang, or Yangtze River. The powerful Chou dynasty lasted for more than 750 years.

The name *China* may have come from Ch'in. This was a family that ruled China from 221 B.C. until 206 B.C. This period was called the Ch'in dynasty. Shih Huang Ti was the first Ch'in emperor. And his empire was the first Chinese empire with a strong central government.

Shih Huang Ti had the Great Wall of China built. The country of China had many natural barriers to keep foreigners out. Mountains and deserts lay all around. The only border that could be easily crossed was to the north. Enemies crossed this northern border to raid Chinese farms. The Chinese of an earlier period had also tried to protect the border. Short walls had been built by the Chou dynasty. Shih Huang Ti decided to connect these walls. He wanted to build one great stone wall. Work on the wall continued on and off until around A.D. 1600.

The Great Wall of China is the only man-made structure on Earth that can be seen from outer space! It is about 4,000 miles long, the longest structure ever built! The Great Wall is 25 feet high and about 15 feet wide at the top. It helped to protect the northern borders from invaders, especially those on horseback. It also further **isolated** China from the rest of the world.

Shih Huang Ti had built a wall that would last for thousands of years. Unfortunately, the Ch'in dynasty only lasted a few years. It was expensive to build the wall. So Shih forced people to pay very high taxes. Many people began to hate the Ch'in dynasty. Soon after Shih died, in 210 B.C., a civil war broke out. The Ch'in dynasty quickly collapsed. By 202 B.C. the Han dynasty had gained control of China.

The Great Wall of China was built to prevent people from entering China. Another famous wall — the Berlin Wall — was built by East Germany in 1961 to prevent people from *leaving* the country.

GREAT NAMES IN HISTORY: Confucius

Confucius was born in 551 B.C. For more than 2,000 years his ideas were the single strongest influence on Chinese life. Confucius gave people rules to live by. He was most interested in how people treated each other.

"Never do to others what you would not like them to do to you," Confucius taught. He taught that family life was most important. In China large family groups lived together. Grandparents, parents, and children usually shared the same house. So if family members loved and honored each other, the family would enjoy good fortune. Old people were honored. Ancestors were respected. Respect for the ways of the ancestors kept Chinese culture from changing.

Confucius prized scholarship. Only well-educated people could be government officials. The greatest honor came to a family if a son became a scholar. Then he could study to take the government exams. A young man who passed the exams could become an official.

For centuries in China, people had to take tests to hold government jobs. It was the world's first civil service system.

History Practice

Write answers to the following questions on a separate sheet of paper.

1. What is the Indian caste system?

2. Name the three most important things that Confucius taught the Chinese.

3. Why do you think so many civilizations grew up near rivers?

The Americas: Faraway Lands

There were faraway lands that the people of the Middle East knew nothing about. For the most part, these lands were wild, thick woods and deep jungles. They were lands that would one day be known as North and South America.

A few tribes of people lived scattered across the Americas. These people would later be known as Native Americans, or Indians. Many scientists believe that these tribes first came from Asia. They say that the tribes traveled across a bridge of land and ice at the Bering Strait. Such a land bridge would have stretched 56 miles between Asia and Alaska. No trace of a land bridge exists now.

Give one possible reason why the land bridge no longer exists. (Hint: Think about what happened at the end of the Ice Age.)

Why would these people have crossed the land bridge? Perhaps they were following animal herds. Then, over thousands of years, they kept on traveling south. Some stayed in North America. Others continued on to Central and South America.

Possible route to the Americas

Map Skills

Which body of water did the land bridge cross? Which part of the Americas did the tribes from Asia reach first?

For a long time, the people hunted and fished for their food. Then farming settlements began to spring up. This took place about 5,000 years after the people of the Middle East and Asia began farming. The new lands produced new crops. Farmers grew **maize**, or Indian corn. They grew squash and tomatoes and beans.

South American farmers grew cotton as early as 3000 B.C. They raised herds of tall, woolly animals called llamas. They wove the llama wool into beautiful cloth.

The Olmecs

A people called the Olmecs built what might have been the first real city in the Americas. Their city was in Mexico, just west of the Gulf of Mexico. Archeologists have discovered Olmec jade and pottery dating back to 1200 B.C.

The Olmecs carved giant heads out of stone. Some of their carvings are more than nine feet tall. The Olmecs also built **shrines** atop high mounds of earth. The Olmecs did an amazing job. They worked without metal tools and had not invented the wheel.

The Olmecs left some inventions behind. They had a system of counting. And they came up with a simple calendar. The Olmec civilization lasted for more than 1,000 years.

The Mayas

Just as the Olmec civilization ended, the Mayas arose. The Mayan civilization began in southern Mexico and Central America. The Mayas cleared jungles and built towns. They built temples to the gods of rain and of earth.

The Mayas used what the Olmecs had learned. They studied the Olmec calendar. Then they watched the sun, the moon, and the stars. They made their own calendar. It showed many feast days set aside to honor their gods. The Mayan civilization was strongest from about 250 B.C. until A.D. 800.

Mayan temple, Chichen Itza, Yucatan, Mexico

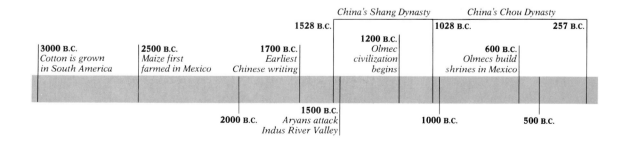

China's Shang Dynasty | *China's Chou Dynasty*

1528 B.C. | **1028 B.C.** | **257 B.C.**

3000 B.C.
Cotton is grown in South America

2500 B.C.
Maize first farmed in Mexico

1700 B.C.
Earliest Chinese writing

1200 B.C.
Olmec civilization begins

600 B.C.
Olmecs build shrines in Mexico

2000 B.C.

1500 B.C.
Aryans attack Indus River Valley

1000 B.C.

500 B.C.

Chapter Review

Chapter Summary

- An early civilization developed along the Indus River Valley in what is now India and Pakistan.

- Aryans conquered the Indus River Valley settlements.

- The Aryans brought a caste system that divided all people into social classes.

- An early Chinese civilization grew up along the Huang Ho, or Yellow River.

- Confucius was born in 551 B.C. His ideas were to influence Chinese life for more than 2,000 years.

- Emperor Shih Huang Ti ordered the building of the Great Wall of China.

- Tribes of people probably crossed a land bridge from Asia to the North American continent. These tribes moved south and settled in Central and South America.

- The Olmecs were one of the earliest civilizations in the Americas. They built a city in Mexico. They carved giant stone heads and invented a simple calendar.

- The Mayas built cities in the jungles of southern Mexico and Central America.

Chapter Quiz

A. Checking Your Facts

Choose the correct word or words to make each sentence a true statement. Rewrite the sentences on a separate sheet of paper.

1. People from whom one is descended are (descendants / ancestors).

2. The word "Aryan" meant (owner of land / maker of cloth).

3. The (Yellow / Yangtze) River became known as "China's Sorrow."

4. The building of the Great Wall of China began during the (Ch'in / Chou) dynasty.

5. Maize, or Indian (rice / corn), was grown by South American farmers thousands of years ago.

B. Think About It!

Write answers to the following questions on a separate sheet of paper.

1. Could a person born in India to a family of farmers hope to go to school and become a teacher? Why or why not?

2. Think about all the different ancient civilizations you have studied. Were some of their inventions the same? Name some that were the same.

3. China remained isolated from the rest of the world for many, many years. What do you think caused this? Do you think it is good or bad for a country to be isolated? Why?

Unit Two Review

Write answers to the following questions on a separate sheet of paper.

1. Name three Sumerian inventions. What did the Sumerians use as money?

2. How did purple become known as a royal color?

3. Do you think the Babylonians were lucky to have Hammurabi as a leader? Why or why not?

4. Why were the Hittites able to conquer cities and build an empire?

5. Name two inventions of the Assyrians. In what ways were the Assyrians cruel?

6. Why was the Yellow River known as "China's Sorrow"?

7. What "rule to live by" did Confucius teach the Chinese people? Do you think this was a good rule? Why or why not?

8. Following Confucius's teachings, how did the Chinese choose their government officials?

9. How do scientists think that people got from Asia to America?

10. Name three crops that were grown in the Americas.

The Origins of Western Civilization: Greece and Rome

Chapter 7

Greece: The Golden Age

The ancient Greeks built the Parthenon on a hill high above the city of Athens. What was the purpose of this building?

Chapter Learning Objectives

- Contrast two different ways that Greek city-states were governed.
- Compare life in Sparta and in Athens.
- Name two Greek gods or goddesses.
- Explain why the time following the Persian Wars is called the "Golden Age."
- Name three Greek thinkers.

Words to Know

athlete   a person trained to take part in competitive sports. The ancient Greek word *athlete* means "one who tries to win a prize in a contest."

citizen   a person who has certain rights and duties because he or she lives in a particular city or town

constitution   the laws and rules of a government

democracy   a government that gives the people the ruling power

jury   a group of people who listen to the facts and decide if a person on trial is guilty or not guilty

military   having to do with soldiers or the armed forces

myths   stories, often about gods or goddesses, that are handed down through the years and sometimes used to explain natural events

plague   a deadly disease that spreads quickly

revolt   to rise up against a government; to refuse to obey the people in charge

tyrant   a ruler who has complete power

The Greeks were people with ideas. Greek thinkers asked questions about everything. They wanted to learn as much about their world as they could.

Most early civilizations were mainly farming societies. But the Greek civilization was different. Greece is a very rocky land with many mountains. Much of Greece made poor farmland. The Greeks could not grow much wheat or other grains. Instead, they raised grapevines and olive trees. And Greece is surrounded by the sea on almost every side. So the Greeks took to the sea and became traders.

The Aegean Sea and the Mediterranean Sea made perfect travel lanes. The Greeks traded with most of the Mediterranean world. Greek traders set up colonies in the lands they visited. Greek culture spread across the seas.

Remember the Phoenicians? Why did they also become sailors and traders?

Ancient Greece

Map Skills

Name three Greek cities. Greece is surrounded by which two bodies of water?

Greek harbors were always busy. The air was filled with sounds. There was the clink of Greek coins and foreign coins. There was the chatter of many different languages as people of the world met. Merchants traded wheat for olive oil. Ships from Egypt unloaded papyrus. Ebony and ivory came in from Africa.

Greek City-States

The earliest people who settled in Greece began to build villages about 1500 B.C. As time passed, the small villages grew into city-states. Through trading, the city-states became wealthy. By about 750 B.C. the Greeks had begun to build colonies in other areas of the Mediterranean. Some Greeks settled on the Greek islands. But many others traveled as far as southern Italy, France, Spain, and Portugal. They built cities there. Naples, Syracuse, Marseilles, and Lisbon began as Greek cities. Cities were also built in western Turkey and on the shores of the Black Sea.

On the Greek mainland, the city-states were becoming more powerful. The city-states were separated from each other by rugged mountain ranges. For this reason there was limited contact between the city-states. Each one developed in its own way.

Each city-state had its own government. And each had its own idea about the way people should live. Some of the city-states were ruled by a **tyrant**, a single powerful man. Some of the tyrants were cruel and unjust. But some of them ruled fairly. Other city-states let citizens vote and have a say in the government. This type of city-state was the earliest example of a **democracy**.

Because the city-states were so different from each other, they often fought among themselves. A tyrant with big ideas would decide that the time had come to expand his rule. He would make plans to attack a nearby city-state. He might convince other city-states to join him. There was a constantly shifting pattern of friendship and hostility between the different city-states. This was a very unstable political situation. It would later lead to a major war between two of the largest city-states, Athens and Sparta.

The Acropolis

Each city-state was made up of a city circled by villages and farms. The farms provided food for the citizens. The city offered protection from invaders.

The Greeks usually built their city-states near a high hill. The hill was called the Acropolis. On that hill, they built special buildings—temples, theaters, and banks.

The people who lived in Athens built a beautiful temple atop their Acropolis. It was built to honor the goddess Athena. The temple was called the Parthenon.

Athens and Sparta

Athens and Sparta were the most powerful Greek city-states. Their citizens spoke the same language. They believed in the same gods. But life in Athens was very different from life in Sparta.

The Spartans lived in a **military** society. Sparta's government was led by a small group of men. They were most interested in keeping Sparta a great military power. Spartan children belonged to the state. A healthy boy was turned over to the government at the age of seven. He was raised to be a soldier. He was taught to fight and to stand up under pain. He had to obey orders without question. Soldiers defeated in battle were not allowed to return home.

Today we use the word *Spartan* to mean harsh or strict.

If a baby boy were born with something wrong, he might be left on a hillside to die. The Spartans only wanted boys who could grow up to be soldiers. And Spartans had little use for girls. Girls and women were seldom seen in public. They kept to their houses. The Spartans were great warriors. But they left the world little in the way of ideas or art or music.

The Spartans, like most of the Mediterranean peoples, kept slaves. Most of the work in the city was done by slave labor. The Spartan army was often kept busy fighting other city-states. At other times it had the job of keeping rebel slaves in line.

Spartan warriors (on left)

Although life was harsh in Sparta, things were very different in Athens. The Athenians gave less thought to warfare. They were more interested in enjoying life.

Athens was a wealthy city. The Athenians decided that their wealth gave them more time to enjoy the beauties of life. They wanted their city to be glorious. They built the Parthenon. Their marble statues show the human body in its ideal form. The Athenians put on plays in huge outdoor theaters. For the first time, plays were written about how people think and act. Some of these plays are still performed today.

The Athenians took time to ask questions about their world. Great teachers, like Socrates, led the Greeks to ask, "What makes people good? What makes people evil?" "Always ask questions," Socrates taught. So the Greeks questioned, and they learned.

Do you think it is ever right for people to own other people? Why or why not?

Some Greeks even questioned slavery. That slavery might be wrong was a brand new idea. Most of the ancient world had slaves as laborers. In Athens, too, work was done by slaves. But a few Athenian thinkers were possibly the first to ask, "Is it right for people to own other people? Is it right to force a person to labor for another?"

LEARN MORE ABOUT IT: Greek Religion

The Greeks believed that people were very important. They celebrated the human mind and the human body. Therefore, their gods were much like humans. The Greeks worshipped many gods and goddesses. They gave each one a name and a humanlike form and personality. The gods and goddesses, according to the Greek storytellers, lived on top of Mount Olympus. This is the highest mountain in Greece. There, they enjoyed life. They laughed and they argued just as humans do. They played tricks on each other and on the humans they ruled.

Zeus was the king of the Greek gods. His wife was Hera, queen of the gods. The Parthenon on the Athenian Acropolis was built to honor Athena. She was the goddess of wisdom and learning.

The Greeks told **myths,** which are stories about their gods. The myths explained things in nature. They told of the doings of the gods and goddesses.

Myths were told about jealous gods and angry gods. And there were gods who fell in love with humans and gods who helped humans. Greek myths made exciting stories.

Democracy

In Athens's early years, government was in the hands of landowners. If a man owned land, he was a **citizen**. He had a voice in running the city-state. As the city grew, many merchants and business people, shippers and traders became wealthy. They did not own land, but they wanted a say in city government. They wanted to be citizens. A **revolt** led to a new government. In 508 B.C. this government drew up an Athenian **constitution**. Under the new laws, all free men were citizens. But women and slaves did not have the rights of citizenship.

A citizen had the right to vote. And he was expected to hold office if called upon, sit on a **jury**, and serve in the army. The Athenian democracy was a government "by the people." The problem was that so many of "the people" (women and slaves) were not allowed to be citizens then.

History Practice

Write answers to the following questions on a separate sheet of paper.

1. What are two different ways that Greek city-states were governed?

2. Why did Greek city-states often fight with each other?

3. What type of buildings did the Greeks build on the Acropolis?

The Persian Wars

As Greek city-states grew strong and wealthy, another land began to look toward Greece. The Persian Empire under Cyrus the Great had become the strongest military power in the world. Around 505 B.C. Persia attacked and conquered the Greek colonies in Lydia. This was along the coast of what is now called Turkey. About 60 years later, the Greeks in Lydia revolted. King Darius I of Persia crushed their uprising. Then he sent his huge army to invade Greece.

In 490 B.C. the Persian armies headed for Athens. On the plain of Marathon, the Athenians beat the mighty Persians! An excited Greek citizen ran 26 miles (40 kilometers) to Athens to spread the good news. An Olympic event of today is named after that run from Marathon to Athens.

But the Persians were not ready to give up. Darius's son, Xerxes, continued the war. About ten years later, Xerxes led an even stronger force into Greece. The Greek city-states put aside their quarrels to fight the common enemy. Xerxes's navy attacked. Spartans fought the Persian invaders long and hard. But the Persians were too strong. Xerxes's men attacked the city of Athens next. They destroyed the Parthenon and burned much of the beautiful city.

Xerxes left Athens thinking that he had won the war. But he was in for a surprise. His men met the Athenian navy off the harbor of Salamis. There was a great sea battle. The Persians were defeated. The Greeks sent the Persians back across the Aegean Sea. And Greece was left to enjoy a time of peace.

If the Persians had conquered Greece, our lives today might be very different. Why do you think this is so?

The Golden Age

The peace following the Persian Wars lasted for about 50 years. During that time, Athens grew in power and strength. It became the greatest city-state in Greece.

Athens collected money from the other city-states. The Athenians insisted that their navy must be kept strong in order to protect all of Greece.

A great Athenian leader named Pericles rose to power in 461 B.C. Pericles helped the Athenians continue their democratic government. He used some of the money collected from other city-states to rebuild the Parthenon.

Athens flowered with Pericles as its leader. It was a time known as the "Age of Pericles," or the "Golden Ages of Athens." The Athenians, at peace now, had time to study science and geography. They wrote their greatest plays and created their finest statues.

Athenians created their greatest art and architecture during the Golden Age.

Athens of the Golden Age was one of the most beautiful cities in the world. Many other Greek city-states followed the Athenians' way of life and their ideas of democracy.

But Sparta continued as a military state. The Spartans did not like the way Athens was building and growing. And they were angry that Athens had been collecting money from the rest of Greece.

The Peloponnesian War

Peace ended in 431 B.C., when Sparta led some of the other city-states against Athens. Sparta was a land power with a strong army. Athens was a sea power. Most of its strength was in its navy. Both cities fought for control of Greece. The war between Athens and Sparta was called the Peloponnesian War. It was named after the Peloponnesus, the part of Greece in which Sparta was located. This war went on for 27 years!

The Spartans tried to cut off supplies to Athens to starve the people. But the Athenians held on even though the Spartans were among the world's best fighters.

Then a terrible **plague** broke out in the city of Athens. One-fourth of the Athenian people died during the plague. Their leader, Pericles, was among those who died.

Athens could no longer hold out against Sparta. In 404 B.C. Athens surrendered to Sparta.

Gifts from the Greeks

Greek thought and Greek works are very much a part of life today. Greek ideas in building show up in modern buildings. Greek statues still influence today's artists. The style of art and architecture the Greeks developed is called the "classical" style.

Today's students still read the works of Greek thinkers like Socrates, Plato, and Aristotle. "Know yourself," the great teachers said. "Ask questions. Search for the truth."

The Greeks were the first people to ask, "What is the world made of? Why is it the way it is?" They developed ideas about the sun, the Earth, and the stars.

"The Earth is round," Eratosthenes said. "The Earth moves around the sun," Aristarchus said. Euclid and Pythagoras helped invent geometry.

We can also thank the Greeks for a model of a democracy. "Our government is called a democracy because power is in the hands of the whole people," said the Athenian leader Pericles.

Greek words and ideas show up in our own language. *Astronomy, biology, geography,* and *geology* are all taken from the Greek language. So are the words *music, theater, drama, comedy,* and *tragedy.*

Classical Greek columns

The word **athlete** comes from the Greeks, too. Our Olympic Games are athletic contests. They are modeled after those played by Greek athletes so long ago.

The first known Olympic games took place in 776 B.C. Early Olympic games were held to honor the gods. They were held every four years at the temple of Zeus in Olympia. All wars in Greece had to stop when it was time for the Olympic games. The athletes came from Athens and Sparta and all the other city-states.

The earliest Olympic games were just foot races. Later the Greeks added boxing, wrestling, jumping, discus throwing, chariot racing, and other sporting events.

Today, just as in early Greece, it is a great honor to win an Olympic event. Winners get medals of gold and silver and bronze. In ancient Greece the winners were crowned with a circle of laurel leaves. The athletes brought glory to their city-state as well as to themselves.

The Greek leader Pericles saw the greatness of Greece in the Golden Age. He was proud of the wonders of his city, Athens.

"Mighty indeed are the marks and monuments of our empire . . . ," Pericles said. "Future ages will wonder at us."

Where do the athletes come from in today's Olympic Games?

The Discus Thrower

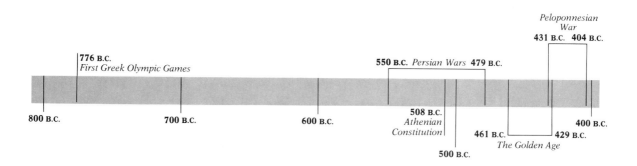

Peloponnesian War
431 B.C. 404 B.C.

776 B.C.
First Greek Olympic Games

550 B.C. *Persian Wars* 479 B.C.

800 B.C.   700 B.C.   600 B.C.

508 B.C.
Athenian Constitution

461 B.C.   429 B.C.
The Golden Age

400 B.C.

500 B.C.

Chapter Review

Chapter Summary

- Most of Greece's wealth came from trading rather than from farming.

- Greece was divided into city-states, each one with its own government.

- Athens and Sparta were two powerful city-states.

- Athens was a democracy.

- Sparta had a military government.

- The Greeks worshipped many humanlike gods and goddesses.

- The Greeks fought the Persians, and they drove the Persian army away.

- Quarrels between Athens and Sparta turned into the Peloponnesian War. Sparta won.

- The Greeks were great thinkers. Because they questioned their world, they learned.

Chapter Quiz

A. Checking Your Facts

Choose the correct word or words to make each of the sentences below a true statement. Rewrite the sentences on a separate sheet of paper.

1. Some Greek city-states were ruled by a (truant/tyrant).

2. The Greek thinker (Socrates/Plato) taught people to ask questions about their world.

3. The goddess (Athena/Hera) was the wife of the Greek god Zeus.

4. In 490 B.C. the Persian ruler (Xerxes/Darius) sent his armies to attack Athens.

5. The Peloponnesian War was the war between Athens and (Salamis/Sparta).

B. Think About It!

Write answers to the following questions on a separate sheet of paper.

1. If you were a Greek of long ago, would you rather have lived in Sparta or in Athens? Give at least two reasons for your answer.

2. Which people could be citizens of Athens? Do you think Athens was as democratic as our own country? Why or why not?

3. Who led the Athenians during the "Golden Age"? Why do you think it was called the "Golden Age"?

Chapter 8

Alexander the Great

Alexander was a king at 20. By the time he died, at age 33, the whole world had heard of him. Why was he called *Alexander the Great*?

Chapter Learning Objectives

- Locate Alexander's empire on a map.
- Explain how King Philip II of Macedonia became ruler of Greece.
- Tell why Alexander was called the "Great Conqueror."
- Explain why Alexander made Babylon the capital of his empire.
- Describe what happened to Alexander's empire after his death.

Words to Know

ambition   the drive to become powerful, successful, or famous
assassinate   to murder a leader or other important person
campaign   a series of battles all aimed at one military end
conqueror   a person who gains control by winning a war
generals   high military officers

King Philip of Macedonia

The Peloponnesian War was over. The Greek city-states were now under Sparta's rule. But they still argued with each other.

To the north was a land called Macedonia. It was ruled by a king named Philip II. Macedonia had always been poor. But things changed when Philip became king. Philip saw to it that Macedonians farmed their good soil. He sent out Macedonian traders. He built new roads. King Philip II had ideas.

Philip built up the Macedonian army. He built war machinery. He taught his men new ways of fighting. Philip soon had a strong army of foot soldiers and soldiers on horseback.

King Philip had an eye to the future. His plan was to conquer the great Persian Empire.

But to do that, Philip needed military strength. He needed more strength than he had with only Macedonia behind him. Philip wanted the power of all the Greek armies.

King Philip told some of the nearby city-states about his plan. They agreed to join him. But Philip needed more power. He needed the largest city-states, Athens and Thebes, behind him. So he used all his military know-how along with his well-trained men and their fine machinery. And Philip conquered Athens and Thebes.

Soon all of Greece fell under Macedonian control. All except Sparta, that is. Philip never conquered Sparta.

Now Philip was ready for war with the Persians. But King Philip II would never lead his men into Persia. By now he had made enemies. There was a plot to **assassinate** him. And before he could begin his **campaign** against Persia, he was killed.

Philip's Son

Philip had a son, Alexander. Alexander was not an ordinary boy. From his father, Alexander inherited **ambition** and a love of power. Philip taught his son all about warfare and leadership. Alexander's mother, Olympias, was said to be very smart and very hot-tempered. Alexander, too, was bright and very easily angered.

As a boy, Alexander seemed almost fearless. Stories tell of the young Prince Alexander taming a certain horse. No other person in the kingdom could ride it. Alexander named that horse Bucephalus. Bucephalus would carry Alexander across an empire!

King Philip always thought highly of the Greek way of life and of Greek ideas. His son, Alexander, was to have the best of teachers—the Greek thinker, Aristotle. At age 14, Alexander began his lessons.

Aristotle taught Alexander to love Greek stories of heroes and adventure. He taught the boy about far-off lands and about other cultures. Aristotle saw to it that

Why do you think that Philip never conquered Sparta?

Do you think it is good to have ambition? Why or why not?

Alexander took part in sports, too. The young boy kept his body and his mind ready and strong.

By the time Alexander was 18, he was able to take a command in his father's army. Alexander was 20 when his father was killed. Now he was ready to take over as king of Macedonia. He was ready to become a **conqueror.**

Aristotle

Alexander, the Great Conqueror

Philip II had planned to conquer an empire. Greece would be the center of that empire. And Greek learning and culture would spread from there. Now that job fell to his son, Alexander.

Since birth, Alexander had been raised to be a ruler and a warrior. He was ready for the job. Alexander and the Macedonian army headed for Persia.

The next two years saw Alexander and his men crossing the Middle East. They conquered one land after another. Then in 334 B.C. Alexander began his campaign against Persia. In 333 B.C. Alexander did battle with the king of the Persian Empire, Darius III. Alexander won the battle, but King Darius escaped.

On through the Persian Empire, on to Syria, swept the conquering Macedonians. They attacked the great Phoenician city of Tyre. Alexander ordered his men to build a raised road over the sea to reach the city. The battle at Tyre was one of his greatest military victories.

Alexander in Egypt

Alexander was out to conquer the whole world! After taking over Phoenicia, he moved south, toward Egypt. Alexander's army easily took that country.

The Egyptians had been under harsh Persian rule. They were glad to have Alexander as their new ruler. Some Egyptians even hailed Alexander as the son of an Egyptian god.

Alexander built a city on the Mediterranean coast of Egypt. He named it after himself, like many other cities he had built. Egypt's *Alexandria* became the most famous of the Alexandrias.

One of Alexander's **generals** was named Ptolemy. Alexander left him to rule as Egypt's king. Ptolemy's family would rule Egypt for 300 years.

LEARN MORE ABOUT IT: Alexandria

Alexander drew up plans for building the city of Alexandria in Egypt in 332 B.C. The Ptolemies continued to carry out Alexander's plan after his death. The city grew rapidly. It became one of the largest and most important cities of the ancient world. Within 200 years after it was founded, more than a million people were living in Alexandria.

It was a beautiful city. Many of its buildings were Greek in style. A giant lighthouse there rose 370 feet high. It was built of white marble and was known as one of the wonders of the world. The huge fire at the top of the lighthouse could be seen by sailors 30 miles away.

Alexandria was also famous for its fine schools and its library. The library contained more than 700,000 scrolls. A *scroll* is a roll of paper or parchment with writing on it. Scrolls were used instead of books in those days. The library of Alexandria was the largest in the world. It became a famous center of learning and culture. The glory of Greece had come to Egypt.

History Practice

Write answers to the following questions on a separate sheet of paper.

1. What did King Philip II of Macedonia need in order to conquer the Persian Empire?

2. How did Philip become ruler of Greece?

3. Why did Philip choose a Greek teacher for young Alexander?

The End of the Persian Empire

Alexander was more interested in conquering than in ruling. Just as with Ptolemy in Egypt, he would set up many more kings to rule other lands. When Alexander felt his work in Egypt was done, he moved on. He still wanted the whole world.

In 331 B.C. Alexander met King Darius III of Persia again. Alexander defeated Darius. And, once again, Darius escaped. But Alexander had no more trouble with his old enemy. King Darius was to die that same year, killed by his own men. With Darius gone, Alexander was the ruler of all the Persian Empire.

The city of Persepolis, in southwestern Persia, was the greatest city of the Persian Empire. Much of the wealth of the Empire was stored in the palaces of Persepolis. Alexander and his army easily captured the city. They killed most of the people who lived there. They took the rest as slaves. The Macedonians took all the treasures and then burned the Persian palaces. In 480 B.C. the Persians had burned Athens. Now Alexander had gotten even.

Then Alexander looked east. What was left for him in the world? India would be next.

Alexander's Empire

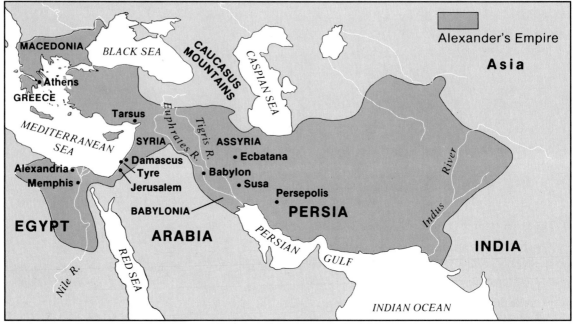

Map Skills

Name three cities in Egypt. Which three rivers did Alexander have to cross to get to India?

Alexander in the Valley of the Indus

Alexander the Great arrived in India. The Aryan rajas along the Indus River battled the Macedonian soldiers. The Aryans rode great, lumbering war elephants. But Alexander's men, riding horseback, were faster. Alexander conquered the Indus River Valley. He then wanted to go on, deeper into India. But his men were tired. Heavy rains had come, and marching was hard. They wanted to go home.

"Back to Greece," they cried.

"On through India," Alexander demanded.

But his armies insisted on turning back. They would go no farther. And Alexander had to give up his campaign.

The Death of Alexander

Alexander was 30 years old when he conquered the Aryan kingdoms in India. He had been fighting and building his empire for 12 years. In all that time he had never lost a single battle!

Alexander made his father's dreams real. He spread Greek culture and ideas over a large part of the world. Alexander's empire was the largest the ancient world had ever known.

Alexander imagined Europe and Asia as one big country, united under his rule. He wanted to blend the two into one. He chose Babylon as his capital city because it was in the center of his empire. He had plants brought in from one continent and planted on the other. Alexander married an Asian woman. And he rewarded his soldiers if they did the same.

Alexander ruled a giant empire from his palace in Babylon. He had big plans for his empire. But in 323 B.C. he fell sick. He had a high fever. No medicines of the day could help him. Within a few days, 33-year-old Alexander the Great was dead. His soldiers placed his body in a gold coffin. It was taken to Alexandria in Egypt to be buried.

After his death, Alexander's lands were divided among some of his generals. The great empire was gone forever, split into separate smaller empires.

But the man who set out to conquer the world had left his mark. The lands Alexander touched would always show something of Greek style and Greek customs.

At a much earlier date, a great ruler of Babylon drew up a code of laws. What was his name?

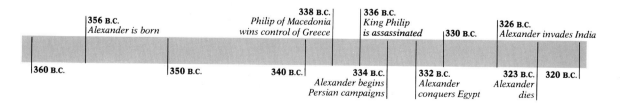

356 B.C. / Alexander is born

338 B.C. / Philip of Macedonia wins control of Greece

336 B.C. / King Philip is assassinated

330 B.C.

326 B.C. / Alexander invades India

360 B.C.

350 B.C.

340 B.C.

334 B.C. / Alexander begins Persian campaigns

332 B.C. / Alexander conquers Egypt

323 B.C. / Alexander dies

320 B.C.

Chapter Review

Chapter Summary

- King Philip of Macedonia planned to conquer the Persian Empire.

- Because Philip needed all of Greece behind him, he first conquered the Greek city-states (except Sparta).

- King Philip died, and his son Alexander led the Macedonian armies into Persia.

- Alexander set out to conquer the world.

- Alexander conquered Persia and then went on to Egypt and India.

- Alexander brought Greek ideas and culture to the lands he conquered.

- Alexander died at the age of 33.

- Alexander's empire split up after his death.

Chapter Quiz

A. Checking Your Facts

Choose the correct word or words to make each of the sentences below a true statement. Rewrite the sentences on a separate sheet of paper.

1. King Philip's plan was to conquer the (Egyptian/Persian) Empire.

2. Philip conquered all of the Greek city-states except (Athens/Sparta).

3. Alexander chose (Ptolemy/Darius) to rule as Egypt's king.

4. The lighthouse at (Babylon/Alexandria) was one of the wonders of the ancient world.

5. Alexander imagined Europe and (Asia/Africa) as one big country, united under his rule.

B. Think About It!

Write answers to the following questions on a separate sheet of paper.

1. What did Alexander learn during his boyhood that made him ready to become a king and a conqueror at age 20?

2. Why were the Egyptians so easily conquered by Alexander?

3. Why do you think Alexander is called "Alexander the Great"?

Chapter 9

The Rise of Rome

This Roman aqueduct was built more than 2,000 years ago. Why did the Romans build aqueducts? What else did they build?

Chapter Learning Objectives

- Describe how the Roman Republic was governed.
- Explain why the Romans thought of the Mediterranean Sea as a Roman sea.
- Name some of the things Julius Caesar did for Rome.
- Name the first Roman emperor, and tell what he did for Rome.
- Explain why the Roman Empire began to fall.

Words to Know

amphitheater   a circular or oval area with sloping sides and seats rising in rows around a central open space

aqueducts   man-made channels that carry flowing water over a long distance

civil wars   wars among people who live in the same country

elect   to choose someone for an office by voting

emperor   a person who rules a group of different countries, lands, or peoples

forum   a public square in an ancient Roman city; lawmakers met there

freemen   people who are free, not slaves, and who have the rights of citizens

gladiators   men who fought animals or other men in the arenas of ancient Rome

governor   a person chosen to run a province or territory

peninsula   a long piece of land almost completely surrounded by water (from the Latin word meaning "almost an island")

provinces   the parts of a country, each with its own local government, much like the states in the United States

representatives   people who are chosen to act or speak for others

republic   a government in which the citizens have the right to elect their representatives to make laws; a democratic government

senate   a governing or lawmaking body

Early Rome

Seven hills rose up along the Tiber River in the center of Italy. Small villages dotted the seven hills. One of those villages was called Rome. It had been built by the Latins around 750 B.C. The Latins, or Romans, were one of several groups of people that had moved down from central Europe. They settled in the Italian **peninsula** around 1000 B.C. Rome was not very important then. But it would one day grow into a great city. That city would become the center of an empire.

From 750 B.C. to 600 B.C., the little Italian villages were ruled by a series of Roman kings. During those years, the Romans lived in peace. They were mainly farmers and herders. But things changed in about 600 B.C. North of the Tiber River lived a warlike people called the Etruscans. They decided to conquer Rome and the other villages. The Romans didn't stand a chance against them.

For about the next 100 years, Rome was ruled by Etruscan kings. The Etruscans had many skills. They built a wall around the city. They drained nearby swamps and laid the first sewer. The Romans even adopted the Etruscan alphabet. Slowly Rome changed from a little farming village into a city-state.

Then, in 509 B.C., the people of Rome rebelled against a very harsh Etruscan king. They took the government of Rome into their own hands and set up a **republic**.

The Roman Republic

In a republic, government is controlled by the people. In a republic, there is no king. Roman citizens **elected** men to make their laws and run their government. Three hundred elected **representatives** met in a **senate**. The Republic was democratic because citizens voted for the people who would represent them. The Roman Republic was a model for our own democratic system of representative government.

Not all Roman citizens had equal rights. Poor people did not win political equality until 287 B.C.

The members of the Roman Senate were usually wealthy landowners. Once elected, they held office for life. Some of the Senate members were very old. The people thought them very wise. The word *senate* comes from the Latin word that means *old*.

The early years of the Republic were not peaceful. At first Rome was attacked by armies from other lands. But Rome grew more and more powerful. After a time, Rome also looked toward gaining more land.

Roman Warriors

The Romans became skilled soldiers. Every Roman male spent some time in the army. Rome's military power grew. The Romans began battling for more land. By about 270 B.C., Rome had taken over the whole Italian peninsula.

One of Rome's greatest enemies was Carthage. Carthage was on the north coast of Africa. It was a city settled by the Phoenicians. Carthage and Rome quarreled over Mediterranean trade routes.

Rome fought three wars with Carthage. These were called the Punic Wars. The first clash between the two city-states came in Sicily. They battled for the city of Messina. Rome finally won this war in 241 B.C., after 23 years of fighting!

GREAT NAMES IN HISTORY: Hannibal

In 218 B.C. a fierce Carthaginian general named Hannibal arrived in Spain. He brought a huge army with him. He led his soldiers over the Pyrenees and the Alps. Many of Hannibal's soldiers rode elephants. The mountains were hard on the huge animals. Many elephants lost their footing on the narrow mountain paths and fell to their deaths. But most of them made it to the Po Valley of Italy. Hannibal was a clever general. He caught the Romans by surprise and beat the Roman army. Thus began the second of the Punic Wars.

For the next 13 years, Hannibal led his army up and down Italy. He won more battles against Roman forces. But little by little the Romans grew stronger. Finally Hannibal was driven out of Italy. Then the Romans invaded Africa and defeated Hannibal's army in 202 B.C.

Hannibal crossing the Alps

Over the next 50 years, Carthage grew strong again. Once more, Rome felt threatened. So Rome declared war and sent its army back to Africa. This time, in the final Punic War, the city of Carthage was totally destroyed.

Name two famous Macedonians you have read about.

During the second war between Carthage and Rome, Macedonia had sided with the Carthaginians. Macedonia was still the most powerful state in Greece. After taking Carthage, Rome sent armies into Greece. Roman armies conquered the Greek city-states. They brought Greek treasures back to Rome, introducing Roman citizens to Greek art and style.

The Romans made slaves of the conquered Greeks. Many of the slaves were used as laborers. But some of the Greek captives were very well educated. They became teachers and doctors in Rome. Many Greek slaves found themselves with kind Roman masters, masters who respected them. Some Greeks were able to earn their freedom. So in many ways, Roman culture was influenced by the Greeks.

By 140 B.C. Rome controlled all of the Mediterranean lands. Citizens of the Republic thought of the Mediterranean Sea as a Roman sea.

The Provinces

Rome conquered many lands. Some of them were very far from the city itself. So the lands were divided into sections called **provinces**. Each province was ruled by its own **governor.** Some people in the provinces accepted the Roman rule. Others were not happy with their new rulers. And they did not like Roman customs.

To keep the people in order, Rome sent large armies to each province. At the head of each of these armies was a general. The soldiers in the provinces were a long way from Rome. They often felt more loyalty to their general than they did to Rome. The generals became very powerful men.

Sometimes the generals and their armies fought among themselves. The most powerful of these generals was a man named Julius Caesar.

Julius Caesar

Caesar is one of the most famous names in history. Who was Julius Caesar, and why is he so famous?

Julius Caesar was the Roman general in the province of Gaul. Gaul was a land to the northwest of Rome. It would one day be called France. People liked Julius Caesar. His soldiers were very loyal to him. The people of Rome admired his success. He won many battles in Gaul and expanded Roman control. But the senators in Rome began to worry. Was Julius Caesar becoming too powerful?

They called him back to Rome. "Leave your army in Gaul," they ordered. Caesar returned to Rome. But he brought his army with him. It was 49 B.C. The common people welcomed Caesar as a hero. Soon Caesar and his army took control of the Roman government.

Some of the other generals were not happy about this. They challenged Caesar's power. This led to **civil wars**, with one Roman army fighting another.

Julius Caesar was always the winner. He won battles in Greece, in Spain, and in North Africa. While fighting in Egypt, Caesar met the beautiful Egyptian princess, Cleopatra. He found time to fall in love with her. He helped her win the throne of Egypt.

By 45 B.C. Caesar controlled the Roman world. The people hailed him as their ruler. For the most part he used his power wisely. He made citizens of many of the people in the provinces. He even allowed some to sit in the Senate. He made sure the governors ruled the provinces fairly. Caesar made more jobs for the people of Rome. He set up colonies where poor Romans could start their own farms.

Julius Caesar

Caesar even improved the Roman calendar. Borrowing from the Egyptians, he changed it to a system of 365 days in a year. He added an extra day every fourth year, creating "leap year." The new calendar was much better than the old one.

And so the people of Rome cheered Caesar. They stamped his picture on Roman coins and built a temple in his name. At the Roman **Forum**, Mark Anthony offered Caesar the crown of king. Mark Anthony was a senator and Caesar's friend. Caesar refused the crown.

Julius Caesar named a month after himself. What do you think it was?

Death to Caesar

But many of Rome's leading citizens were worried. It didn't help that Caesar had not accepted the crown. They were still afraid he planned to make himself a king and put an end to the Republic.

Some of the Roman senators, led by Brutus and Cassius, plotted to kill Caesar. Many of these men had been Caesar's friends. But they did not want to lose the Republic. Their first loyalty was to Rome. On March 15, 44 B.C., Julius Caesar was stabbed to death as he entered the Roman Senate.

Why were some Romans worried? What do you think would happen to Rome if the Republic came to an end?

History Practice

Write answers to the following questions on a separate sheet of paper.

1. Why did the Romans think of the Mediterranean Sea as a Roman sea?

2. Name three things Julius Caesar did for Rome.

3. Who was the Egyptian princess with whom Caesar fell in love?

The Emperor Augustus

Even though Julius Caesar was dead, the days of the Roman Republic were numbered. Most of the people had been happy under Caesar. They wanted a ruler who would continue with Caesar's policies and plans.

Once again there was a struggle for power, and civil wars shook Rome. First Brutus and Cassius fought against Mark Anthony and Octavian. Mark Anthony and Octavian had remained loyal to Caesar. When Octavian and Mark Anthony won, they turned against each other.

Mark Anthony fell in love with none other than Egypt's Cleopatra. They were determined to rule Rome together. But they were defeated by Octavian. The defeat led Anthony and Cleopatra to kill themselves.

Now Octavian ruled all the Roman world. It was the beginning of a new age for Rome. It was the start of the Roman Empire. Octavian became Rome's first **emperor.**

An emperor had even more power than a king. To his people, he was only one step below a god. In 27 B.C. the Roman Senate gave Octavian the title of "Augustus." The title meant that he was above all other men. He was to be worshipped.

Do you think it is a good idea to allow one man to have complete power? What would happen if he were not a wise ruler?

The Roman Senate continued to meet, but the Republic was as dead as Caesar. Augustus chose new senators to make his laws. Augustus, indeed, held complete power.

Under Emperor Augustus the Roman Empire flourished as never before. Augustus ended the civil wars. The time of peace that he brought about was called the *Pax Romana* (Roman Peace).

Augustus chose good, honest men as government leaders. He built roads connecting all the provinces with Rome. He improved harbors and made trade easier. Life became better for most people.

The Roman Empire under Augustus

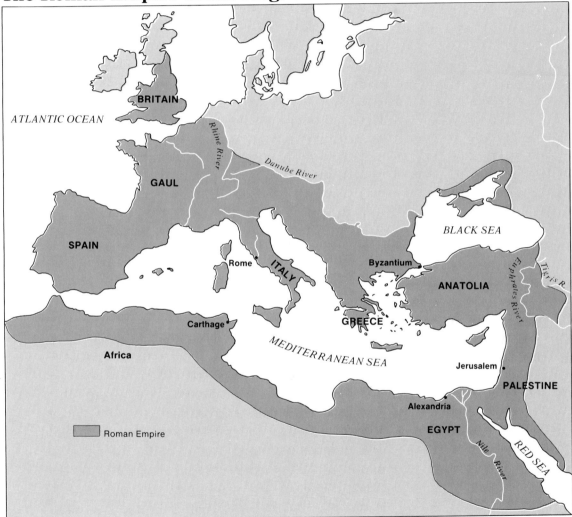

Map Skills
Name five lands bordering the Mediterranean Sea that were ruled by Rome. Which two rivers formed the northern border of the Roman Empire?

Life in Rome

Rome was a busy place. A million people lived in or near the city. Rome had come a long way from that tiny village on a hill. It was a fine and beautiful place. The wide main streets were paved with stone. Fresh water came to the city through overhead **aqueducts.** The water was piped into houses and public fountains.

The Romans built beautiful temples to their many gods. There were 300 temples in Rome alone. One of the most famous of these was the Pantheon.

The Roman Forum was a gathering place. It was there that the Senate met in the Senate House. Columned temples lined the edges of the Forum. Merchants built shops there.

The Romans also built huge public baths. They were more than a place to bathe in hot and cold pools. The baths were also a center of social life. The baths held libraries, gymnasiums, and even small theaters. The public baths were free to everyone.

Wealthy Romans lived in big houses. These houses had swimming pools and large dining halls for parties. Many rich people also had country homes. They hired workers to live there and look after the land.

The average Roman family lived in a small house or apartment. The poorer people lived in tiny rooms in big apartment buildings. They often had to struggle for enough to eat.

In many places today it is possible to enjoy free entertainment. Give an example.

But rich and poor alike enjoyed the free entertainment provided by the emperors. The Romans celebrated many holidays—to honor their gods or to honor military heroes. On these days they often held chariot races. These exciting races took place at a sports stadium called the Circus Maximus. The Romans loved to watch these events. They also enjoyed a much more violent form of entertainment.

YOU ARE THERE: The Colosseum, Rome, A.D. 100

You are sitting high up in the stands. A crowd of more than 45,000 people fills the huge **amphitheater**. The contests are about to begin. First there is a fight between a lion and a tiger. Then some slaves are sent into the arena and forced to fight lions. But the slaves have no weapons! You cannot bear to watch as the lions jump on the slaves and kill them. Most people seem to enjoy the sight, however. The crowd roars in excitement.

Next the gladiator Demetrius has to fight four other **gladiators** at the same time. It is to be a sword fight to the death. Demetrius is a brave fighter and is a favorite with the crowd. He is a slave, as are most gladiators. But some gladiators are **freemen** who fight for money and glory. The four gladiators close in on Demetrius. It seems to you that this is a very unfair fight. But Demetrius battles furiously and manages to kill one gladiator after another. Only one man, Glycon, still faces Demetrius.

By now the sand on the floor of the arena is red with blood. Suddenly Demetrius falls backward. The crowd gasps in horror. Glycon leaps on top of Demetrius and knocks the sword out of his hand. This looks like the end for Demetrius. You and the others in the stands shout that Demetrius must live. Glycon hesitates and looks up at the emperor's box. The emperor usually gives in to the wishes of the crowd. He stands up and signals thumbs up. The crowd is happy. Demetrius will live!

Roman Builders

The Romans admired the Greeks. They put up statues taken from Greek city-states. They copied Greek style in statues of their own. Many of the great buildings in Rome were also based on Greek style and form.

Roman builders liked to use arches. Arches spanned streets, supported bridges, and held up great aqueducts. Visitors often passed under a great arch to enter a Roman city.

The Romans wanted their art and architecture to be useful. The 14 aqueducts that carried water into Rome were certainly beautiful. But they were also useful. And they were built to last. Some aqueducts, built more than 2,000 years ago, still stand today.

Some roads of ancient Rome are still in use today, too. "All roads lead to Rome," a famous saying goes. That means that Roman highways, paved layer upon layer, linked all the provinces to Rome. The Romans were fine builders. They built a sewer system to serve ancient Rome. Parts of it are still being used in the modern city.

Roman Language and Law

Italian, French, Spanish, Portuguese, and Rumanian are all called Romance languages. They all come from Latin, the language of the Romans.

There are many words that we have taken from the Romans. We have *colosseums* today. Our government has a *senate*. The Russians changed the word *Caesar* to *Tzar*, the Germans to *Kaiser*.

"Justice for all!" was an idea that came from the Roman Senate. Many of our ideas about laws and courts of law came from the Romans. Roman laws and lawmaking served as a model for many other nations.

The End of the Empire

Not all of the emperors that followed Augustus were wise and good. Indeed, some were mad with power. Some were greedy. Royal families often fought among themselves over who would get the throne. But there were always skilled men to do the actual work of running the empire. The *Pax Romana* lasted for two centuries. During that time there were no serious threats to Rome's power.

But around A.D. 180, things began to go wrong. The Roman world faced invaders from northern Europe. Rome had to double the size of its army to protect the empire. A bigger army meant higher taxes—taxes that people could not pay! Prices of goods rose. Trading fell off. People were out of work. Life in the city was no longer good. More and more wealthy people left Rome to live in the country.

The Roman Empire did not fall in a day, or in a month, or even in a year. But the empire grew weaker with each passing year. Its fall was coming.

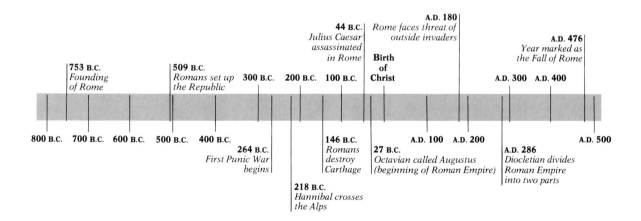

Chapter Review

Chapter Summary

- In the Roman Republic, laws were made by elected representatives. There was no king.

- Roman armies were mighty. They conquered many peoples, including the Carthaginians and the Greeks.

- Conquered lands became Roman provinces.

- Julius Caesar was a powerful general in the province of Gaul.

- Caesar became the leader of the Roman Republic.

- Some senators killed Caesar because they feared he had too much power.

- Civil wars ended with Octavian as head of the Roman Empire.

- The people called Octavian the Emperor Augustus.

- Two hundred years of peace and growth began with Augustus's reign.

- The ancient Romans are known as great builders and lawmakers.

Chapter Quiz

A. Checking Your Facts

gladiators	aqueducts	amphitheater	peninsula	forum

Complete each sentence below. Use the correct word from the box. Rewrite the sentences on a separate sheet of paper.

1. The Romans settled in the Italian _____ around 1000 B.C.

2. Temples lined the edge of the Roman _____ , and merchants built shops there.

3. Fresh water came to Rome through overhead _____ .

4. A huge _____ in Rome could hold more than 45,000 people.

5. The men who fought in the Colosseum were called _____ .

B. Think About It!

Write answers to the following questions on a separate sheet of paper.

1. In what ways was the Roman Republic like the government of Athens? How was it different?

2. If Brutus and Cassius were Caesar's friends, why did they murder him?

3. What happened to the Roman Senate after Augustus was named emperor?

Chapter 10

The Birth of Three Major Religions

Paul traveled far to tell people about the teachings of Jesus Christ. Why do you think people were willing to listen?

Chapter Learning Objectives

- Explain why Jesus' teachings appealed to poor people and slaves.
- Tell how the Romans persecuted the Christians.
- Describe how the Emperor Constantine helped the Christian religion grow in Rome.
- Explain why Mohammed's teachings appealed to poor people and slaves.
- Explain why Buddhism is called a "gentle" religion.

Words to Know

bishops   high-ranking church officials; from the Latin word that means "overseer." A *bishop* oversees the churches in his district.

converted   changed from one religion to another

crucifixion   the putting to death of someone by nailing or tying that person to a cross

enlightened   knowing the truth

idols   images of a god that are used as objects of worship

paradise   a place or condition of perfect happiness; heaven

persecute   to treat in a cruel way, to hurt or injure

pope   the head of the Roman Catholic Church

prophet   a religious leader who claims to speak for God; one who tells what will happen in the future

reincarnation   a belief that living beings are reborn in a new body

vision   something seen in the mind or in a dream

Religion played a large part in shaping world history. Three major religions—Christianity, Islam, and Buddhism—began with men who spoke of equality and brotherhood. Over the years the teachings of these men attracted more and more followers. These religions grew into powerful forces. Today these religions still play a big part in the lives of hundreds of millions of people.

Jesus

Look at any one of the time lines in this book. Each shows how important a man named Jesus was to the history of the world. All the dates before the birth of Jesus Christ are labeled B.C., or "Before Christ." All the dates after the birth of Christ are labeled A.D.

The letters A.D. stand for the Latin words *Anno Domini*, or "in the year of our Lord."

The Christian religion began with Jesus. Jesus was a Jew. He lived during the time of the Roman Emperor Augustus. He was born in Bethlehem, a little town south of Jerusalem. This was in a far-off province of the Roman Empire. Much of what we know about Jesus comes from the Bible. The first four books of the New Testament are about his life. These books are called the Gospels. The Gospels contain stories passed down over the years.

The Gospels say that Jesus taught people to love one another, to do good deeds, and to love God. If people were good, Jesus taught, they would be rewarded in an afterlife.

The teachings of Jesus were most popular with poor people and slaves. These teachings offered some hope for happiness, if not in this life, then in the next. Other religions, including the Egyptian religion, also spoke of an afterlife. But those religions said that princes would remain princes. And commoners would keep their lowly station—even after death. Jesus spoke of a happy afterlife for everyone who was good on Earth.

And so his followers called Jesus a "Christ," or savior. Jesus was about 33 years old when he was sentenced to death. But the **crucifixion** of Jesus was certainly not the end of his teachings. In the next years, the Christian religion spread through many lands.

One man who carried word of the Christian religion was named Paul. Paul spent almost 30 years of his life traveling the Mediterranean world. He told people about Jesus Christ's teachings. Paul could speak Greek. So he took Christian beliefs to Athens and to other Greek cities. Paul started churches wherever he traveled. Even in Rome, Paul found people willing to listen. People were ready to accept a new religion that spoke of equality and hope.

Jesus Christ

Christianity in the Roman Empire

The Roman Empire had many religions. At first, one more religion did not seem too important. The emperors allowed the Christians to worship as they pleased.

But the Christians would not bow down to the Roman emperor. They would not call the emperor a god. The Roman government decided that the Christians were a threat. So the Roman emperors began to **persecute** the followers of Christ. They blamed the Christians for everything that went wrong.

A terrible fire burned in Rome in A.D. 64. This was the time when Nero was emperor. "The Christians started the fire!" Nero shouted. So, many Christians were executed. Paul, one of the men who had carried Christ's word, was one of those killed.

Name a group of people who have been persecuted in modern times.

The Romans persecuted the Christians for 300 years! Christian men and women were forced into Roman arenas to fight wild animals. Some of the emperors worried more about Christianity than others. Sometimes the Christians were safe; other times they were in danger.

Why do you think so many people risked their lives to follow the Christian religion?

Christians often held secret church meetings. They met in tunnels, called *catacombs,* deep under the city of Rome. It was dangerous to follow the Christian religion. But even though it could mean death, people continued to join the Christian religion. At first it was only the poor Romans and slaves who turned to Christianity. But, after a time, some of the Roman leaders became interested, too.

The Emperor Constantine

Constantine became emperor of Rome in A.D. 306. In A.D. 312 a Roman general named Maxentius threatened to seize the throne. One night, Constantine dreamed that he saw a cross in the sky. He thought it was the Cross of Christ. He dreamed that if he carried that cross into battle, he would win a great victory. So Constantine rode into battle against Maxentius. He carried a flag that pictured the cross. And he won that battle. Maxentius was defeated.

At the time Constantine became emperor, he had to share power with others. The Roman Empire had been divided into an eastern and western part. In A.D. 286 the Emperor Diocletian decided the empire had grown too big to be ruled by just one man. He set up a system of shared rule.

Constantine was not happy with this arrangement. In A.D. 324 he clashed with Licinius, the ruler of the eastern part of the empire. That same year, Constantine became the sole ruler of the Roman Empire. In A.D. 330 he set up a new capital at Byzantium in the east. He renamed the city Constantinople. Today this city is known as Istanbul.

The Eastern Roman Empire and the Western Roman Empire

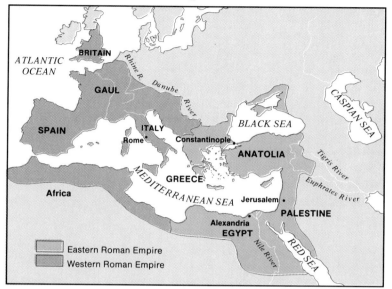

Map Skills

Name three countries in the Eastern Roman Empire. Name four countries in the Western Roman Empire. The city of Constantinople is near what sea?

Constantine **converted** to Christianity and became the first Christian emperor of Rome. In A.D. 313 he made Christianity legal. Christians were no longer persecuted. More and more Romans now turned to the religion. Constantine built the first great Christian cathedral in Rome. He then built churches in Constantinople and in other cities.

The Roman government and the Christian church became very much a part of one another. Officials of the church were powerful men. The largest churches chose **bishops** as their leaders. The bishop of the Church of Rome became the **pope.** While the government of the Roman Empire was weakening, the Christian church was gaining power.

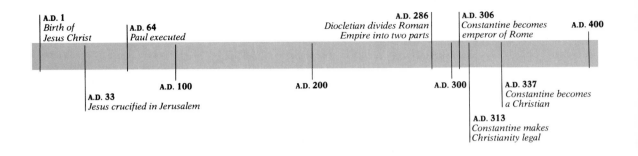

A.D. 1
Birth of
Jesus Christ

A.D. 64
Paul executed

A.D. 286
Diocletian divides Roman
Empire into two parts

A.D. 306
Constantine becomes
emperor of Rome

A.D. 400

A.D. 33
Jesus crucified in Jerusalem

A.D. 100

A.D. 200

A.D. 300

A.D. 337
Constantine becomes
a Christian

A.D. 313
Constantine makes
Christianity legal

History Practice

Write answers to the following questions on a separate
sheet of paper.

1. Why did Jesus' teachings appeal to poor people and
   slaves?

2. How did the Romans persecute the Christians?

3. Why did the Emperor Diocletian divide up the Roman
   Empire into an Eastern and Western Empire?

Mohammed

Southeast of the Mediterranean Sea is a vast desert
kingdom. Tribes of nomads lived on the edges of the
desert in tent camps. They drove caravans of camels
across the sands. Wealthy people lived in fine homes
in the cities of the kingdom. They dressed in rich silks
and wore bright jewels.

It was not a peaceful land. Bands of thieves rode
into the cities, waving swords. They looted and killed,
taking riches off into the desert. And the nomadic
tribes fought among themselves. There was more and
more trouble throughout the kingdom. Trade became
harder, and the people became poorer. Fewer lived in
fine palaces; more struggled for even enough to eat.

This desert land was called Arabia. Today this kingdom is called Saudi Arabia. The people were Arabs. Most of the Arabs believed in many gods. They worshipped **idols** made of gold and silver.

Desert travel

Around the year A.D. 570, in the Arabian city of Mecca, a man named Mohammed was born. Not much is known about Mohammed's early life. But Mohammed was to become a religious figure who would change the shape of the world.

When Mohammed was 40 years old, it is said, he had a **vision**. Mohammed believed he saw an angel on a hillside outside of Mecca. The angel spoke to him, saying that Mohammed was a **prophet** of God. "Teach your people," the angel said, "that there is one God, and that God is Allah."

Like Jesus, Mohammed became a teacher. He tried to teach people that Allah was the one true god. Most Arabs would not listen. They still worshipped their many gods.

But some people did follow Mohammed. They heard his words about Allah. Allah would reward people for good deeds with a wonderful life after death, Mohammed promised. Poor people listened. Slaves listened. Just as they had listened to Jesus, people whose lives were hard or sad listened to Mohammed.

The powerful leaders of Mecca began to worry. They had laughed at him at first, this man called Mohammed. But he was growing popular. What if he stirred the commoners into a rebellion? So they began to persecute Mohammed and his followers.

The Moslems, Mohammed's followers, were forced to flee the city of Mecca. In A.D. 622 Mohammed took his people to the Arabian city of Medina. Still, the number of Moslems grew. New converts became soldiers for Mohammed. With an army of followers, Mohammed returned to Mecca and took the city.

In A.D. 632 Mohammed died. By the time of his death, the prophet Mohammed had done his job. Arabia was united under one religion. The religion of the Moslems was called Islam. The Islamic religion promised that any followers who died battling for Allah would go straight to **paradise**. This idea alone created huge armies of enthusiastic soldiers. The Moslem soldiers were ready to carry the word of Allah throughout the world.

The Spread of Islam

Then came one of the greatest series of conquests the world had ever seen. Arab armies swept through Syria, Persia, and Egypt. The Arab conquests continued for hundreds of years. Arab lands would stretch from North Africa and Spain to the Indus River.

The Moslem Empire, about A.D. 750

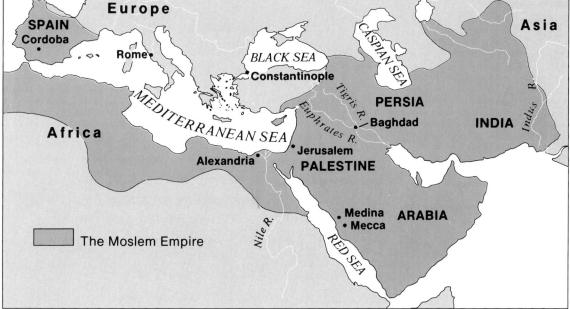

Map Skills
The Moslem Empire extended across parts of which three continents?

Some of the conquered people welcomed the new religion with its hope of paradise. But the Arabs gave them little choice. The people must become Moslems or die. Only Jews and Christians were allowed to keep their own religion. The Moslems respected those who also worshipped one god and followed the words of a holy book.

Early Arabic numerals. Each one was drawn with as many strokes as the number it represented.

Indeed, Mohammed had been influenced early in his life by the Jews and Christians he knew. His God, Allah, was the one God of the Jews and Christians. According to Mohammed, God revealed himself to man through his chosen prophets. He thought the major prophets were Adam, Noah, Abraham, Moses, Jesus, and, finally, Mohammed. God gave the Ten Commandments to Moses, the Gospels to Jesus, and the Koran to Mohammed. But even the Christians and the Jews were forced to pay tribute to the new Arab rulers.

The conquering Arabs brought their culture as well as their religion. They built fine cities and new schools. Their language and writing became part of world culture. And so the Arabs made their mark on the world. The numerals that we use now in America, for example, are Arabic numerals.

Today Islam is one of the world's great religions. Most Moslems live in the Middle East, Pakistan, India, parts of Southeast Asia, and North Africa. They live in lands that the Arabs conquered during the seventh and eighth centuries.

Mohammed Ali Mosque, Cairo, Egypt

WORDS FROM THE PAST: The Koran

Islam is based on Mohammed's writings. These are found in a holy book called the Koran. In it, Mohammed wrote that there is only one true God, Allah. He wrote that all people will be judged on the day they die. If people did good deeds and followed Allah, paradise awaited them.

There are several things a good Moslem must do, according to the Koran. A Moslem must pray five times a day, facing toward Mecca. A Moslem must give to the poor. A Moslem must not eat or drink during daylight hours of one special month called Ramadan. A Moslem should, if at all possible, make one visit to Mecca.

"There is no God but Allah," a Moslem declares, "and Mohammed is His prophet!"

Today Moslem pilgrims from many lands still journey to the holy city of Mecca.

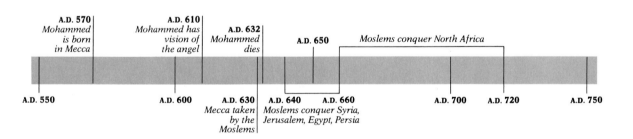

A.D. 570 — Mohammed is born in Mecca
A.D. 610 — Mohammed has vision of the angel
A.D. 632 — Mohammed dies
A.D. 650
Moslems conquer North Africa

A.D. 550
A.D. 600
A.D. 630 — Mecca taken by the Moslems
A.D. 640 — Moslems conquer Syria, Jerusalem, Egypt, Persia
A.D. 660
A.D. 700
A.D. 720
A.D. 750

Buddha

The man who would one day be called *Buddha* was born in about 563 B.C., long before Jesus or Mohammed. He was the son of a wealthy Hindu in India. His father was a raja, or prince. And so the boy, Siddhartha Gautama, also was considered a prince. His life should have been one of riches and plenty. But Gautama chose a different path.

Buddha and his followers

He saw many of his people living in poverty and sorrow. He saw beggars in the streets. Gautama felt sorry for the unhappy people. Human life was full of suffering. The rich had so much; the poor had so little.

When he was a young man, Gautama gave up his own wealth. He left his father's palace and went to live in the forest. For about six years he lived simply, wandering around India. He spent his time thinking about how life could be better for mankind.

It is said that the truth came to Gautama one day as he sat under a fig tree. "The sorrows of the world are caused by selfishness," Gautama decided. If people could put aside their desire for riches, Gautama thought, the world would be a better place. So he developed a new religion, Buddhism, based on brotherly love. Gautama was called Buddha, which means the "**enlightened** one."

The Buddhist Religion

The Buddhist religion is known as a gentle religion. It teaches that the secret of life is found in unselfishness. People who get rid of all greed and selfishness will reach a state of mind known as *nirvana*. Buddhists also believe in **reincarnation**. They believe that living beings, even animals, are reborn in another form after death. They see life as a continuing cycle of death and rebirth. A person can only break the cycle of death and suffering by reaching nirvana. Buddhists hope to reach nirvana someday, just as Christians hope to go to heaven.

After Alexander the Great had left northern India, a new empire was created. It was called the Maurya Empire. The third of the Maurya emperors was named Asoka. Asoka's rule began in 273 B.C. He followed Buddha's teachings about brotherly love. Asoka made Buddhism the state religion. He taught that all people, and even animals, were to be loved.

Buddha's teachings were very different for the Indians. They were accustomed to Hindu ways. But the Hindu caste system weakened during Asoka's rule. New laws treated all people more equally.

Do you think that Asoka was a wise ruler? Why or why not?

India's Maurya empire came to an end in about 185 B.C. Then one foreign land after another invaded India. Most Indians went back to the Hindu religion. But Buddhism had spread. Followers of Buddha had carried their ideas to China, Japan, and other parts of Asia. Beautiful Buddhist temples and pagodas are still standing today. They show that the "gentle religion" became an important part of Asia's culture.

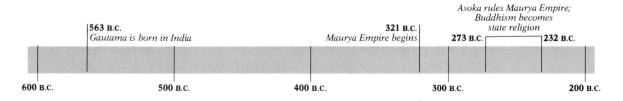

563 B.C.
Gautama is born in India

321 B.C.
Maurya Empire begins

Asoka rules Maurya Empire; Buddhism becomes state religion

273 B.C. ┌──────┐ 232 B.C.

600 B.C.   500 B.C.   400 B.C.   300 B.C.   200 B.C.

Chapter Review

Chapter Summary

- The Christian religion is based on the teachings of a man named Jesus.

- Christians believe that good deeds in life are rewarded with a place in heaven.

- Some Roman emperors persecuted the Christians.

- Constantine was the first Christian emperor of Rome.

- Mohammed, born in Arabia, taught that the one true god was Allah.

- Followers of Mohammed were called Moslems. Their religion was Islam.

- Moslems conquered many lands, spreading Islam and the Arabic culture.

- An Indian prince, Gautama, gave up his wealth to teach a religion of brotherly love.

- Gautama became known as Buddha, the "enlightened one."

- The Buddhist religion was first practiced in India. Then it spread to other parts of Asia.

- Christianity, Islam, and Buddhism all spoke of equality and promised rewards for good deeds.

- All three religions attracted poor people as the first followers.

Chapter Quiz

A. Checking Your Facts

Choose the correct word to make each of the sentences below a true statement. Rewrite the sentences on a separate sheet of paper.

1. Jesus lived during the time of the Roman Emperor (Constantine/Augustus).

2. The Roman emperors blamed the (Christians/Greeks) for everything that went wrong.

3. In A.D. 312 a Roman general named (Diocletian/Maxentius) threatened to seize the throne.

4. In A.D. 570 in the Arabian city of (Mecca/Medina), a man named Mohammed was born.

5. (Asoka/Gautama) made Buddhism the state religion.

B. Think About It!

Write answers to the following questions on a separate sheet of paper.

1. Why do you think wealthy, powerful people at first feared Christianity, Islam, or Buddhism?

2. How did the Emperor Constantine help the Christian religion grow in Rome?

3. Why did the young prince Gautama give up his wealth and go live in India's forests?

Unit Three Review

Write answers to the following questions on a separate sheet of paper.

1. What was the "Acropolis" in Greek city-states, and what was it used for?

2. What kind of life did a young boy in Sparta have to look forward to? What was the role of women in Sparta?

3. The Peloponnesian War, which began in 431 B.C., was between which two city-states? Who was the winner of the war?

4. What was so special about the city of Alexandria in Egypt, which was built by Alexander the Great?

5. In what way was the Roman Republic similar to the government of Athens? In what way was it different?

6. Name three things that Augustus did for Rome.

7. Name two things the Romans did for entertainment.

8. Give two reasons why the Roman Empire began to fall.

9. Why did Mohammed's teachings appeal to poor people and slaves?

10. Why is Buddhism called a "gentle" religion?

Unit 4

The Middle Ages

Chapter 11

The Barbarians and the Vikings

In A.D. 793 Vikings sailed down from the north and began raiding the coasts of Europe. Which lands did these "Northmen" come from?

Chapter Learning Objectives

- Explain why the barbarians invaded the Roman Empire.
- Name three Germanic tribes.
- Describe what happened to the city of Rome.
- Tell why Charlemagne proved to be a fine ruler.
- Explain why people were afraid of the Vikings.

Words to Know

barbarians   uncivilized primitive people; people living outside Greece or Rome in the days of the Roman Empire

exiled   forced to live away from home in a foreign land

frontiers   lands just beyond the border of a country

Middle Ages   the period of European history extending from the Fall of Rome in A.D. 476 to about A.D. 1450

plundered   stole, took by force

sagas   long stories of brave deeds

uncivilized   savage; primitive; without training in arts, science, government

Vandal   a member of a Germanic tribe that invaded the Roman Empire. A *vandal* is a person who damages or destroys things.

The Roman Empire was growing weaker. The tribes that lived beyond the northern borders were growing stronger. The day was coming when these tribes would sweep across the borders. The empire would be destroyed. New people would come into power. And these were people with cultures very different from the Roman culture. A new period in history was being born—the **Middle Ages**. This period would last about 1,000 years.

The Germanic Tribes

Tribes of nomads lived along the northern **frontiers** of the Roman Empire. These people were known as Germans. The Romans described them as tall, light-haired people who loved to drink and gamble. The Romans called the Germanic tribes **uncivilized**. The tribesmen wore clothing of rough cloth and animal skins. They carried spears, swords, and battle-axes.

Do you think there are any people in today's world who are uncivilized?

Under which system of laws would there be more justice—the German or the Roman? Why?

The Germans' tribal laws were different from the well-ordered Roman system of law. An assembly of men ruled each German village. If a villager broke the law, the assembly would ask, "Guilty or not guilty?" If the villager said he was not guilty, a test was used to prove his innocence. For example, his hand might be thrust into boiling water. If the burn healed easily, his innocence was proven. If not, he was guilty. The gods had spoken! This was not at all like the Roman courts of justice.

Germanic tribes often fought each other. The men took pride in their bravery in battle. And they had fierce loyalty to the tribal chief. "I am a man now!" a German boy would shout when he received his first spear and shield. To lose his shield in battle would be his greatest dishonor.

The Romans called these German outsiders **barbarians**. Today this word is used to describe any uncivilized person. The Roman frontiers were protected from the barbarians by natural boundaries such as rivers and mountains. Where there were no natural boundaries, the Romans built forts and stone walls. The Roman Emperor Hadrian, who ruled between A.D. 117 and A.D. 138, built a huge wall. Hadrian's wall stretched across northern England.

But the Germanic tribes lived just on the edge of the frontier. They were bound to cross over the borders. So the cultures mingled. The Germans learned to use Greek and Roman letters to write their own language. The Romans began to wear furs, as the Germans did. Many Roman women wore blond wigs made from German hair.

The Romans recognized the barbarians' war skills. Some Germans joined the Roman armies. German soldiers sometimes married Roman women. It was all very neighborly at first. But the barbarians would not be friendly neighbors for long.

Barbarian Invasions

The tribes from the north grew restless. They wanted adventure. They wanted power of their own. They saw that they could take power, and riches too, from the weakening Roman Empire. So barbarian armies poured across the frontier.

Besides being driven by greed, the Germans were fleeing an enemy of their own. A tribe of wild horsemen, called Huns, had swept out of Asia. They were led by their fierce leader, Attila. They took more and more German lands. They forced the German tribes into the Roman Empire.

Barbarians attacking Rome

A barbarian tribe called the Goths marched into Italy. Germans who had become Roman soldiers left their armies to join the Goths. In A.D. 410 the Goths, led by Alaric, entered Rome. The city was weak. The Goths took Rome with little trouble. They destroyed much of the city and stole what they could. Then they went on, leaving the ruins of Rome behind them.

Now other tribes of Germans swept through the Roman Empire. In A.D. 455 the city of Rome was attacked—this time by the **Vandals**. Like the Goths, they looted and destroyed everything in their path. Then they moved on into Spain and northern Africa.

Another army of Goths settled in Italy and Spain. Then the Angles, Saxons, and Jutes invaded the island of Britain. The Angles gave England its name. Their language would be called English. A tribe known as the Franks were on the move, too. They settled in Flanders, just north of the province of Gaul.

The Roman Empire fell. Many Romans buried treasures—art and religious objects. They tried to save things from the barbarians. Long after that, people were still finding remains of the great empire. The treasures of Rome were buried in the fields and pastures of Europe.

The days of the Western Roman Empire were over. In A.D. 476 the German chief Odoacer overthrew the last of the Roman emperors. The fine cities were gone. There were no new schools. No one studied art or literature or science. Barbarians set up new states. Their kings ruled, blending Roman law with tribal law. The Latin language changed. It became different in each of the different states. Only the Christian church kept its power and its organization.

History Practice

Write answers to the following questions on a separate sheet of paper.

1. How did the Romans describe the people living beyond the northern frontiers of the Roman Empire?

2. Why did the Emperor Hadrian build a wall across northern England?

3. Name two barbarian tribes that attacked Rome.

The Byzantine Empire

The Western Roman Empire fell to the barbarians. The Eastern Empire, with Constantinople as its capital, resisted attack. The Eastern Empire was known as the Byzantine Empire. It would last for almost 1,000 years after German tribes took the Western Roman Empire. Life in the Western Empire was grim. But the Byzantine Empire put up fine buildings trimmed in gold. A new university was built there. The people grew wealthy from trading.

The language of the Byzantine Empire was Greek. This became the official language of the Eastern church. In A.D. 1054 the Christian church split into two sections. The church in the west was called Roman Catholic. The church in the east was called Eastern Orthodox.

The Franks and Charlemagne

"A giant of a man! About seven feet tall! He had blond hair and a merry face." That is the way a writer of the time described Charles the Great, or Charlemagne. Charlemagne was king of the Franks, the German tribe that took Flanders. The Franks had continued their conquests. They ended up ruling all the lands that would one day be France.

Do you think Charlemagne was a fine ruler? Why or why not?

Charlemagne being crowned by the pope

Charlemagne's father was called Pepin the Short. He had died in A.D. 786. Charlemagne proved to be a fine ruler when he became king of the Franks. He conquered more land—much of Germany and part of Italy. He showed an interest in education and in the Christian religion, and won favor with the pope.

On Christmas Day, A.D. 800, the pope crowned Charlemagne. He gave him the title *Emperor of the Holy Roman Empire.* Although the empire was called "Roman," Charlemagne was still a barbarian. He dressed in the Frankish style and spoke the language of the Franks. His was a Germanic land rather than a Roman one.

Charlemagne's empire was good while it lasted. Charlemagne built schools and encouraged artists. He learned to read Latin and worked closely with the church.

When Charlemagne died, his empire went to his son, Louis I. The empire began to crumble. It was finally divided among Charlemagne's three grandsons—Charles the Bald, Lothair, and Louis the German. The divided lands would one day become France, Germany, and part of Italy.

Raiders from the North

People called the attackers Northmen because they sailed down from the north. They came from lands that are today Norway, Sweden, and Denmark. The Northmen were adventurers. They loved sailing and fighting. Their ships, powered by oars and sails, were swift. The sailors set their course by the stars and by the sun. They called themselves Vikings.

The Viking raids began in A.D. 793. Norwegian Vikings attacked an island off the east coast of England. This was followed by a wave of raids against England, Scotland, and Ireland. During the mid-800s Norwegian Vikings burned and looted towns on the coasts of France, Spain, and Italy.

YOU ARE THERE: A tiny coastal village in England, A.D. 800

All of the people from the village are gathered inside the small stone church. It stands on a rocky hill above the sea. The people's heads are bowed in prayer. All around you, people are saying, "Lord, deliver us from the fury of the Northmen."

Everyone is scared. A short while ago, one of your neighbors had spotted the long, narrow ships out at sea. He had run from house to house warning everyone. You have heard what happened to other towns along the coast. The Northmen plundered and they destroyed. They killed the men of the towns and stole away the women. Then they left as quickly as they came.

You get up and run outside the church. You look toward the sea. Your heart sinks! The long ships are getting closer. You want to run away, but you can't move. You watch as the ships approach the shore. The ships' prows are decorated with fierce-looking dragon heads carved from wood. The ships have bright-colored purple, blue, red, and yellow sails.

On board each of the ships are about 30 men. They are tall, blond-haired men, tanned from the sun and sea winds. The men come ashore. Now they are running toward the village, waving their swords and battle-axes. You can hear them yelling. You turn and run.

The cruelest Viking warrior was called a *berserker*. Today we use the word *berserk* to describe wild, out-of-control behavior.

Viking Settlers and Explorers

For many years the Vikings kept on the move. They **plundered**, then sailed back home. Later, they settled in the lands that their ships reached.

Swedish Vikings settled in Russia. Danish Vikings found homes in England and along the coast of France. The Vikings in France became known as the Normans. And their new land was called Normandy.

Several hundred Icelanders followed Eric the Red to Greenland.

Norwegian Vikings sailed the Atlantic Ocean and set up colonies in Iceland. In about A.D. 982, the red-bearded Viking, Eric the Red, was **exiled** from his home in Iceland. So Eric sailed to Greenland to set up a colony.

Eric had a son named Leif Ericson. In A.D. 1000 Ericson sailed as far as the east coast of North America. The Vikings only spent a short time there. They made wine from the grapes they found. So Ericson called the land Vinland (or Wineland).

The Vikings never returned to America, as far as we know. And they had to give up their colony in Greenland during the 1400s. By that time, the climate had become much colder.

Songs and stories of Leif Ericson, Eric the Red, and other Viking heroes are called **sagas**. Much of what we know about the Vikings comes from these sagas. They tell of Viking gods like Odin and Thor. They tell of Valhalla, the hall of the gods, where dead Viking warriors live forever.

The Normans

The Vikings in France, the Normans, set out to take more land. In 1066 William, the Duke of Normandy, decided to make himself King of England. He waited for fair breezes to blow his ships across the English Channel. At last the moment came.

There was a savage fight known as the Battle of Hastings. William killed the English king, Harold. William became King of England. He became known as William the Conqueror.

Gifts of the Vikings

With new settlements and new languages, the Vikings turned to a new religion. They became Christians, leaving behind the Norse gods of the sagas.

The Vikings kept sea trade alive and booming. They used their fine ships and sailing skills to travel oceans and rivers. Their art is found throughout Europe. They decorated buildings, as well as ships, with carved dragon heads and carved animals.

Because they settled in so many lands, the hardy, adventurous Vikings left their mark on many cultures.

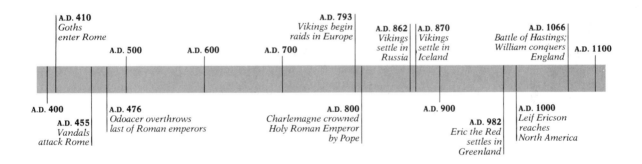

A.D. 410 Goths enter Rome

A.D. 500

A.D. 600

A.D. 700

A.D. 793 Vikings begin raids in Europe

A.D. 862 Vikings settle in Russia

A.D. 870 Vikings settle in Iceland

A.D. 1066 Battle of Hastings; William conquers England

A.D. 1100

A.D. 400

A.D. 455 Vandals attack Rome

A.D. 476 Odoacer overthrows last of Roman emperors

A.D. 800 Charlemagne crowned Holy Roman Emperor by Pope

A.D. 900

A.D. 982 Eric the Red settles in Greenland

A.D. 1000 Leif Ericson reaches North America

Chapter Review

Chapter Summary

- Tribes of Germans lived along the northern frontier of the Roman Empire.

- The Romans called those people barbarians.

- Barbarians attacked and conquered the Western Roman Empire.

- The Eastern Roman Empire, or Byzantine Empire, did not fall for another 1,000 years.

- The pope crowned Charlemagne, a Frank, as Emperor of the Holy Roman Empire.

- Vikings sailed to other parts of Europe from Norway, Denmark, and Sweden.

- The Vikings settled many of the places they raided.

- Vikings also had colonies in Iceland and Greenland.

- The Viking Leif Ericson visited America.

- William the Conqueror was a Viking Duke of Normandy who conquered England.

- The Vikings influenced many cultures during the Middle Ages.

Chapter Quiz

A. Checking Your Facts

Choose the correct word or words to make each of the sentences below a true statement. Rewrite the sentences on a separate sheet of paper.

1. In A.D. 410 the Goths, led by (Attila/Alaric) attacked Rome.

2. In A.D. 476, the German chief (Odoacer/Hadrian) overthrew the last of the Roman emperors.

3. The Eastern Roman Empire was known as the (Holy Roman/ Byzantine) Empire.

4. (Latin/Greek) became the official language of the Eastern church.

5. On Christmas Day, A.D. 800, (Pepin the Short/the pope) crowned Charlemagne.

B. Think About It!

Write answers to the following questions on a separate sheet of paper.

1. Describe two differences between German culture and the Roman culture.

2. Why do you think Charlemagne won favor with the pope? What would lead you to believe that Charlemagne was interested in education?

3. Why do you think the Vikings began to attack the countries of Europe?

Chapter 12
The Lords and the Serfs

Feudal manor houses were actually huge castles. Why do you think these buildings had high stone walls?

Chapter Learning Objectives

- Describe the life of the lord of a manor.
- Describe the life of a serf.
- Name the three classes in feudal society.
- Tell how a boy became a knight.
- Explain the role of religion in feudal life.

Words to Know

clergy   people trained or ordained for religious work

estate   a large piece of land with a large home on it

feudalism   the political and military system of Europe during the Middle Ages; the system of exchanging lands for services

homage   a pledge of loyalty; a promise to serve, made to kings and lords during the Middle Ages

jousts   fights with lances between two knights on horseback

knights   high-ranking soldiers of the Middle Ages who received their titles from a noble

manor   the lands belonging to a medieval lord, including farmland, a village, and the home of the owner

medieval   belonging to the Middle Ages

nobles   people of high social rank

serfs   people legally tied to the land; farm workers who were almost slaves

vassals   nobles who received land from a king in return for their loyalty and service

---

The Feudal System

When the Roman Empire fell, the period of European history known as the *Middle Ages* began. Most people in Europe moved from the cities to the country. The splendor of the great cities faded. After a time, some towns no longer existed. Trade all but disappeared. People no longer used money. Education and learning became less and less important. Only in the church was there an effort to continue the reading and writing of Latin. The church also saved the writings of many ancient thinkers.

Life was now organized under a new system called **feudalism**. A king ruled a whole country. He divided the land among important men, or **nobles**. These nobles were called **vassals** of the king. In exchange for land, the nobles paid **homage** to the king. This meant that they promised to serve the king. They swore to fight for him and protect him.

A noble, or lord, lived in a huge castle or **manor** house on a country **estate**. The estate included a small village and fields for growing crops. Freemen and **serfs** lived on the feudal estate. They depended on the ruling noble and his land for their living.

The manor fields were divided into strips of land. Freemen were allowed to buy and farm their own strips. But they had to pay the lord of the manor a part of their crops. Also, they had to promise to fight for the lord. A noble always had to worry about attacks by neighboring estates.

The serfs did not own their own land. They worked for the lord of the manor, farming his land. Serfs were tied to the land on which they were born. They could not leave the estate, even if they wanted to.

The serfs provided every service for the manor lord. They grew his food and gathered his wood. They took care of his lands and his castle. In the feudal system, each class owed loyalty and service to the class just above it.

Life on a Feudal Estate

Very little trade went on under the feudal system. Each feudal estate had its own village and met its own needs. Each village had a blacksmith to make tools and weapons. Each village had a miller who ground grain into flour. The serfs had to use the services of the manor. And they had to pay whatever price was asked for these services.

Did the serfs have any rights under the feudal system?

The nobles and their families lived in great houses made of stone. The **medieval** manor houses were real castles. But they were still very cold and often gloomy. They had no glass in the windows. They had no running water. They were dimly lit by burning torches made of twigs. The damp, shadowy castles were really cold fortresses. There the noble families could be safe from enemies.

Many of the manor lords had several manors. They lived part of the year at one and part of the year at another. The lords chose managers to oversee the land when they were away.

While the noble family lived in the castle, the villagers lived in small, smoky huts. They ate from wooden bowls and sat on backless, three-legged stools. They could not read or write. Their only contacts from outside the manor came when the village held a fair. Then merchants from around the countryside might bring their wares.

A manor lord could treat his serfs however he pleased. "Between you and your serf there is no judge but God," was a medieval saying. No laws protected the people from their lord's treatment.

Even rich people lived under harsh conditions during the Middle Ages.

History Practice

Write answers to the following questions on a separate sheet of paper.

1. What jobs did the serfs have to do for the lord of the manor?

2. Describe the houses that the nobles and their families lived in.

3. Where was the only place that education and learning were carried on during the Middle Ages?

Men of the Church

Medieval society was a Christian society. Higher officials in the church were nobles much as the lords of the manor were. Large pieces of land were often given to the **clergy.** The highest-ranking clergymen were as wealthy and powerful as the most important lords.

Men who wished to devote their lives to serving God lived in monasteries. There they spent their days studying, praying, and taking part in religious services.

Knights

Except for the Church leaders, every important man in the feudal society was a fighting man. Even the kings were warriors. The estates fought each other. There were bands of robbers to be controlled. Tribes of people from other parts of the country often came looking for new lands.

So men were trained to fight. Warriors of the noble class were known as **knights**. Knights fought to defend their own manors. And they fought for their king as they had promised to. They also fought to protect Christianity from the Moslem threat.

Knights were expected to be brave, courteous, and kind. This code of behavior was called *chivalry.*

LEARN MORE ABOUT IT: Knights in Armor

Being a knight was a costly business. Armor and weapons were elaborate and expensive. The serfs had to work very hard to pay for their lord's fancy armor, many horses, and fine weapons. If a boy wanted to grow up to be a knight, he began training at age seven. He started out as a page. He learned to fight and to have the proper knightly manners.

The next step in becoming a knight was acting as a squire. A squire served a knight. He helped the knight with his armor and weapons. And the squire rode with his knight into battle. When he was 21, a worthy squire was "knighted" by a nobleman. The young squire became a knight when a sword was tapped on his shoulder.

Knighthood was both a military and a religious honor. A young man spent the night before he was knighted in a church. There he kept watch over his armor, as he knelt and prayed. He thought about the honor he was about to receive.

Knights kept their fighting skills ready by entering tournaments, or **jousts**. Two knights on horseback would fight each other with long lances. Their goal was to knock the other knight off his horse. The winner's honor was not only for himself. It was also for his favorite "lady," whose ribbon he wore into battle.

Jousting knights

A Hard Life!

The feudal way of life was most widespread during the 1100s and 1200s. Life on a feudal manor was hard. There were floods and years of bad crops. There were always battles to fight. And there were plagues.

In A.D. 1348 a ship from the East docked at an Italian port. Some sick sailors came ashore. They brought with them a terrible plague. This disease became known as the Black Death. It got its name because it caused spots of blood to turn black under the skin.

Little was known about medicine during the Middle Ages. There were few doctors. And those doctors did not understand the causes of diseases or how diseases were spread. The villages were not very clean. There was a large population of rats that lived off the garbage. Doctors today think that bites from infected rat fleas caused the plague. But doctors in the 1300s didn't know much about prevention or treatment of disease. They had little to offer. As a result, nobles and serfs alike fell sick and died. By the end of 1351, one-fourth of the entire population of Europe had died from the Black Death.

Feudal society lasted for almost 700 years. But by A.D. 1400 the great manors had almost disappeared. Trade had picked up. Money had come back into use. Nobles no longer received land for services. People moved back to the towns.

New methods of warfare were being developed. Gunpowder and new weapons such as cannons were now available. And foot soldiers were being used more effectively. Because of these changes, knights were no longer useful.

But for hundreds of years, the picture of life in Europe had been the feudal manor. It was a world where everyone fit into one of three classes: nobles, clergy, or workers. "Some fight," a medieval bishop wrote. "Others pray. And others work."

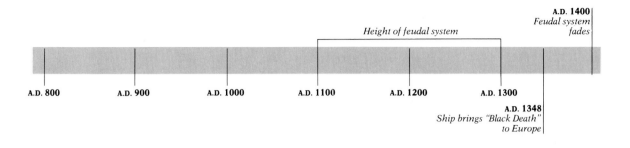

A.D. 800 | A.D. 900 | A.D. 1000 | A.D. 1100 | A.D. 1200 | A.D. 1300

Height of feudal system

A.D. 1400
Feudal system fades

A.D. 1348
Ship brings "Black Death" to Europe

WHICH CAME FIRST?

Use the time line to choose the event, year, or period of time that came first. Write your answers on a separate sheet of paper.

1. Ship brings "Black Death" to Europe *or* Feudal system fades?

2. Feudal system fades *or* Height of feudal system?

3. A.D. 1100 *or* A.D. 1000?

4. Height of feudal system *or* Ship brings "Black Death" to Europe?

5. A.D. 1348 *or* A.D. 1300?

Chapter Review

- During the Middle Ages people lived under the feudal system.

- In return for land, nobles paid homage to their king.

- Medieval manors included a manor house, a village, and fields.

- The lord of the manor was the absolute ruler of his feudal estate.

- Each feudal estate took care of its own needs. Very little trade went on.

- Serfs worked the land for the lord of the manor.

- Except for the clergy, every important man in feudal society was a warrior.

- Knights were warriors of the noble class.

- Knighthood was both a military and a religious honor.

- Medieval society was divided into three classes: the nobles, the clergy, and the workers.

- A plague called the Black Death killed one-fourth of Europe's people in the Middle Ages.

Chapter Quiz

A. Checking Your Facts

Choose the correct word or words to make each of the sentences below a true statement. Rewrite the sentences on a separate sheet of paper.

1. Men who wished to devote their lives to God lived in (manor houses/monasteries).

2. Warriors of the noble class were known as (knights/squires).

3. Medieval manor houses were lit by (gas lamps/burning torches).

4. (Serfs/Vassals) were tied to the land and were not allowed to leave the estate.

5. Feudal society lasted for almost (1700/700) years.

B. Think About It!

Write answers to the following questions on a separate sheet of paper.

1. Do you think that the life of a medieval serf was any different than that of a slave? Give at least two reasons for your answer.

2. "Between you and your serf there is no judge but God," was a medieval saying. What do you think this saying means?

3. Why do you think men during the Middle Ages trained to become knights?

Chapter 13

The Crusades

The crusaders journeyed all the way from Europe to the Holy Land. What do you think the crusaders hoped to accomplish?

Chapter Learning Objectives

- Give four reasons people went on the Crusades.
- Explain how the Crusades affected European trade.
- Name three new developments in farming in the Middle Ages.
- Describe what life was like in a medieval town.
- Tell why the Magna Carta was important.

Words to Know

apprentices   people who learn a trade under a master

fallow   land not used for farming during a season

guild   a medieval organization formed to protect the interests of workers in one craft or trade

harness   leather straps that fasten a horse to a plow, cart, or wagon

journeyman   a person who has finished his apprenticeship and receives wages, but who is not yet a master

justice   fairness according to the principles of right and wrong; what is deserved; the administration of law

migrate   to move away from one country or region to settle in another

pilgrimages   visits to a holy place

plowshare   the broad blade of a plow

population   people living in a place, or the total number of those people

surplus   more than what is needed

truce   a time when enemies agree to stop fighting

The Middle Ages is often thought of as a time of darkness, of little forward movement. But there were changes going on in medieval Europe. The Crusades, or Holy Wars, brought new ideas and new interests to Europeans. There were changes happening on medieval farms and in towns. Some people began recognizing that kings had too much power. People could see that their rights were being denied. Europe changed very slowly during the Middle Ages, but it did change.

Christian Pilgrims

During the Middle Ages, the Christian religion was the strongest force in Europe. People made **pilgrimages** to show their faith. From Germany, France, England, and Italy they traveled to holy shrines. Thousands of pilgrims went on foot and on horseback. They crowded Europe's roads.

Moslems also made pilgrimages. Which city did they journey to?

Pilgrims traveled east to the Holy City of Jerusalem. Jerusalem had been a holy city for the Jews since the days of Solomon's splendid temple. Now it was a holy city for the Christians as well. Christian pilgrims flocked to Jerusalem. They went to see the place where Jesus had lived and taught.

The Moslems called Jerusalem a holy city, too. And Jerusalem was then under Arabic control. The Arabs respected the Christian religion. They allowed Christian pilgrims to visit the Moslem city.

But, in 1071, the Seljuk Turks took power in Jerusalem. The Turks were Moslems, too. But they were not as friendly to the Christians. The Turks would not allow Christians to visit their city. They would not let them worship at the holy shrines.

The Soldiers of Christ

An angry pope, named Urban II, stirred Europeans to action. He spoke before a gathering of important people. He reminded them that the Turks held Jerusalem. He told them that Christians there were in danger. It was their Christian duty, he said, to free the Holy Land.

People listened. Feudal nobles, knights, and commoners were all moved to action. Word spread across Europe. Soon armies of Christians were ready to travel to the Holy Land. They wore a cross sewed on their clothing as a symbol of this mission. Then the Christian armies set forth on the Crusades. The Holy Wars they started were to last for 200 years.

The Crusades

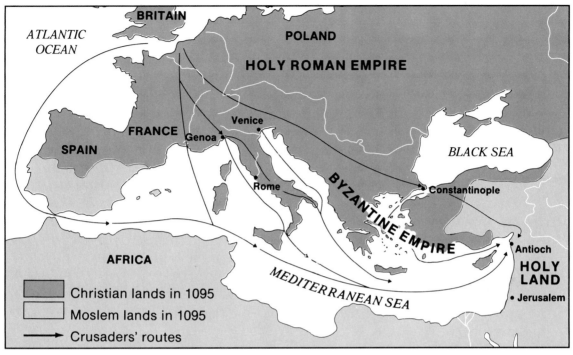

Map Skills
Which bodies of water did the crusaders cross on their way to the Holy Land? According to the map, did the Holy Land belong to the Moslems or Christians in 1095?

Many crusaders marched because of strong religious feelings. But some went on the Crusades for other reasons. Some were looking for adventure. Others were looking for wealth in new lands. Soldiers wanted military glory. Merchants wanted new markets for their goods. Criminals wanted a safe place to hide.

Crusaders came from every social class—kings and nobles, knights and lords. The serfs saw a chance to escape feudal manors. They joined the march, too. They all set out to take Jerusalem from the Moslems.

If you were a Christian during those days, would you have wanted to go on the Crusades? Why?

The earliest Crusade, in 1096, was led by a man called Peter the Hermit. These first crusaders were a ragtag bunch of unorganized peasants. They started out for the Holy Land before the huge armies of knights did. They did not do very well. They had to steal food along the way to keep from starving. The Turks had little trouble defeating them. Most were killed before they ever reached Jerusalem.

In the autumn of 1096, several armies of knights set out from Europe. Nobles from France led the march. It was a hard trip. Over the next two years, many died from hunger and from disease. The knights had to fight many battles along the way. But those who made it to Jerusalem were ready for another fight. They started a bloody battle. It lasted six weeks. When it was over, the crusaders had taken Jerusalem from the Moslems. The crusaders had killed many of the people who lived there—Jews as well as Moslems. The year was 1099.

The noblemen from Europe set up several small states in the Holy Land. Christians back home were pleased. The Holy Land was under Christian control. Most of the crusaders returned to Europe.

Then European leaders in Jerusalem began to quarrel among themselves. The Turks launched new attacks. So more crusaders went off to help protect the Holy Land.

A Truce

The Moslems had a leader who was said to be strong and wise. His name was Saladin. Saladin's troops won back the city of Jerusalem in 1187.

Then European rulers joined together to fight for the Holy City. Three of them set off on a Crusade. They were the German emperor, Frederick I (called Barbarossa), King Philip II of France (called Philip Augustus), and King Richard I of England (Richard

Off to the Crusades

the Lion-Hearted). Together they went to fight for Jerusalem.

The German emperor, Frederick, accidentally drowned on the trip to the Middle East. King Philip of France returned home before the Crusade was over. He claimed he was too sick to fight. It was up to Richard the Lion-Hearted to face Saladin.

Richard and Saladin were both great leaders and brave warriors. They had much respect for each other's skills. When they met in battle, Saladin's forces gained the upper hand. Then word came that Richard was needed back in England. Saladin agreed to a five-year **truce**. Under the terms of the truce, Christians would be allowed to visit Jerusalem. And they could also keep control of a few cities on the coast.

The Holy Land Falls to the Ottomans

But Saladin died, and the truce weakened. By 1291 the Moslems again held all of the Holy Land. In 1453 the Ottoman Turks took power in Turkey. The Holy Land fell under their rule. The Ottomans also put an end to the Byzantine Empire. They changed the name of their capital city, Constantinople, to Istanbul. By 1500 the Ottomans would rule over a huge empire. The Middle East, North Africa, and much of eastern Europe fell to the Ottomans. The Ottoman Empire would last for hundreds of years.

Europeans found the Crusades costly in many ways. It took a lot of money to equip the warriors and send them such great distances. And the Crusades were also costly in terms of lives. Many people, both Christians and Moslems, died bloody deaths fighting for the Holy Land. In the name of God, people had looted, burned, and killed.

In the beginning, people thought the Crusades would lead them to glory. But the Holy Wars only caused suffering and misery. And this was all in the name of religions based on brotherhood and love.

LEARN MORE ABOUT IT:
The Children's Crusade

One of the saddest of the Crusades became known as the Children's Crusade. In 1212 an army of 30,000 French boys and girls set out to fight. Most of them were twelve years old or younger. They were gathered together and led by a shepherd boy named Stephen.

At first it must have seemed like an adventure for the children. But it ended badly. Nearly all of the 30,000 children died. Most fell sick along the way, or they starved to death.

Another army of German youths headed for Jerusalem. Led by a boy named Nicholas, these 20,000 children never saw the Holy Land either. When seven ships offered to take them to Jerusalem, they accepted. How lucky, they thought, to get a ride!

But it turned out to be bad luck indeed. Two of the ships were wrecked in storms. All of the children aboard drowned. The rest of the ships were not headed for Jerusalem at all. The children had been tricked. The ships took them to Egypt where they were sold as slaves.

The Crusades Bring Change to Europe

By 1291 the Christians had lost all of the lands they once held in the Middle East. But the crusaders brought back Middle Eastern ideas. And crusading merchants brought home new products. The Crusades created a new Europe.

The merchants introduced Europe to foods like lemons, rice, apricots, and melons. New spices such as ginger and pepper, cloves and cinnamon, now seasoned European food. The merchants brought fine cloth. Europeans began wearing brightly dyed silks. With the new trading, Europe's whole economy became stronger.

When the crusaders left Europe, their journeys gave them fresh ideas. There was a new interest in travel and exploration. People learned to make better maps. All the fighting that went on encouraged even more interest in warfare. Crusaders returned with new weapons and better battle skills.

The feudal society had kept medieval people tied down to the manors. The Crusades sent them out into the world. The Crusades were sad and costly. But they increased trade and brought a sharing of cultures.

History Practice

Write answers to the following questions on a separate sheet of paper.

1. Give four reasons why people went on the Crusades.

2. Name the Moslem leader who agreed to a truce with Richard the Lion-Hearted.

3. What effect did the Crusades have on European trade?

Changes in Agriculture

The world's first agricultural revolution had taken place long ago. It occurred along the Mediterranean Sea when people began planting seeds and raising animals. During the Middle Ages another farming revolution was going on. Now people were learning new and better methods of growing food. And these changes in agriculture changed society as a whole.

The Emperor Charlemagne had opened new iron mines. With more iron available, farm tools improved. Now there were new metal axes and hoes.

But the new tool that most changed farming in the Middle Ages was the **plowshare**. Early plows had been little more than large sticks. These sticks were dragged across the ground by one or two oxen. They only scratched the earth. It took hours and hours of work to break up even a small field.

Remember Charlemagne? What else did he do to improve life in the Middle Ages?

Medieval farming

The new plowshare was made of sharp, curved iron. The plow itself was fastened to a heavy, wheeled frame. It took eight oxen to pull the plowshare. With the new, heavier equipment, farmers could till even the heaviest soil. Working in long, narrow strips, they could plow the land more quickly.

The plowshare meant that more land could be farmed and more food could be grown. People did not have to eat all that they grew. They had a **surplus** of food now. And they could use this surplus to trade for other goods.

Medieval farmers discovered that horses were better workers than oxen. Horses could work longer without rest. They moved faster. With more iron around, it was easy to make enough horseshoes.

The farmers invented a new kind of **harness** for their horses. It fit over the horse's shoulders instead of across its chest. Now the horse could breathe easier and could pull heavier weights. It took fewer horses than oxen to pull the new plowshare.

Farmers learned to get more out of their fields. They maintained three fields now. They planted one field in the autumn and one in the spring. A third field lay **fallow** each season. Each field was given a season to be fallow. This let the soil rest and grow rich again.

The three-field method of crop rotation worked well. If one crop failed, there was always a second crop to rely on. More food was produced.

The Population Grows

During the 1000s Europe's **population** began to grow. But more people meant a need for even more farmland. Farmers cleared forests and drained swamplands in England and in France. People began to **migrate** eastward. Germans colonized new lands in eastern Europe. So changes in agriculture meant that people lived in new places.

As farm production increased, workers had more food to trade for goods. Beginning in the 1000s, craft workers and traders began to settle in medieval villages. They moved there to sell their goods. In addition to the blacksmith and the miller, there were now new shops in the villages. The villages grew into towns.

Medieval towns were usually surrounded by stone walls. Their narrow streets were often just mud. Sometimes the streets were paved with cobblestones. The towns were often dirty and dark.

With walls closing them in, the towns were small and crowded. People threw their garbage into the streets. There were no fire departments, no police departments, no health services. Most of the houses were just huts made of wood. With these conditions, there was always a danger of fire and of disease. The town of Rouen in France burned to the ground six times between 1200 and 1225! It is easy to see how the plague spread so quickly in such crowded, dirty towns.

But the medieval towns grew. And as they did, the workers, merchants, and craftsmen became more specialized.

People used money more often now. On the manors, services had been exchanged for goods. Now people paid money for new leather shoes, a pottery bowl, or a tasty cake.

Serfs saw the town as a place to win freedom from manor lords. Sometimes serfs ran away and hid within the walls of a town.

"Live free for a year and a day," the rule went, "and go free."

A serf who could manage to escape his lord for that long became a free man.

The Feudal System Weakens

During the late Middle Ages, business and trade increased. As the towns became stronger, and the merchants became richer, the feudal system weakened. The towns wanted to govern themselves—to be free of the manor.

Some feudal lords sold charters of freedom to the towns. No longer were so many people "tied" to the land. Most towns were dirty and crowded. But people were freer than they had been on the feudal estates. So they wanted to live in the towns.

Guilds

The towns offered opportunity. Peasants could work their way up in the world. They could learn a trade or a craft.

How do people learn a trade or craft today?

Each trade and craft had its own group, or **guild**. The guild helped set prices. And it set standards for workmanship. The guilds decided how long shops should stay open each day.

The guilds also offered a chance to learn. Boys and girls could become **apprentices** and go to work for a guild member. The apprentice lived in his master's house and worked in his shop. He received no pay.

An apprentice served for seven years. Then he could become a **journeyman** and earn wages. When he became skilled enough, a journeyman made one special piece of work for his master. It was called a "masterpiece." If the masterpiece was good enough, the journeyman joined the guild.

Streets in medieval towns often were named after different guilds. *Tailors Row* and *Boot Street*, for example, were typical street names.

Big Cities

Most people lived in the small, walled towns during the Middle Ages. But there were a few fine, wealthy cities. Trade flourished in those cities. There were theaters and hospitals, schools and libraries.

There were cities like Constantinople, capital of the Byzantine Empire. One million people lived there. As many as one thousand ships might dock at Constantinople's harbor at the same time.

There were cities like Baghdad, center of the Islamic world. There, scientists studied mathematics and astronomy. Doctors made new discoveries in medicine. Geographers mapped the world.

There were cities like Cordova, Spain. It was called the *Lighthouse of Learning*. Spanish Moslems and Spanish Jews studied there.

And there were cities like Venice and Antwerp. Trade and manufacturing made these places wealthy.

All these cities grew during the Middle Ages. Trade kept them powerful and rich. They were centers for art, science, and education.

Progress in Human Rights: The Magna Carta

There was little concern with human rights during the early Middle Ages. A lord could treat his serfs any way that he pleased.

When King John ruled England, he showed no interest at all in anyone's rights. He didn't even treat the nobles very well! Suppose that King John didn't like a certain noble. Or suppose he thought that noble was becoming too powerful. He might very well have the noble put to death.

Do you think that King John did the right thing by signing the Magna Carta? Why or why not?

The Signing of the Magna Carta

Noblemen were angry. In 1213 a group of powerful men met in England. They drew up a list of rights that they wanted the king to grant them. They also listed some rights that they would grant to freemen. Because they included the commoners in their demands, all of England supported the nobles.

King John didn't want to give up any of his power. He refused to sign the list. In 1215 the nobles sent an army after him. King John saw that he couldn't defeat the army, so he finally gave in. At Runnymede, on the banks of the Thames River, King John signed the list of rights. It became known as the *Great Charter*, or the *Magna Carta*.

WORDS FROM THE PAST: The Magna Carta

The Magna Carta listed 63 demands. Some were very important. These rights led the way toward English democracy.

The Magna Carta said that:

A freeman had to be tried by a jury of his equals before he could be sent to prison.

Taxes would be collected by legal means, not by force.

Justice would not be denied to freemen.

The Magna Carta did not bring instant democracy to England. It really gave more privileges and rights to the nobles. All men were still far from equal. But it did limit the power of the king. And it set a basis for the modern jury system. Hundreds of years would go by before everyone would benefit from the justice mentioned in the Magna Carta.

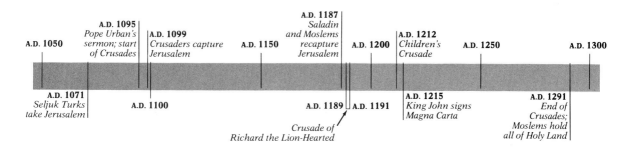

A.D. 1050

A.D. 1095
Pope Urban's sermon; start of Crusades

A.D. 1099
Crusaders capture Jerusalem

A.D. 1150

A.D. 1187
Saladin and Moslems recapture Jerusalem

A.D. 1200

A.D. 1212
Children's Crusade

A.D. 1250

A.D. 1300

A.D. 1071
Seljuk Turks take Jerusalem

A.D. 1100

A.D. 1189

A.D. 1191
Crusade of Richard the Lion-Hearted

A.D. 1215
King John signs Magna Carta

A.D. 1291
End of Crusades; Moslems hold all of Holy Land

Chapter Review

Chapter Summary

- Christian crusaders fought to win Jerusalem from the Moslems.

- The Christians won the Holy Land for a time, but the Moslems got it back.

- The Crusades were bloody wars fought in the name of religion.

- The crusaders brought back new ideas, new products, and new plans for trade in Europe.

- A medieval revolution in agriculture meant new tools and better methods of farming.

- The population of Europe grew, and many people migrated eastward.

- Medieval towns saw an increase in craftsmen and merchants.

- The craftsmen formed guilds.

- Most towns in Europe were crowded and dirty, but there were some fine, big cities.

- In 1215 King John signed the Magna Carta, giving new rights to Englishmen.

Chapter Quiz

A. Checking Your Facts

| apprentices | pilgrimages | journeyman | plowshare | harness |

Complete each sentence below. Use the correct word from the box. Rewrite the sentences on a separate sheet of paper.

1. The new tool that most changed farming in the Middle Ages was the _____ .

2. Christians made _____ to holy shrines to show their faith.

3. If a _____ made a good enough masterpiece, he could join a guild.

4. Medieval farmers invented a new kind of _____ for their horses.

5. _____ served for seven years.

B. Think About It!

Write answers to the following questions on a separate sheet of paper.

1. How did the growth of towns weaken the feudal system?

2. Why do you think the Magna Carta was important? Under the Magna Carta, what happened to a person accused of a crime?

3. Would you have liked to live in a medieval town? Give at least two reasons for your answer.

Unit Four Review

Write answers to the following questions on a separate sheet of paper.

1. What high position did Charlemagne hold? Who named him to that position?

2. Name three places that the Vikings settled. What are three words you might use to describe the Vikings?

3. Name three ways in which feudal life was hard.

4. Describe a medieval castle.

5. Who were the "soldiers of Christ"? After the Crusades were over, who ended up controlling the Holy Land?

6. Name three changes that the Crusades brought about in European life.

7. Name three new developments in farming tools and methods during the Middle Ages.

8. Compare training for a medieval trade to training for knighthood. How was it the same? How was it different?

9. Name two changes that took place in Europe because of the agricultural revolution.

10. Did the Magna Carta bring instant democracy to all English people?

The Renaissance

Chapter 14

New Ideas: The Renaissance

Galileo made many discoveries about the heavens with his telescope. How did this affect people's thinking about the universe?

Chapter Learning Objectives

- Explain what the word *Renaissance* means.
- Tell how the invention of movable type helped in the spread of knowledge.
- Name four important men of the Renaissance.
- Explain what the Reformation was.
- Name two leaders of the Reformation.

Words to Know

astronomy the study of stars, planets, and other heavenly bodies

heretics people who are against the teachings of a church

humanism a concern with the needs and interests of human beings rather than religious ideas

monk a man who has taken religious vows and usually lives in a monastery

patrons wealthy people who support artists

pendulum a weight hung so that it swings freely back and forth; often used to control a clock's movement

protest to speak out against or act against something

reform to change for the better

Renaissance the revival of art, literature, and learning in Europe in the fourteenth through sixteenth centuries

scholars people who have learned much through study

sculptor a person who makes statues out of wood, stone, marble, or other material

theory an explanation of how and why something happens, usually based on scientific study

During the Middle Ages the culture and learning of the Greeks and Romans were all but forgotten. For most people it was as if Greece and Rome had never existed. For this reason the Middle Ages, especially the early part, is sometimes called the Dark Ages. There was an increase in trade and travel toward the end of the Middle Ages, around A.D. 1300. It was as if a light had been turned on in Europe. It was the light of reason and thought. That is why the period after the Middle Ages became known as the Renaissance. **Renaissance** means *rebirth* or *awakening*.

The Renaissance lasted about 200 years.

The Renaissance was a time of new ideas. During the Middle Ages the Catholic church was all-powerful. Thinking centered on God. And most **scholars** were also men of the church. During the Renaissance, people began to think about themselves as well as about God. People used to worry about whether or not they would go to heaven after they died. Now they thought more about making a good life on earth. This new belief in the importance of human beings became known as **humanism**. The spirit of humanism sparked new ideas in art, in science, in literature, and in philosophy.

LEARN MORE ABOUT IT: The Humanists

Humanists were scholars whose main interest was in human beings. They began to question the church and its leaders. A Dutch scholar, Erasmus, eyed the church critically.

"It seems," Erasmus decided, "that the church is more concerned with wealth and power than with helping men find God."

Erasmus wrote books that questioned the church's practices. He believed that simple ways were best. There was too much ritual and ceremony in the church, he said. Erasmus was a humanist. He believed that if people were just shown what was right, they would live that way. Erasmus was among the first Renaissance scholars to criticize the church. But he certainly was not the last.

Renaissance Art

The Renaissance began in Italy. Then it spread northwest across Europe. More and more people began to appreciate beautiful things. The work of Italian craftsmen became very fine. People thought of it as art. Europeans showed a new interest in the civilizations of ancient Greece and Rome.

"Perhaps," people said, "that is when civilization was at its best!"

"Look at the art that came out of Greece," they said. "Look at the beautiful statues and the paintings. Look at the fine architecture of the Romans." At first Italian artists tried to copy the work of the ancient Greeks and Romans. Then they began to improve on it.

During the Middle Ages most paintings were of religious scenes. The people in these pictures were not very lifelike. Renaissance artists studied the human form. They tried to make the people in their pictures look more like real people. For the first time, artists used live models.

A craftsman could make a good living from his work. But it was harder for an artist to earn a steady wage. Wealthy Italians served as **patrons** for promising young artists. A patron provided food, housing, and enough money for the artist to live on. Because of their patrons, artists were able to work and study to improve. Some of the world's finest artists lived during the Renaissance.

The spirit of humanism led Renaissance artists to make the people in their pictures lifelike.

Michelangelo Buonarroti

One of the most famous artists of the Italian Renaissance was Michelangelo Buonarroti. During the Renaissance, people were encouraged to be good at many things. Michelangelo, in true Renaissance spirit, was more than just a fine painter. He was also a **sculptor**, a poet, and an architect.

Michelangelo was a poet as well as an artist. He was a true *Renaissance* man.

He earned his greatest fame for his sculptures. Michelangelo studied the human body. He studied the human form at work and at rest. Michelangelo even cut up dead bodies. This helped him understand the lines of bone and muscle. His sculptures seem alive and real. Each muscle is perfect. Each position is totally lifelike.

Michelangelo was born in A.D. 1475 in a mountain town in Italy. He began showing artistic talent as a young boy. A wealthy Italian, Lorenzo de' Medici, noticed Michelangelo's brilliance. He became Michelangelo's patron.

Pietà **by Michelangelo**

At age 24 Michelangelo created his first masterpiece. It was a huge statue called the *Pietà*. Michelangelo sculpted it for St. Peter's Church in Rome. In the *Pietà* the body of Christ is shown held in his mother's arms. The word *Pietà* came from the Italian word for pity.

Michelangelo's statue of *David* is another of his most famous works. Completed in 1504, it is a perfect example of the Renaissance interest in the human form. "David" is strong and looks alive. The statue is 18 feet high and made of solid marble. Michelangelo's *David* is very heavy. It took 40 men to move it from the workshop to a central square in Florence, Italy.

Pope Julius II hired Michelangelo to paint the ceiling of the Sistine Chapel in Rome. Michelangelo painted a series of pictures showing events in the Bible. Over 300 figures from the Bible appear on the 60-foot-high chapel ceiling. Michelangelo had to paint the scenes lying on his back. He lay on a platform held by ropes. He worked on that ceiling for four years.

Later in his life, Michelangelo turned to architecture. He worked on the rebuilding of St. Peter's Church. He took no pay then. He believed it was a task that would please God.

Michelangelo died when he was 90. He had a long life in which to sculpt, to paint, and to build. His art brought light and beauty to all of Europe.

Education and Learning

All writing was done by hand during the Middle Ages. Books were copied on parchment made of animal skin. So books were expensive and few in number. Only wealthy people could own books of their own. Most books were written in Latin, the language of the church. The only scholars were clergymen. The church was the only place where any studying went on.

Why did Latin, the language of ancient Rome, become the language of the church? (Hint: Where did Christianity first become the official religion?)

The famous Gutenberg Bible wasn't discovered until 1760. It was found in Paris.

Then, about A.D. 1450, things started to change. Secrets of making paper were brought to Europe from China. They were introduced by the Moors, or Spanish Moslems. Then a new invention made books available to everyone! A German printer named Johannes Gutenberg discovered how to use movable type for printing.

With movable type, letters were molded onto small metal blocks. The letters could be moved around to spell different words. When inked and pressed onto paper, the movable type printed a whole page at one time.

Now books could be made quickly at low cost. Now everybody could read the stories of the Greeks and Romans and tales of travel. The ideas of the past and the present were there for everyone. Books were translated into the languages of the common people, not just that of Latin scholars.

Johannes Gutenberg reading the first sheet from his printing press

With the *Gutenberg Bible* Europeans could read the Bible for themselves. People did not have to rely on the church to tell them what the Holy Book said. The Bible was translated into English, Italian, French, and German.

It became important to be able to read. More schools opened. Schools that taught Greek and Latin grammar were called "grammar" schools. There were new universities. Studies went beyond religious thought. People studied the world. And they studied about their own place in the world.

How important is it to be able to read in today's world?

Science and Invention

The Renaissance was a time for progress. There were some important changes during the Middle Ages. But change had come slowly. Now new books—and new ideas—were available for anyone who could read. Universities were growing. With the spirit of the Renaissance, change came rapidly.

People explored new ideas. Gutenberg's printing press was just one of the new inventions. Inventors discovered how to make springs. Then they made watches that were small enough to be carried in a pocket. Before, the only clocks had been huge ones on public buildings. Now people could keep time at home.

New instruments helped sailors find their way on the open seas. New maps improved travel. People experimented with metals. Soon they came up with cast iron to replace expensive bronze.

In medicine, the English doctor, William Harvey, discovered that the heart pumps blood throughout the body. And in 1600 the microscope was invented. It led to a new look at the world. Suddenly people learned that there were tiny creatures—smaller than the eye could see!

The Center of the Universe

Some of the greatest scientific discoveries of the Renaissance came in the field of **astronomy**. These new ideas changed people's thinking in many ways. Not only were there new ideas about the way the Earth and stars moved. Now there was also a new way of seeing mankind's place in the whole system. These ideas shook up the scientific world and shook up the church, too.

For hundreds of years people had believed that the Earth was the center of the universe. They believed that the sun, moon, and stars all moved around the Earth. Then in 1543 the Polish astronomer, Nicolaus Copernicus, wrote a book. He said that the planets, including the Earth, revolve around the sun.

Most people would not believe him!

Why do you think people weren't willing to believe Copernicus?

Galileo Galilei

The invention of the telescope challenged more old ideas. Now scientists could get a better look at the sky. An Italian scientist, Galileo Galilei, took up where Copernicus had left off. Galileo was born in Pisa in 1564. He made his first important scientific discovery at the age of 20. Galileo watched a great lamp swing from the ceiling of the cathedral in Pisa. Then he came up with the idea of the **pendulum**.

Later, he discovered the "law of falling bodies." Galileo found that gravity pulls all bodies to the Earth at the same speed, no matter what their weight. Galileo climbed to the top of the Leaning Tower of Pisa to prove his **theory.** Then he dropped a ten-pound weight and a one-pound weight. He showed that they both hit the ground at the same time.

Some people were angry. They were shocked that Galileo would dare to challenge the ideas of the wise Greek, Aristotle. Galileo's discoveries would bring him a lot of angry words.

The invention of the telescope brought another breakthrough. Galileo was not its inventor. But he was the first to use the telescope to study the heavens. With his telescope, Galileo discovered that the moon did not have its own light. It reflected light. He discovered moons around Jupiter and the mass of stars in the Milky Way. All of Galileo's discoveries led him to support Copernicus's theory. The Earth was not the center of the universe. The Earth was just another planet revolving around the sun!

No matter how well Galileo proved his theory, the church would not hear of it. They ordered members of the church not to read Galileo's books. The church sent Galileo warnings. He was not to teach his theories. In 1632 Galileo was called to a church hearing. There was a long trial. Galileo had to promise that he would give up his belief in Copernicus's theory. The church forced him to say that the Earth was the center of the universe. Church officials watched Galileo closely for the rest of his life. He became a prisoner in his own home.

History Practice

Write answers to the following questions on a separate sheet of paper.

1. What is the meaning of the word *Renaissance*?

2. How would you describe Michelangelo's sculptures?

3. What is the name of the famous ceiling that Michelangelo painted? What did he paint on the ceiling?

The Renaissance Person

A well-educated Renaissance person was supposed to have many skills. Michelangelo could paint, sculpt, write poetry, and build. Galileo studied medicine, physics, and astronomy.

Do you think it is possible to be a *Renaissance* person today? Do you know anyone like that?

A Renaissance person was expected to enjoy art, to write poetry, and to play a musical instrument. Renaissance education taught people to read and write Latin and to speak several other languages. People were expected to understand the politics of the day. They were supposed to ride well on horseback and to be good at sports.

A Renaissance man should be able to put up a good fight if necessary. And a Renaissance person had to learn proper manners of courtesy and grace. Great importance was placed on being well educated and very well rounded. One of the best examples of the perfect Renaissance person was Leonardo da Vinci.

Leonardo da Vinci

A list of what Leonardo da Vinci could *not* do would very likely be shorter than a list of what he could do! Italian-born da Vinci was a Renaissance genius in not one field, but many. He was one of the world's greatest artists and scientists. Leonardo was a painter, a sculptor, an architect, and a musician. He was an inventor, an astronomer, and a geologist. He was one of the first to show an interest in "flying machines."

Leonardo's sketchbooks show drawings of many different flying machines. His ideas were based on the flight of birds. These sketches also show great understanding of the human body and of engineering.

He had a sure sense of the way things worked. He understood the way parts joined together to form a whole. This great knowledge helped make Leonardo such a good artist.

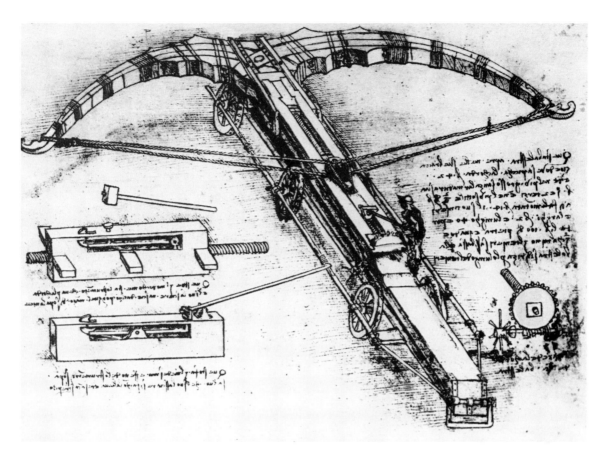

Details from Leonardo da Vinci's sketchbook

His *Mona Lisa* is a painting of a woman with a mysterious smile. It is one of the world's most famous masterpieces. Today it hangs in the Louvre Museum in Paris.

For 17 years Leonardo served the Duke of Milan. He worked as a painter, sculptor, and as an engineer. He was then hired as a painter by the government of Florence. For the last two years of his life, Leonardo lived in France at the invitation of King Francis I.

Mona Lisa by Leonardo da Vinci

Leonardo, the Renaissance man, used one talent to benefit another. His scientific studies helped him understand people and the world. Because of this, his paintings seemed all the more real. He had a desire to know more about everything. It was curiosity like Leonardo's that made the Renaissance a time of new ideas and new inventions.

The Reformation

During the Middle Ages most of the people in western Europe were Roman Catholics. The Catholic church held great power. It owned lands and collected taxes. Popes and priests were wealthy men.

But during the Renaissance, more people went to school and learned to read. They began to question the ways of the church.

Was it right for the clergy to be so interested in wealth? Was it right that church officials should have so much power? Some people also questioned the ceremonies and rituals that filled church services. What had become, they wondered, of the simple ways taught by Jesus?

The movement that questioned the practices of the Catholic church was called the *Reformation*. Some Europeans set out to **reform**, or change, the church.

Martin Luther

A German **monk** named Martin Luther became a leader among the reformers. Luther was born a German peasant. He grew up as a Roman Catholic. He studied at a university and became a monk. But the more Luther studied religion, the more he worried. His concern was that the Catholic church was headed in the wrong direction.

A person did not need fancy rituals or pilgrimages to find God, Luther said. He began to criticize the Catholic church in public sermons. In 1517 Martin Luther wrote a list of 95 complaints about the church. He nailed it to the door of the Castle Church in Wittenberg, Germany.

Luther continued to question church practices. In 1521 he spoke out against the power and authority granted the pope. This did not please the pope. Luther was told to *recant*, or take back, what he had said. Luther refused. He said that unless the Bible itself proved him wrong, he would not recant.

Luther challenged the supreme authority of the pope.

Luther was thrown out of the Catholic church. Emperor Charles V declared Luther an outlaw. He said that anyone could kill Luther without punishment.

Several German princes supported Luther and his feelings about the church. One prince hid him in a castle. The church could not take him prisoner. Soon Luther had so many supporters that before long he was able to set up a whole new church.

The new church, based on Luther's ideas, simplified religion. Religious practices would be based only on what was found in the Bible. In 1529 the Catholic church declared that no one should practice Lutheranism. Lutheran princes decided to **protest**. Because of this, they were called *Protestants*.

Other leaders across Europe also protested against Catholic practice. Other Protestant churches were started. The Reformation was underway.

Other Protestants

A man named John Calvin developed his own version of Protestantism in Switzerland. He set up strict rules for Christians to live by. Calvin's teachings were followed in many parts of Europe.

French Calvinists were called Huguenots. But most Frenchmen were Catholic. They began to resent the Huguenots. On St. Bartholomew's Day, in August of 1572, the Catholics carried out a plot. They murdered all the Protestants they could find in the city of Paris. The killing then spread throughout France. Thousands died during the next few days.

In Spain the Inquisition was at work. The Inquisition was a special court. It had been set up by the Roman Catholic church to punish **heretics**. Besides Spain, the Inquisition was also going on in France, Germany, and Italy. The Inquisition hunted down anyone who was not a practicing Catholic. It forced people to confess their beliefs, often by torturing them. Those who would not accept the Catholic religion were burned to death. In Europe blood was again being shed in the name of religion.

The Inquisition held secret trials, and people on trial weren't told who their accusers were.

The Counter Reformation

Many people who wanted change had turned away from the Catholic church. Others hoped to make changes within the church itself. The movement for reform within the Catholic church was called the Counter Reformation.

In 1545 the pope called a meeting of clergymen at Trent in Italy. The Council of Trent looked for ways to keep the Catholic church from losing followers. The Council clearly spelled out the beliefs of the Church and insisted that people obey them. To reawaken faith among the people, church leaders approved of some new religious orders. One of these was the Society of Jesus.

St. Ignatius Loyola

St. Ignatius Loyola was one of the most powerful leaders of the Counter Reformation. Loyola had once been a Spanish soldier. He was crippled when a cannonball hit his leg. While recovering, he read a book about the life of Jesus. After his recovery he decided to hang up his sword. He began a spiritual life. He went to the University of Paris and studied to become a priest.

In 1534 Loyola gathered six followers and formed the Society of Jesus. Its members were called Jesuits. The society quickly gained many more members. Their mission was to win Protestants back to the Catholic church. The Jesuit order, with ex-soldier Loyola at its head, was run much like an army. Jesuits were expected to obey without question.

The Jesuits did stop the spread of Protestantism in Germany. They carried Catholic ideas to far-off lands. Loyola died in 1556. By then the Jesuit order was well established.

Throughout the Reformation, Catholics and Protestants competed for religious control of Europe. Kings and queens of Spain, of England, and of France became caught up in the struggles of the Reformation. Religion played an important part in shaping Europe's history.

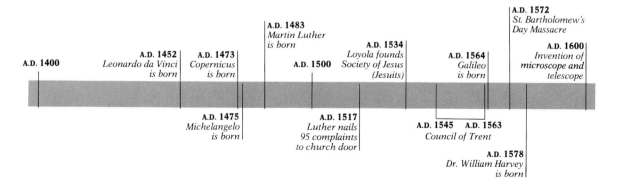

A.D. 1400

A.D. 1452
Leonardo da Vinci
is born

A.D. 1473
Copernicus
is born

A.D. 1483
Martin Luther
is born

A.D. 1500

A.D. 1534
Loyola founds
Society of Jesus
(Jesuits)

A.D. 1564
Galileo
is born

A.D. 1572
St. Bartholomew's
Day Massacre

A.D. 1600
Invention of
microscope and
telescope

A.D. 1475
Michelangelo
is born

A.D. 1517
Luther nails
95 complaints
to church door

A.D. 1545   A.D. 1563
Council of Trent

A.D. 1578
Dr. William Harvey
is born

Chapter Review

Chapter Summary

- Renaissance means "rebirth" or "awakening."

- Renaissance Europeans became interested in the art and ideas of the ancient Greeks and Romans.

- During the Renaissance, great work was done in art and in science.

- Books became available to all people.

- Renaissance people celebrated human beings and the human form in pictures and statues that looked real.

- Ideal Renaissance people, like Leonardo da Vinci, had many talents and many interests.

- The Catholic church had grown powerful and wealthy. During the Renaissance some people began to question the church's practices.

- Martin Luther led the Reformation. He wanted to reform, or change, the Catholic church.

- People who protested against the Catholic church were called Protestants.

- Protestants struggled with Catholics for freedom to practice their religion.

Chapter Quiz

A. Checking Your Facts

Choose the correct word or words to make each of the sentences below a true statement. Rewrite the sentences on a separate sheet of paper.

1. Lorenzo de' Medici became Michelangelo's (teacher/patron).

2. Europeans were able to read the (Wittenberg/Gutenberg) Bible for themselves.

3. On St. Bartholomew's Day the (Catholics/Huguenots) carried out a plot to murder Protestants.

4. The Spanish Inquisition hunted down anyone who was not a practicing (Protestant/Catholic).

5. The movement for reform within the Catholic church was called the (Reformation/Counter Reformation).

B. Think About It!

Write answers to the following questions on a separate sheet of paper.

1. Why was the Renaissance called a time of "awakening"?

2. How did the invention of movable type help in the spread of knowledge? Do you think books are just as important today as they were during the Renaissance? Why or why not?

3. Name three things a well-rounded Renaissance person was expected to do. Imagine that you are a "Renaissance" person in today's world. Make a list of the skills you would be likely to have and the jobs you would be good at.

Chapter 15

Kings and Queens

London's Globe Theater was built in 1599 during the reign of Queen Elizabeth I. Why was she called "Good Queen Bess"?

Chapter Learning Objectives

- Describe the goal of King Philip II of Spain.
- Describe the Spanish Armada and tell what happened to it.
- Name the good things that King Henry IV did for France.
- Explain why King Henry VIII set up a Church of England.
- Explain why the English people called Queen Elizabeth "Good Queen Bess."

Words to Know

annul   to cancel; to make something no longer binding under law

declines   periods of increasing weakness

fleet   a group of warships under one command

galleons   large Spanish sailing ships of long ago, having many decks

loyal   faithful and true to one's country or to a person

monarchs   rulers, like kings, queens, or emperors

nationalism   love of one's nation; patriotism

Parliament   England's body of lawmakers

reign   the rule of a monarch; or to rule as a king, queen, or emperor

The Age of Monarchs

Spain, France, and England had each become unified into nation-states. Now a separate government ruled each of these three lands. The rulers were **monarchs**—kings and queens who held power over a whole nation.

The people of each nation were **loyal** to their rulers. They felt a bond with their country and with each other. Within a country everyone spoke the same language and followed similar customs. This feeling of pride and loyalty toward one's nation is called **nationalism**. Nationalism and religious beliefs became very important. Both were powerful forces that shaped sixteenth-century European history.

The monarchs of Spain, France, and England followed different religious teachings. Some were Roman Catholics. Some were Protestants. One ruler even started his own church. Because of their separate beliefs, the monarchs led their people into wars. They led them through times of peace, through cultural growth, and into national **declines**.

Do you believe that people should be loyal to their rulers? Why or why not?

The history of each nation affected each of the others. The religions and the personalities of the monarchs changed the lives of the people of western Europe.

Spain

Do you think that Ferdinand and Isabella were wise rulers? Why or why not?

In the late 1400s King Ferdinand and Queen Isabella ruled Spain. They were Roman Catholics. They wanted no one but Roman Catholics living in their nation.

There weren't many Protestants in Spain, but there were Jews and Moslems. Spanish Moslems were called Moors. Ferdinand and Isabella called upon the Inquisition to hunt down anyone who was not Catholic. Many Jews and Moors were tortured and killed. Those who were lucky enough to escape the Inquisition had to flee the country. The Jews left for other European countries and the Middle East. Many of the Moors fled to North Africa.

King Philip II

King Philip II ruled Spain from 1556 until 1598. He began his rule as the most powerful monarch in all of Europe. At that time, Spain was the strongest European nation. It held many other provinces. And it controlled rich colonies in the New World. But Philip's **reign** marked the beginning of Spain's decline.

Like Ferdinand and Isabella, Philip II was a Catholic. He also supported the Inquisition and its methods. King Philip saw himself as a man with a job to do. He wanted to see not only Spain, but all of Europe, under the Catholic church. King Philip's goal was to crush Protestantism.

King Philip and the Netherlands

Spain ruled the Netherlands. Many Protestants lived there. Philip II would not stand for Protestants living under his rule. He issued a royal command: "People of the Netherlands will accept the Catholic religion!"

But Philip did not count on the spirit of the Dutch people. They wanted to worship as they chose. Even the Dutch who were Catholics didn't like King Philip. He was a Spaniard, not Dutch. He expected them to send too much tax money to Spain.

The proud people of the Netherlands rebelled. A Dutch prince, William of Orange, led the rebellion in 1568. Things looked grim. But the Dutch would not give in to Spain. In 1581 the Dutch declared independence. The Netherlands was on its way to freedom from Philip and from Spain.

King Philip and England

King Philip was not alone in his dream of a Catholic Europe. Before he became king, Philip had married Queen Mary I of England. Mary was a loyal Catholic, too. She hoped to see all Protestants converted to Catholicism. Mary and Philip would fight together under the sign of the cross.

But Queen Mary only reigned for five years. When she died, the English throne went to her Protestant half-sister, Elizabeth. Although Philip had been her brother-in-law, Elizabeth saw him as England's enemy. She sent aid to the Netherlands in its fight for freedom from Spain. She gave English ships permission to attack Spanish ships on the world's seas. Queen Elizabeth I was definitely getting in the way of Philip's plans to unite Europe under Catholicism.

LEARN MORE ABOUT IT: The Spanish Armada

King Philip II decided to go to war with England. Philip built up a mighty **fleet**. It was called the Armada. The Armada was the largest fleet of ships that Europe had ever seen. In 1588, 130 Spanish ships set out against England. They were giant ships. There were crosses on their billowing sails. King Philip thought that his Armada could not be beaten.

The Armada reached the English Channel. English ships sailed out to meet it. The English ships were much smaller than the Spanish ships. At first it looked as if they would not stand a chance. But the English crafts were fast. They could dart among the heavy Spanish **galleons**, firing from all sides. The English had skilled captains like Sir Francis Drake. They kept King Philip's Armada busy. The Spanish giants could not stop the quick, little English ships.

The fighting lasted for more than a week. Most of the Spanish ships were damaged. The crippled Armada fled to the North Sea. It escaped the English by sailing north around the British Isles. Heavy winds wrecked many ships off the coast of Ireland. What was left of Philip's once-glorious Armada headed back to Spain. Only 67 ships returned home.

Philip's dream of a Catholic Europe ended with the destruction of his Armada. He had lost many soldiers. The Armada had cost Spain much money. Instead of conquering Europe, King Philip had sent Spain into a decline.

English ships attacking the Spanish Armada

History Practice

Write answers to the following questions on a separate sheet of paper.

1. What did the Spanish Inquisition do to the Moors and Jews in Spain?

2. What was the goal of King Philip II of Spain?

3. What was the Spanish Armada? What happened to the Armada when it reached the English Channel?

France

France had problems of its own. There, too, wars broke out because of religion. Civil wars had torn the country apart for more than 30 years. The Protestant Reformation had started all the trouble. French Protestants, the Huguenots, fought the Catholics. King Philip of Spain and the pope supported the Catholics. England's Queen Elizabeth sent aid to the Huguenots. In 1572, thousands of Protestants died in the Massacre of St. Bartholomew's Day.

France's Catholic king was assassinated in 1589. Before he died, he named Henry of Navarre as the next king. Henry of Navarre became King Henry IV. And Henry IV was a Huguenot!

"Good King Henry"

The French Catholics were in an uproar. A Huguenot was king! Henry IV had to fight to keep his throne. He won several battles. But he could not bring peace. Frenchmen, especially those in Paris, would not accept a Protestant as king.

To keep the peace, Henry IV declared himself a Catholic. Most Frenchmen welcomed this move. Henry IV was then officially crowned king of France. At last he was able to restore peace to the country.

But King Henry IV did not turn his back on the Huguenots. In 1598 he issued the Edict of Nantes. This gave religious freedom to the French Protestants. It was better, Henry said, than seeing France torn apart by civil war.

King Henry turned out to be a good king. Once there was religious peace, Henry worked hard to make France rich and strong. He passed laws to help the farmers. He built new roads. And he encouraged trade and manufacturing.

King Henry sent French explorers out on the seas. Under Henry's reign the first French colony was founded in North America. It was called Quebec. Feelings of nationalism grew. The French called their king "Good King Henry."

But their "good king" was assassinated in 1610. However, the religious freedoms that he had brought to France lasted long after his death.

England

In England in 1485, a man named Henry Tudor became King Henry VII. His reign ended years of civil war. He was the first of several monarchs from the Tudor family.

Henry VII was not a very colorful character. But his people liked him. He kept England out of wars. He was a good businessman and built up the country's economy. King Henry VII saw to it that everyone, especially the nobles, paid their taxes.

King Henry VIII

When Henry VII died, his son became king of England. King Henry VIII was the second Tudor monarch. He had a more colorful personality than his father. He is well remembered for having six wives.

King Henry VIII

The story of Henry VIII and his wives is all mixed up with religion. To begin with, Henry VIII was a Catholic. The people liked him. His father had been a good king. And the new King Henry seemed good-humored and kind.

Problems began when Henry no longer wanted to be married to his wife, Catherine of Aragon. Catherine had only been able to have one child. That child was a girl, the princess Mary, who later married King Philip of Spain. Henry wanted a son to follow him on the throne.

Anne Boleyn

Henry showed an interest in Anne Boleyn. She had been one of his wife's maids of honor. Anne, he thought, was beautiful. She would make him a fine wife. And she might give him a son.

King Henry asked the pope to **annul** his marriage to Catherine. The pope refused. So Henry VIII took matters into his own hands. In secret he married Anne Boleyn in 1533. His marriage to Catherine was annulled by the man who would become the Archbishop of Canterbury. Henry then broke with the Roman Catholic church. In 1534 England's **Parliament** passed a law making Henry head of the Church of England.

The new Church of England was still Catholic in its practices and beliefs. But it was not subject to any control by Rome. Henry's break with the church also increased his own power and wealth. He seized all the lands, all the gold, and all the silver that had belonged to the Roman Catholic church in England.

But things did not go so well for King Henry VIII and his new wife, Anne Boleyn. Anne, too, gave him a daughter, the princess Elizabeth. But Henry still wanted a son. He wanted a new wife, too. He accused Anne of being unfaithful. He had her imprisoned in the Tower of London. She was sentenced to death and beheaded in 1536.

Henry married a third wife, Jane Seymour. At last Henry got that son, Prince Edward. Henry married again after Jane Seymour died. In fact, he married three more times. One wife, he divorced. Another, he ordered killed. The sixth and last wife outlived Henry.

"The Boy King"

Prince Edward was Henry's only son. When Henry died, Edward took the throne of England. He became the monarch Edward VI at the age of ten.

Under Edward's rule, the number of Protestants increased in England. Protestantism, in fact, became the state religion. Edward was very young. So the affairs of his country were handled by his uncle, Duke Edward Seymour.

Edward was called "The Boy King." He died after reigning for only six years. Now two women were next in line for the throne of England. They were Henry VIII's two daughters, Princess Mary and Princess Elizabeth.

"Bloody Mary"

The oldest of Henry's daughters, Mary, reigned after Edward's death. Queen Mary I was a strong Catholic. She was determined to make England Catholic again. First she struck down all the religious laws passed under Edward VI. She made new laws enforcing Catholicism. Mary married Philip II of Spain. Together they planned to put an end to Protestantism in Europe.

History calls Queen Mary "Bloody Mary." She persecuted Protestants. She had more than 300 Protestants burned to death.

The English Parliament did not like it when Mary married Spain's King Philip. They were afraid of Spanish power. They refused Queen Mary's request to make Catholicism the state religion.

Queen Mary I died after reigning for five years. Her spirit was broken because she never saw Protestantism crushed.

"Good Queen Bess"

The next Tudor on the throne of England was Mary's half-sister, Elizabeth. Elizabeth declared that the Church of England was Protestant. The country became firmly united under the one church.

Imagine that one day you wake up to find that our country has a president who is ten years old. Describe what changes might happen.

What might have happened in England if "Bloody Mary" had ruled for 25 years instead of five?

Queen Elizabeth I

Elizabeth reigned for 45 years until her death in 1603. Her reign became one of the most glorious periods in English history.

Nationalism grew during Elizabeth's reign. Trouble with Spain only served to strengthen that spirit. England's defeat of the Spanish Armada caused all of England to cheer.

Queen Elizabeth I did have her faults. She was said to be hot-tempered. She was also called vain. But the English people loved Elizabeth. And Queen Elizabeth, despite any other faults, loved her England!

Queen Elizabeth never married. Her reign ended the Tudor line. But Englishmen remember her as "Good Queen Bess." She had brought a bright age to England.

Elizabeth's England

The reign of Queen Elizabeth became known as the Elizabethan Age. Great writers like William Shakespeare, Edmund Spenser, and Frances Bacon lived in England then. London's Globe Theater was built in 1599. Many of Shakespeare's plays were first performed at the Globe.

Elizabeth helped make her people wealthier and England's cities safer. Except for fighting the Spanish Armada, she kept her country out of expensive wars. So there was more money to spend on other things. Elizabeth made new laws. These gave work to the poor and shelter for those who could not work.

There were ship captains like Sir Walter Raleigh. They brought new products back to England. They brought tobacco and potatoes from America. Daring sailors like Sir Frances Drake captured treasures from Spanish ships. In Elizabeth's name, English sailors went out to explore the world.

You may have read or seen one of Shakespeare's plays. *Romeo and Juliet*, *Hamlet*, and *Macbeth* are some of Shakespeare's most famous plays.

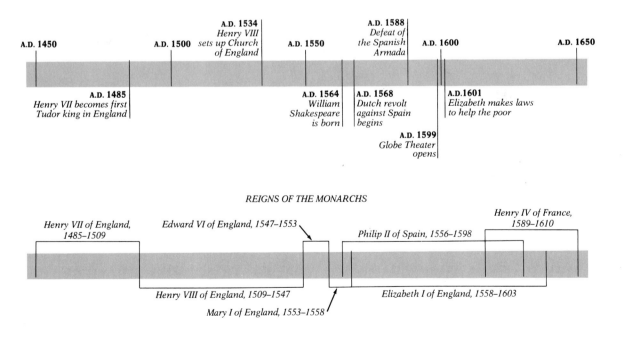

A.D. 1450   A.D. 1500   A.D. 1550   A.D. 1600   A.D. 1650

A.D. 1534 *Henry VIII sets up Church of England*

A.D. 1588 *Defeat of the Spanish Armada*

A.D. 1485 *Henry VII becomes first Tudor king in England*

A.D. 1564 *William Shakespeare is born*

A.D. 1568 *Dutch revolt against Spain begins*

A.D. 1601 *Elizabeth makes laws to help the poor*

A.D. 1599 *Globe Theater opens*

REIGNS OF THE MONARCHS

Henry VII of England, 1485–1509

Edward VI of England, 1547–1553

Henry IV of France, 1589–1610

Philip II of Spain, 1556–1598

Henry VIII of England, 1509–1547

Elizabeth I of England, 1558–1603

Mary I of England, 1553–1558

Chapter Review

Chapter Summary

- King Philip II of Spain wanted to make all Europeans Catholic.

- Philip II sent his Armada out to conquer England. But quick, smaller English ships sent the Armada home in defeat.

- King Philip's reign sent Spain into a decline.

- The French King Henry IV converted to Catholicism to keep peace in France.

- Henry IV passed laws giving religious freedom to the Protestants in France.

- The Tudors ruled England from 1485 until 1603.

- King Henry VIII of England broke from the Roman Catholic church and set up a Church of England.

- The last Tudor monarch was Queen Elizabeth.

- Elizabeth made the Church of England Protestant, and she encouraged English nationalism.

- During the Elizabethan Age there were many famous writers in England.

Chapter Quiz

A. Checking Your Facts

monarchs	nationalism	declines	Parliament	galleons

Complete each sentence below. Use the correct word from the box. Rewrite the sentences on a separate sheet of paper.

1. The feeling of pride and loyalty to one's nation is called _____ .

2. Some rulers led their people into periods of national _____ .

3. _____ are kings and queens who hold power over a whole nation.

4. The ships in the Spanish Armada were called _____ .

5. England's _____ passed a law making Henry VIII head of the Church of England.

B. Think About It!

1. Do you think King Henry IV was "good" for France? Name at least three good things he did for his country.

2. Different kings handled the question of religious freedom in different ways. How did King Philip II of Spain deal with it? How did King Henry IV of France deal with it?

3. Which of the Tudor monarchs do you think was the most interesting? What do you remember about that ruler?

Unit Five Review

Write answers to the following questions on a separate sheet of paper.

1. Where did the Renaissance begin? What part did the ancient Greeks and Romans play in the Renaissance?

2. Name two Renaissance artists who studied, painted, or sculpted the human body.

3. Why was the Catholic church angry at Galileo?

4. What was the Reformation? Why did some people want to break away from the Roman Catholic church?

5. Where did the Lutheran religion begin? What was one thing Martin Luther wanted to change about the Catholic church?

6. How did King Philip of Spain's Armada boost the English spirit of nationalism?

7. Why did King Henry VIII set up a Church of England?

8. Why was King Edward VI called the "Boy King"?

9. Why was Queen Mary called "Bloody Mary"?

10. Why did the English people call Queen Elizabeth "Good Queen Bess"?

The Age of Exploration and Conquest

Chapter 16

To the East; To the West

The Taj Mahal in Agra, India, is one of the most beautiful buildings in the world. What was its purpose?

Chapter Learning Objectives

- Name three Chinese inventions.
- Name the lands conquered by Genghis Khan.
- Describe the role of samurai and shoguns in Japanese society.
- Tell what religion the Moguls brought to India.
- Explain how the Aztecs worshipped their gods.

Words to Know

acupuncture treating pain or illness by putting needles into certain parts of the body

bartered traded goods or services without using money

forge to work into shape by heating and hammering

hermit one who lives alone, away from others

junks flat-bottomed Chinese sailing ships

missionaries people sent by a church to other countries to spread a religion

mosaic a design made by putting together small pieces of colored stone, glass, or other material

samurai a class of warriors in the Japanese feudal system

In China . . .

European nations battled each other. Empires rose and fell. But Chinese culture continued over the centuries with little change.

The Chinese invented many things. But China was isolated. The rest of the world would not learn about Chinese discoveries for hundreds of years to come. The Chinese kept their secrets.

Papermaking first began during the Han dynasty. The Chinese made paper from wood ash and cloth pulp. The Chinese also knew how to melt iron and how to **forge** it. They knew how to mine salt. They learned to use **acupuncture** to cure pain and disease.

Later, the Chinese used wood blocks with carved characters to print books. Chinese sailors developed compasses. And gunpowder was invented in China. It was first used for fireworks. Not until A.D. 1161 were the first explosives used in actual battle.

Do you remember why China was isolated for so many years? It was surrounded by deserts and mountains—and the Great Wall also kept outsiders away.

The Silk Road

A route known as the *Silk Road* was China's only link to the Western World. A few traders traveled this road. They made their way across deserts and over mountains. They brought Chinese goods to the West. Many Europeans were fascinated with Chinese art and style. They especially liked the fine silk cloth. It was made from threads spun by silkworms.

People still like fine silk cloth. But today it is made in many places in the world.

The Silk Road was not a one-way road. Chinese products came out of China. And new ideas filtered into China along this road. Buddhism came to China from India in the second century A.D. In the next centuries it spread across China.

Mongol Invasion

To the north of China are the vast plains of central Asia. The people who lived there then were called Mongols. They were nomads, loosely organized into tribes. They wandered over their lands with their horses, sheep, camels, oxen, and goats. The Mongols were expert horsemen. And they were skilled at using the bow and arrow. In their camps they lived in felt tents called "yurts."

In A.D. 1206 a great chief took power over all the Mongols. His name was Genghis Khan. *Khan* was a title given to rulers. And Genghis Khan believed that he was destined to rule a great empire. He built up a huge army of Mongol soldiers. They conquered lands including parts of China, Russia, Persia, and India.

Genghis Khan had little education. But he was clever and ruthless. With his soldiers on horseback, he swept across the countryside. The thunder of the hooves of Mongol horses was a terrifying sound. The Mongols were among the most savage conquerors in history. If any city in their path tried to put up a fight, the Mongols showed no mercy. Every single person in the city would be killed.

GREAT NAMES IN HISTORY: Kublai Khan

Perhaps the greatest of the Khans was Kublai Khan. He was a grandson of Genghis Khan. Kublai Khan completed the conquest of China. Chinese farmers were no match for the Mongol armies. The Mongols ruled China from A.D. 1260 until A.D. 1368.

Kublai Khan ran his empire well. He was a Buddhist, but he allowed religious freedom. He saw to it that roads were good and trips were pleasant. There were stones to mark the way. And trees were planted to give shade to travelers.

Kublai Khan developed a postal service. He wanted to make it easy for people throughout his empire to communicate. Horsemen carried messages along China's Great Wall. A post house stood every 25 miles along the wall. At each post house messengers could change horses. And travelers could rest. The Grand Canal was built to transport goods from north to south. Chinese boats called **junks** carried goods along the 850 miles of waterway.

Marco Polo

Marco Polo was a trader and a traveler. He lived in Venice, Italy. Marco Polo traveled to China with his father and his uncle. They went to see Kublai Khan. His palace was in the capital city of Peking.

Kublai Khan welcomed the traders. He allowed Marco Polo to travel about his empire. The young Italian stayed in China for 17 years. Marco Polo saw sights that no other European had ever seen.

Kublai Kahn's kingdom was huge. It extended as far as Russia.

Then Marco Polo returned to Italy. He got caught up in a war. The fight was between Venice and another Italian city, Genoa. He was taken as a prisoner of war. He was thrown into jail in Genoa. There he told some amazing tales to a fellow prisoner who helped to write them down. The tales became a book, *Description of the World.* The book contained stories of the great Chinese civilization and of the empire of Kublai Khan.

Many people did not believe Marco Polo's tales. But the stories later proved to be true. He had written a good description of his adventures in China.

Marco Polo had found China a rich land. He found that travel in China was quite easy.

Marco Polo and Kublai Khan

Marco Polo was impressed with all he saw in China. The Chinese were using gunpowder and compasses. They used coal for heat. Marco Polo wrote that coal was "a sort of black stone, which they dig out of the mountainside. . . ." He was interested in their use of paper, especially for money. Europeans were still using heavy, metal coins.

Marco Polo's stories gave Europeans their first glimpse of life inside of China.

The End of Mongol Rule

In the 1300s the Chinese revolted against Mongol rule. It was the end of any foreign rule in China. The Mongols were driven away. The Ming dynasty reigned.

Blue and white Ming porcelain is still much admired.

Ming emperors lived in Peking in a great palace known as the *Forbidden City*. The Mings ruled there for nearly 300 years. Chinese art and literature thrived during this period. Europeans found Ming art beautiful. But the Chinese did not want European goods in trade. China would only accept payments of gold and silver.

In Japan . . .

Japan is a group of islands off the coast of China. Very little is known about the early history of Japan. Why? Because the ancient Japanese had no system of writing. Writing first came to Japan from China during the fifth century A.D. Customs, crafts, arts, and ideas of government and taxes also came to Japan from China. The Japanese adapted the Chinese calendar system and the ideas of Confucius. About A.D. 552 Buddhism came to Japan from China and Korea.

The Japanese visited China. The Chinese came to Japan. The Japanese began to model their way of life after the Chinese ways. In the seventh century one Japanese emperor was especially drawn to Chinese ways. He *ordered* changes in Japanese life to make it more like Chinese life.

Samurai warrior, Japan

Japan's Feudal System

What were the European feudal warriors called? How were they similar to the samurai?

Europeans of the Middle Ages lived under a system of feudalism. At the same time so did the Japanese. Japanese feudal society was divided into classes. Nobles were at the top. A class of warriors fought for the nobles. Japanese feudal warriors were called **samurai**. Samurai were given many privileges.

The nobles gave them wealth and land. The samurai were respected as an upper class. In return, samurai warriors pledged loyalty and protection to their nobles.

The samurai were highly trained soldiers. They were expected to die, if necessary, for their noble. Samurai fought with huge, two-handed swords. Before attacking, a samurai would first shout his own name. Then he would shout of the bravery of his ancestors. This was meant to scare his enemy.

The nobles and samurai made up the upper classes of Japanese feudal society. But most of the population were peasants. They raised the food for the nobles and warriors.

Japanese society also included craftsmen and a few traders. Traders were looked down upon. Buying and selling goods was not considered honorable.

Feudal clans, or families, later united into larger groups. In time, Japan became a nation-state under one emperor. The emperor was called the Mikado. Japanese people honored their Mikado. But he had no real power. The country was actually ruled by a warlord, a military leader.

One of those warlords was a man called Yoritomo. In A.D. 1192 he began to use the title of *Shogun*. This meant "great general." For almost 700 years one powerful shogun after another ruled Japan. Highly trained samurai enforced the shogun's rule. Shogun rule lasted until 1867.

The shoguns were so powerful they actually took over leadership from the emperors.

Kublai Khan, the Mongol emperor, tried twice to conquer Japan. He launched attacks in 1274 and in 1281. Both times, his fleet was forced to flee because of a fierce storm. The Japanese called these raging storms *Kamikaze*, or "Divine Wind."

Kublai Khan's fleet approaches Japan

The Hermit Nation

A **hermit** is someone who lives alone, away from others. Japan under the shoguns could be called a hermit nation. Japan showed little interest in the rest of the world. For years it remained isolated, like China.

The Italian traveler Marco Polo first told Europeans about Japan. He called the country *Cipango*, land of gold and riches. Europeans liked the sound of "gold and riches"! Traders began to travel to Japan.

At first the Japanese allowed the trade. They even welcomed Christian **missionaries**. But soon the shogun began to worry. He thought that Christianity and European ways might upset the Japanese culture. So the ruling shogun, of the Tokugawa family, closed the doors to Japan. Only the Dutch were allowed to continue a little trade. Just one Dutch ship a year could come to the port of Nagasaki.

The Japanese were strict about their rules. Stories tell of foreign sailors shipwrecked on Japanese shores being put to death. Their crime was that they had dared to set foot on Japanese soil!

The shogun also forbade the Japanese to travel outside of their country. Beginning in about 1600, Japan was totally separated from the rest of the world. For about the next 250 years, Japan remained alone.

History Practice

Write answers to the following questions on a separate sheet of paper.

1. Name three Chinese inventions.

2. Name the lands conquered by Genghis Kahn.

3. What was the role of the shogun in Japanese society?

In India . . .

For a long time India was divided into different kingdoms. Wealthy princes ruled each one. The people followed the Hindu religion. But in 273 B.C., Asoka became emperor. He converted to Buddhism. Most of India's people turned away from the Hindu religion with its strict caste laws. They turned to the gentle teachings of Buddha.

But later, the Hindu religion became popular in India again. Hindu believers flocked to the Ganges River to wash away their sins. The Hindus believed that all rivers came from the gods. They thought that the Ganges was especially holy.

The Moguls Invade India

In the eighth century A.D., Moslem warriors began a series of invasions into India.

The first Moslems came from Arabia. Three hundred years later, the invaders came from Persia and Afghanistan. The city of Delhi was captured several times. In 1206 Moslems set up a government in Delhi. Then in 1398 the conqueror Tamerlane and his army from central Asia raided India. Delhi was captured once again.

In 1526 a Moslem prince of Afghanistan named Babar invaded India. He was a direct descendant of Genghis Khan. Babar conquered most of northern India. He established the Mogul empire and made himself emperor.

Do you agree that Akbar was a wise ruler? Why or why not?

The greatest Mogul emperor was Babar's grandson, Akbar. He extended Mogul rule to most of India. He was a wise ruler. He was a Moslem. But he let others worship as they pleased. He tried to bring all religions together to live in harmony. Most of the empire remained Hindu.

The Mogul Empire lasted for about 200 years. These were good years. The strong central government provided a time of peace. The arts thrived. A special blend of Middle Eastern and Indian culture developed. The Moguls left fine buildings. One of these is the famous Taj Mahal. It was built by Shah Jahan as a tomb for his wife, Mumtaz Mahal. Shah Jahan was the grandson of Akbar.

It took 20,000 workers 20 years, from 1630 to 1650, to complete the building of the Taj Mahal.

Shah Jahan had a son called Aurangzeb. In 1658 Aurangzeb took the throne. He threw his father in prison. Aurangzeb was a harsh ruler. He made Hindus pay a special tax. He destroyed many Hindu temples. He tried to force people to convert to Islam. In central India the Hindus revolted. The empire was weakened. Aurangzeb died in 1707. Shortly after, the Mogul Empire began to break up.

In the Americas . . .

Until the end of the fifteenth century, most Europeans did not know about the Americas. Only the Vikings knew that land existed across the western sea. But one day the Europeans would call these lands the New World.

Name the Viking who had reached the shores of North America.

Mound Builders and Cliff Dwellers

Groups of Indians lived in different parts of the Americas. From about 100 B.C. to A.D. 500, the Hopewell Indians lived in the Ohio River Valley. They built huge burial mounds. As many as 1,000 people were sometimes buried in a single mound. Other Indians lived along the Mississippi River. They too built giant mounds of earth around A.D. 1000. They built their temples on top of the mounds. These Indians were called Mississippians. They lived mainly by farming.

To the west, in what is now New Mexico, Arizona, and Colorado, lived the cliff dwellers. These Indians were called Anasazi. The Anasazi are also called Pueblo Indians, from the Spanish word for *town*. Around A.D. 1000 they began building villages on the sides of cliffs. All building was done with sandstone blocks and mud. Some homes were on protected ledges. Others were in hollow spaces in the cliff walls. Most homes were two or three stories high. As many as 1,500 people lived in one of these villages. But the Anasazi moved on by about A.D. 1300. By then their villages were empty. Perhaps the climate had become too dry to allow farming.

These Indians did not have a system of writing. What we know about them comes from the findings of archeologists.

Early civilizations of North America

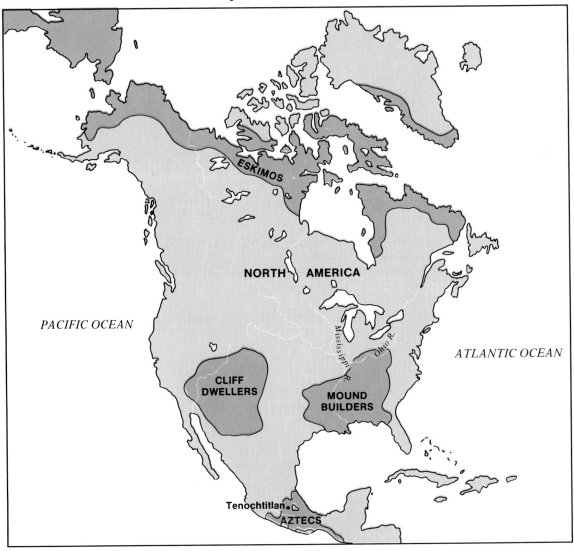

Map Skills
Name four early civilizations of North America. The Mound Builders were located near which two rivers?

The Eskimos

Far north on the continent of North America lived the Eskimos. Eskimos ate the meat of caribou, seals, whales, and birds. They also ate fish from icy northern waters. They had no greens to eat. They got their vitamins by eating every part of an animal. They often ate the meat raw. The word *eskimo* is an American Indian word. It means "eater of raw meat." The Eskimos call themselves *Inuit*, which means "people."

The Eskimos lived in one of the coldest places in the world. They made tools and weapons to fit their cold land. They traveled in sleds made of driftwood and leather. The sleds were pulled by teams of furry dogs. In the summer the Eskimos lived in tents made of animal skin. In winter they lived in houses made of blocks of snow. These houses were called *igloos*.

Eskimos loved feasts and celebrations. Their medicine men danced and sang to the spirits of the earth and the air.

The first Europeans to meet Eskimos were the Vikings. Eskimos arrived in Greenland about A.D. 1100. They found Vikings living there.

The Aztecs

In Chapter 6 you read about the Olmecs and the Mayas. They were the earliest civilizations in the Americas. They had built their cities in the jungles of Mexico and Central America.

The Aztecs were another American Indian people. In the 1200s they settled in a large valley in Mexico. The Aztecs built one of the most advanced civilizations in the Americas.

"Find a place where a great eagle sits on a cactus," Aztec priests declared. "The eagle holds a snake in its beak. At that place you shall build your temple."

The Aztecs followed the words of their priests. Th[ey]
believed that these words came from the gods. So th[is]
is how they decided on a site for the capital. Where
they found the eagle, they built the city of
Tenochtitlan. Modern-day Mexico City is on the same
site as Tenochtitlan, the ancient Aztec capital.

The Aztecs were a warlike people. They were feared
by other Mexican tribes. During the 1400s, Aztec
warriors conquered all the lands around Tenochtitlan.
More conquests followed. Montezuma II came to the
throne in 1502. He ruled the mighty Aztec empire
from the capital city.

The Aztecs were always waging war. And they were
always collecting tributes from those they conquered.
The tributes came in the form of gold and silver,
craftwork, food, and human prisoners. Young men and
women were taken to the temples. They were offered
as sacrifices to Aztec gods.

Human sacrifice was the worst part of Aztec
civilization. The Aztec religion called for constant
sacrifices to keep the gods happy. Aztec priests cut
the hearts out of their living victims. They offered the
hearts to the gods. Huge piles of skulls of the Aztecs'
victims were displayed in a public square.

In spite of their cruel religious practices, the Aztecs
had a well-ordered society. They invented a simple
form of picture writing. They also developed a system
of numbers to help them keep track of what they
owned. They had a calendar stone that recorded time.
They built temples and buildings in a pyramid style.

The Aztecs had no need of money since they
bartered for goods. Chocolate was a favorite drink. So
cocoa beans were often traded. Our word *chocolate*,
in fact, comes from the Aztec language.

The Aztecs made some beautiful craftwork.
Archeologists have found **mosaic** masks made of
turquoise and jade. Aztecs also used colorful feathers
to make headdresses and cloaks.

**Name an invention of
the Olmecs and the
Mayas.**

The Aztecs liked games and contests of athletic strength and skill. One of their favorite games was called *tlachiti*. It was a combination of handball and basketball. The players had to put a very bouncy rubber ball through rings at either end of a court.

The Aztec empire came to a bloody end in 1521. Cortez and his army had arrived in Tenochtitlan in 1519. They were amazed at what they found. Tenochtitlan was larger than any Spanish city of that time. The Spaniards were welcomed in friendship. The Aztecs may have believed that Cortez was a long lost Aztec god. The god was supposed to have sailed away across the sea. And he was expected to return someday. But then Cortez captured the emperor, Montezuma, and made him a prisoner. The Aztecs rebelled in 1520 and drove the Spanish away. Montezuma died during the fighting. The next year Cortez returned and destroyed Tenochtitlan.

The Incas

The earliest history of the Incas is only legend. What we know for sure is that the Incas lived in the mountains of what is now South America's Peru. Around A.D. 1200 they began to spread out and build their empire. In time, the Incas conquered much of western South America. They took over the rest of Peru and parts of what is now Colombia, Bolivia, Ecuador, and Chile.

One man ruled the entire Inca Empire. He was called the *Inca*. His people worshipped him as a direct descendant of the sun. The sun was their most powerful god. The Inca's word was law. He had many officials to see that his laws were obeyed.

The Inca ruled over a giant empire from his capital at Cuzco. More than 6 million people lived under his rule. Communicating with all these subjects was a problem. So the Incas built a fine network of roads.

Ruins of the Inca city of Machu Picchu, Peru

These roads connected all corners of the empire. The Incas also built bridges of twisted vines to stretch across steep jungle ravines. They had no horses or wheeled vehicles. All traveling was done on foot. Llamas carried their goods.

Swift runners raced along the Inca roads to deliver messages. The Incas had no system of writing. So messages were passed by word of mouth. Runners also carried *quipus*. These were different colored ropes with knots to stand for numbers. They used the quipus to keep track of things.

The Incas built rest stops along their roads. At each stop a tired runner could tell his message to a fresh runner. Then that messenger would hurry to the next stop. This relay system kept communication moving across the empire.

The Incas were fine builders. They used huge stone blocks. They fit the blocks together very carefully. They needed no mortar or cement of any kind. Some of the stones fit together so tightly that the blade of a knife cannot slide between them! Inca buildings still stand at Cuzco today, even after earthquakes have destroyed modern structures.

The Incas had plenty of gold and plenty of silver. Their temples were decorated with both of the valuable metals. Inca artists made beautiful objects of solid gold. These were often inlaid with precious jewels.

It is no wonder that the Spanish explorers were drawn to the Incas. In 1532 tales of great wealth brought Francisco Pizarro to South America. His visit was the beginning of the end of the Inca civilization.

We don't know how the Incas were able to do such amazing work with huge stones. Does this method remind you of any other ancient builders?

Two Worlds Meet

For centuries the rest of the world did not know about the Americas or the people living there. Then the Vikings landed in North America. But they left no lasting colonies. Much later, European explorers found the continent by accident. What they were really looking for was a quicker route to India and the Far East. The place they found seemed like a land of wealth and plenty. It seemed well worth exploring and conquering. The next chapter in world history would be an exciting time of exploration and discovery.

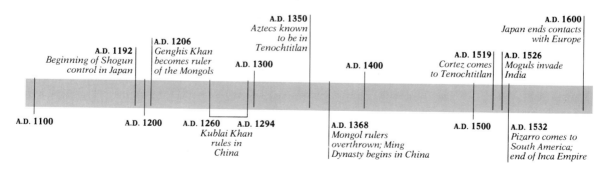

A.D. 1192
Beginning of Shogun control in Japan

A.D. 1206
Genghis Khan becomes ruler of the Mongols

A.D. 1350
Aztecs known to be in Tenochtitlan

A.D. 1300

A.D. 1400

A.D. 1519
Cortez comes to Tenochtitlan

A.D. 1526
Moguls invade India

A.D. 1600
Japan ends contacts with Europe

A.D. 1100

A.D. 1200

A.D. 1260
Kublai Khan rules in China

A.D. 1294

A.D. 1368
Mongol rulers overthrown; Ming Dynasty begins in China

A.D. 1500

A.D. 1532
Pizarro comes to South America; end of Inca Empire

Chapter Review

Chapter Summary

- The Chinese used paper, printing, and gunpowder long before the Europeans did.

- Mongols from the north invaded China and ruled an empire there for nearly 100 years.

- Marco Polo, an Italian trader, visited China and took home stories of his travels.

- The Japanese lived under a feudal system similar to the one in Europe.

- The samurai were Japanese warriors, and shoguns were ruling warlords.

- In the early 1600s Japan's shogun forbade travel and trade outside Japan.

- Moslem invaders brought the Moslem religion to India.

- Until the late 1400s most Europeans did not know that the Americas existed.

- The Aztecs developed a large, warlike civilization in Mexico.

- The Incas made their homes in the mountains of Peru.

- The Incas' empire spread throughout much of western South America. It was linked by a fine system of roads and bridges.

Chapter Quiz

A. Checking Your Facts

Choose the correct word or words to make each of the sentences below a true statement. Rewrite the sentences on a separate sheet of paper.

1. Marco Polo wrote a book called (*Description of the World/ Around the World in Eighty Days*).

2. Samurai belonged to the (upper/lower) classes of Japanese feudal society.

3. In A.D. 1192 Yoritomo began to use the title (Kamikaze/ Shogun).

4. Hindu believers in India thought that the (Ganges/Indus) River was especially holy.

5. The Taj Mahal was built by (Aurangzeb/Shah Jahan).

B. Think About It!

Write answers to the following questions on a separate sheet of paper.

1. Kublai Khan ruled his empire well. Do you agree or disagree with this statement? Give reasons for your answer.

2. Why did the shoguns forbid Japan to trade with the outside world? Do you think that this was good for Japan? Why or why not?

3. Why do you think the Aztecs welcomed the Spaniards in friendship? If you were an Aztec living in Tenochtitlan, how would you have felt about Cortez and his men?

Chapter 17

Explorers, Traders, and Settlers: An Expanding World

Pilgrims and Indians enjoyed the first Thanksgiving dinner in the New World. Why do you think the Pilgrims came to America?

Chapter Learning Objectives

- Tell how Columbus came to discover the New World.
- Identify the Spanish conquistadors and the lands they claimed.
- Describe how the Spaniards treated the Indians.
- Explain how the slave trade developed.
- Name the groups of Europeans who settled the east coast of North America.

Words to Know

conquistadors   Spanish conquerors

insurance   a guarantee that a person or company will be paid money to cover losses

interest   money paid for the use of other people's money

investments   money lent to businesses in order to get even more money back

piracy   the robbing of ships on the ocean

Puritans   members of a sixteenth- or seventeenth-century English group of Protestants; they wanted to make the Church of England simpler and stricter

shareholders   people who own one or more parts (shares) of a business

stock   shares in a business

trappers   people who trap wild animals for their furs

Christopher Columbus

Christopher Columbus set sail from Spain in August of 1492. He was not out to prove that the world was round, as stories often tell. He was not out to conquer new lands. Columbus was looking for a water route to India. He believed that by sailing west he might find a shorter route to the treasures of India. He had convinced Queen Isabella of Spain to support his voyage. So Queen Isabella and King Ferdinand gave Columbus three ships: the *Niña*, the *Pinta*, and the *Santa Maria*.

Columbus sailed westward. But instead of reaching India, Columbus landed on an island in the Bahamas. There it was: a new world where no land should have been! Columbus claimed the land in the name of Spain. And he named the land San Salvador.

Early voyages of exploration

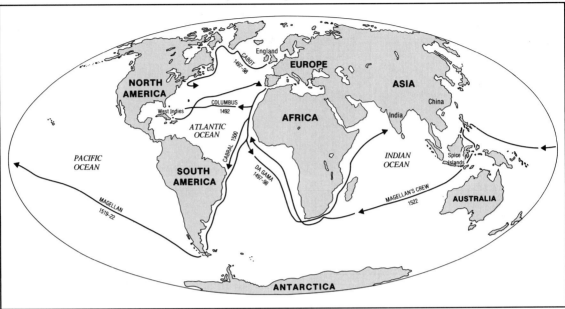

Map Skills
Which ocean did Columbus cross? Describe da Gama's route to India.

Columbus thought he had reached an island off the coast of India. So he called the peaceful natives "Indians." It was not too many years before people realized Columbus was wrong about the land's location. But natives of the Americas are still called Indians. And those islands that Columbus discovered are called the "West Indies."

Many places in the Americas have been named after Columbus. But the word *America* comes from the name of another explorer, Amerigo Vespucci. Columbus had reached the West Indies. But Vespucci claimed to be the first European to reach the mainland of South America, in 1497.

Portuguese Explorers

Other explorers searched for that water route to India. The Spaniards and the Portuguese led the way in voyages of discovery.

In 1497 Vasco da Gama sailed around Africa's Cape of Good Hope. Vasco da Gama was a Portuguese nobleman and sailor. He became the first explorer to reach India by a sea route.

Another Portuguese explorer, Pedro Cabral, set out for India in 1500. He sailed wide of Africa and found Brazil. Thanks to Cabral, Brazil was claimed in the name of Portugal.

Why were so many explorers trying to find a route to India?

In 1519 the Portuguese navigator Ferdinand Magellan began a voyage around the whole world. His own king had refused to back his trip. But the Spanish king agreed to supply five ships and 241 men.

Magellan sailed around South America and across the Pacific. However, Magellan himself did not make it all the way. In 1521 he was killed by natives in the Philippine Islands. Only one of the ships, the *Victoria*, completed the trip around the world. With only 18 survivors, it returned to Spain in 1522. This was the first ship to have sailed completely around the world. This voyage was the first proof that the Earth is round.

Now people would not be afraid to sail across the ocean. Nor would they worry about falling off the edge of the world.

The Conquerors

Europeans quickly realized what a prize they had found in the new lands. No matter that people already lived there. No matter that the natives had civilizations and cultures of their own. Europeans thought the new lands were theirs for the taking.

How would you feel about taking something that belonged to other people?

When the Spanish **conquistadors** arrived in Mexico and South America, they found great civilizations. But the natives were no match for the greedy Europeans. The conquistadors brought guns and horses to help them claim gold.

Cortez conquering the Aztecs

Hernando Cortez attacked the Aztec capital of Tenochtitlan in 1521. The Spaniards soon conquered all of Mexico. They called it New Spain.

In South America, Francisco Pizarro attacked the Inca Empire in 1532. Again the natives were no match for the new enemy they did not understand. The Spaniards tried to make the Indians accept the Christian religion. Many Indians who refused were burned to death!

The Spaniards treated the Indians cruelly in other ways, too. They used the Indians as slaves, working them harder than animals. After all, many Europeans thought, these people were only savages.

And the Europeans caused the Indians to suffer in yet another way. The Europeans brought their diseases with them to the Americas. Thousands of natives died from the new diseases.

Many people think the Indians would have been better off if the Spaniards had never set foot in the Americas. What do you think?

LEARN MORE ABOUT IT: The Slave Trade

In Africa, too, Europeans were treating people like work animals. The Europeans discovered that there was money to be made in slave trade. The Spanish and Portuguese brought ships full of Africans to the New World. The Africans were sold as slaves.

For a time the Spanish and Portuguese controlled the slave markets. Soon England and France joined the slave trade, too.

An Englishman, Sir John Hawkins, was one of the more famous slave traders. In the 1560s Hawkins made three voyages. On each he stopped in Africa to kidnap the strongest, healthiest men he could find. Then Hawkins carried the Africans to Spanish colonies in the New World. There he sold them as slaves. How could any decent person do such a thing, we might wonder. Yet Hawkins was known as a hero in England. Slave-trading led the way in setting up trade between England and the New World.

History Practice

Write answers to the following questions on a separate sheet of paper.

1. How did Columbus discover the New World?

2. Where does the word *America* come from?

3. How did the Spaniards treat the Indians?

Pirates

When the English and French set sail for the New World, they were a little late. South American land had already been claimed. So they often resorted to **piracy** to claim their share of the treasures of South America.

Sir Frances Drake was an Englishman. He was the first Englishman to sail around the world. The English called him an explorer. The Spanish called him a pirate! Drake made daring attacks on Spanish ships and towns in the West Indies. He brought his treaures home to England.

The English loved Drake. But the Spaniards feared his piracy. They called him "The Dragon."

Do you think Drake was an explorer or a pirate?

Settlers

The Spanish and Portuguese had already set up colonies in South America. So the English and French settled in North America. But this was hardly a blessing for the natives of North America.

The first Europeans landed on the east coast of North America. There they found hundreds of tribes of natives living peacefully. Each tribe had its own customs and culture. Most of the tribes lived in small villages. They lived by growing corn and other vegetables. But they didn't fit in with the newcomers. The Europeans brought new ways, new religions, and new diseases. The Indians became strangers in their own land.

In 1607 a group of English colonists settled in Jamestown in Virginia. Another group of English, the Pilgrims, arrived on the sailing ship *Mayflower* in 1620. They landed at Plymouth, Massachusetts. They were seeking religious freedom. Another religious group from England was the **Puritans**. They built several settlements on Massachusetts Bay in the 1630s.

The 13 original colonies

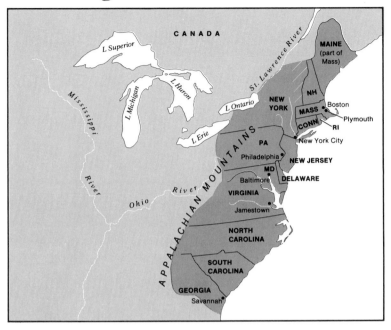

Map Skills
The colonies bordered on which mountain range? Name the 13 colonies.

More Europeans came. They were after religious freedom, a better life, and some adventure.

Most of the colonists were farmers. In the south, tobacco became a money-making crop. Slave traders brought black slaves from Africa to help on the tobacco plantations.

The settlers on North America's east coast formed 13 colonies. The colonies were under the control of the English government. Trade with Europe helped the colonies grow. Port towns like Boston sprang up.

The Indians and the Europeans did not live side by side. Slowly, the Native Americans were driven westward. Over time they lost their lands to the newcomers.

Traders

Not all of the people who came to America were interested in settling and farming. There were also the **trappers**. These men made their living hunting animals and selling the furs. Many Frenchmen trapped along the Mississippi River. They explored the area, claiming lands in the name of France. Other French trappers went north to Canada. Hunting was good there, and fishing too.

The English also held land in Canada. This land had been claimed by John Cabot in 1497. Sometimes fights over Canadian land broke out between the French and the English. In 1608 the French founded the Canadian settlement of Quebec. In 1759 the English captured that settlement. By 1763 the English had taken all of Canada from the French.

Trading Companies

Trade between Europe and the New World became big business. Merchants set up trading companies. The trading companies offered shares of their **stock** for sale. Sea voyages were expensive. So the **shareholders' investments** helped pay for the trips. Profits from successful trips were divided among the shareholders. In 1613 the Amsterdam Stock Exchange was built. This was the first building meant just for the buying and selling of stocks.

Three European countries became leaders in trade: Holland, England, and France. These were the trading powers of the 1600s. Banks were set up to help pay for trading trips. They lent money to the merchants and charged a fee called **interest**. London and Amsterdam became important banking cities.

Today many countries have stock exchanges where people can buy and sell stocks.

Shipping could be a risky business. There were storms and shipwrecks and lost cargoes. Although merchants could make a lot of money, they could also lose everything. So the merchants paid **insurance** companies a fee to protect their businesses. Then if their ships were lost at sea or attacked by pirates, the insurance companies covered the losses.

Three trading companies became powerful forces in the growing trade between Europe and the East Indies. These were the English East India Company, the Dutch East India Company, and the French East India Company. They brought home ships loaded with spices and rice, diamonds and ivory.

The New Middle Class

European merchants became very wealthy. They often lived in the style of noblemen. They built grand houses in the cities or settled on country estates.

With their new-found wealth, many became vain and greedy. They were interested only in money and fashion and fine living. Other merchants used their own good fortune to help others. They paid to set up hospitals, orphanages, and schools.

Successful trade ventures created a new, rising middle class in Europe.

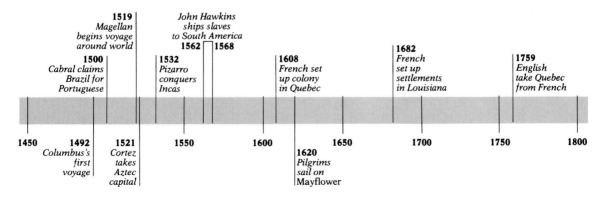

Chapter Review

Chapter Summary

- Columbus was looking for a sea route to India when he discovered the New World.

- The Spanish and Portuguese led the way in early explorations.

- Spanish conquistadors like Cortez and Pizarro claimed lands and gold for Spain.

- Africans were brought to the New World to be sold as slaves.

- While the Spanish and Portuguese set up colonies in South America, the English and French settled in North America.

- French trappers explored the Mississippi River and lands in Canada.

- England and France fought over lands in Canada.

- Holland, England, and France set up big trading companies.

- Successful trade created a new, wealthy middle class in Europe.

Chapter Quiz

A. Checking Your Facts

Choose the correct word or words to make each of the sentences below a true statement. Rewrite the sentences on a separate sheet of paper.

1. Vasco (Vespucci/da Gama) was the first European explorer to reach India by sea.

2. Hernando Cortez attacked the Aztec capital of (San Salvador/Tenochtitlan).

3. Sir John Hawkins was a famous (trapper/slave trader).

4. (Sir Frances Drake/John Cabot) was called "The Dragon" by the Spaniards.

5. Ferdinand Magellan was killed by natives in the (Philippine Islands/West Indies).

B. Think About It!

Write answers to the following questions on a separate sheet of paper.

1. Why did Columbus call the natives of the New World "Indians"? Why do you think American Indians are called "Native Americans"?

2. Why do you think that Europeans considered Africans and American Indians "savages"? Do you think the Indians would have been correct to call the Europeans "savages"?

3. How was European life affected by trade with the New World?

Unit Six Review

Write answers to the following questions on a separate sheet of paper.

1. Where did Japan get its system of writing and many of its early ideas?

2. How did the Mogul emperors treat Indians who were not Moslems?

3. Why did certain groups of North American Indians build giant mounds?

4. How did the Aztecs worship their gods?

5. How did the Incas communicate across their empire?

6. Why were the Spaniards so interested in the Incas and their South American lands?

7. What happened to the Aztecs and the Incas?

8. How did the American colonists treat the Indians?

9. What European countries were the trading powers of the 1600s?

10. Why did trading companies buy "insurance"?

The Birth of Democracy

Chapter 18

The Struggle for Democracy in England and in America

Americans declared their independence on July 4, 1776. Why do you think America wished to be free from English rule?

Chapter Learning Objectives

- List three main ideas from the Age of Reason.
- Tell why a civil war began in England in 1642.
- Explain how the Glorious Revolution gained more power for Parliament.
- List the main complaints that colonists in America had against King George III and England.
- Name five freedoms and rights that Americans won.

Words to Know

commonwealth a nation in which the people hold the ruling power; a republic or democracy

council a group of people that meet to decide something or to give advice

declaration a public statement

divine of or having to do with God or a god; like a god

independence freedom from control by others

patriots people who are loyal to their own country and show a great love for that country

petition a written request, often with many signatures, to a person or group in authority

representation sending one or more people to speak for the rights of others before a body of the government

---

"People have certain natural rights! They are entitled to life, liberty, and property!"

"Man is born free! A monarch's right to rule is given to him not by God but by the people!"

"If a monarch rules badly, throw him out!"

Whoever heard of such wild ideas! These were shocking things to say in seventeenth-century Europe. And it took brave people to say them. Yet in the 1600s and 1700s, such ideas *were* being written and spoken in Europe. It was a time called the *Enlightenment* or the *Age of Reason*.

Remember Socrates? He also taught people to question everything.

Philosophers at that time believed that every person is born with the ability to reason. Everyone had the power to decide what was true or false, or good or bad. And they said that people should use their abilities to question things. Why were things the way they were? How might they be better? Why should one person have so much power over others?

Questions like those were asked by the Englishman John Locke and the Frenchmen Voltaire and Jean Jacques Rousseau. These men were thinkers. They believed in freedom of thought, of action, and of speech. Their writings spread ideas of democracy and equality throughout the world. Their questions sparked flames of revolution in Europe and in America.

"Our lives could be better," people said. "Give us power over our own lives!"

The Road to Revolution in England

In 1215 King John of England was forced to sign the Magna Carta. This document limited certain powers of monarchs, and it granted certain rights. Mainly, it served to ensure the rights of nobles. It did little for the common people. Yet the ideas in the Magna Carta marked the beginning of democracy in England.

The words *Magna Carta* mean *great charter*.

Now a king or queen could not simply go ahead and order new taxes. He or she first had to bring the matter before a **council** of nobles. That council was called the Great Council.

In 1272 King Edward I became King of England. In 1295, when Edward needed more money to fight a war, he called the Great Council into session. But Edward made some changes. He invited not only nobles to the Council, but also merchants, knights, and rich landowners. Now more people had a voice in the king's decisions.

Parliament

The Great Council became known as Parliament. The word *parliament* comes from a French word, *parler*. It means *to speak*. Members of Parliament could speak out, advise the king, and affect his decisions.

After 1295 Parliament was divided into two parts. One group, called the House of Lords, was made up of nobles. Members of the middle class were people such as merchants and rich farmers. They met in a group called the House of Commons. For those first few hundred years, the House of Lords held the most power. But the day would come when the House of Commons became the real law-making body.

King Charles I Does Away with Parliament

The power of Parliament grew and grew. Some kings didn't like it! King Charles I ruled England from 1625 until 1649. He did not want Parliament limiting his power.

In 1603 the line of Stuart kings had begun with the reign of James I. King Charles I was the son of James. He believed in the "**divine** right" of kings. He believed that God gave him the right to rule. He also thought he should rule with absolute power.

Should any ruler ever be allowed to claim that he or she rules by "divine right"? Why or why not?

King Charles decided to ask people to pay higher taxes. When people did not pay the high taxes he demanded, he had them thrown in jail.

Parliament did not like it. "What about the Magna Carta?" they asked. "Rulers must have our approval on new taxes!"

In 1628 Parliament presented King Charles with a **Petition** of Right. The petition said that a king could not demand new taxes without Parliament's consent. It also said the king could not throw people in jail without a jury trial.

King Charles agreed to the petition. But he did not keep his word. He kept raising taxes. When Parliament protested, Charles I disbanded the whole group. King Charles ruled without a Parliament from 1629 until 1640.

Then trouble developed with Scotland. Charles I had been forcing the Scottish to follow the English religion. Scotland rebelled. So Charles called Parliament back into session in 1640. He wanted money to go to war with Scotland.

Again Parliament tried to put reins on the king's power. Charles I reacted by arresting five of the leading members of Parliament. His troops marched right into a session of Parliament and made the arrest!

It was too much. The people rebelled.

Cromwell at the Battle of Marston Moor

Civil War in England

In 1642 a civil war began in England. It lasted until 1649. The nobles who supported the king were called *Royalists*. The greatest supporters of Parliament were the Puritans. They were called *Roundheads* because they cut their hair short.

A man named Oliver Cromwell became a leading figure in the civil war. Cromwell was a member of Parliament. He led the Puritan army against the king.

Cromwell's military victories meant the end of King Charles's reign. In 1649 Charles I was captured and tried by Parliament. He was found to be a "public enemy of the nation." Charles I was beheaded.

History Practice

Write answers to the following questions on a separate sheet of paper.

1. Where did the word *Parliament* come from? What were the two houses of Parliament?

2. Why did a civil war begin in England in 1642?

3. Who were the *Roundheads*? How did they get that name?

The Commonwealth and Oliver Cromwell

Parliament set up a republic. The republic, known as the **Commonwealth** of England, lasted from 1649 until 1660. Under the Commonwealth, England had no monarch. The country was governed by a committee of Parliament and its leader, Oliver Cromwell.

But Cromwell fought with Parliament. To solve the arguments, he put an end to Parliament in 1653. For the rest of the Commonwealth period, Cromwell ruled England alone.

Cromwell dissolving Parliament

Cromwell had believed in freedom. He had refused the title of king when Parliament once offered it to him. He had been against the total power of kings. Now he had sole power in England. Cromwell's official title was Lord Protector of the Commonwealth. During his rule, he brought Ireland and Scotland under English control.

Oliver Cromwell died in 1658. His son Richard tried to carry on his father's policies. But Richard was not as strong as his father. And the people of England were ready to return to the royal Stuart line.

Even though he refused the title of king, Cromwell ruled as a king with total power.

The Glorious Revolution

In 1660 Charles II became king. He restored Parliament, and things were quiet for a while. But new problems came up when James II came to the throne.

Parliament was unhappy with King James II. He asked for too much power. So Parliament sent word to James II's daughter Mary and her husband William of Orange. Parliament asked them to come from Holland and take over James II's throne.

Did this anger King James? Did it cause another war? No. James II left the throne quietly. It was a bloodless takeover. Parliament persuaded William and Mary to sign over many of their royal rights and powers. The change came to be called the *Glorious Revolution*.

In 1689 William and Mary signed a Bill of Rights. This Bill stated that the ruling monarch could act only after consulting Parliament. With that, England took another big step toward true democracy. Now Parliament was truly the main force in government.

One day the Americans would write their own Bill of Rights. The English Bill of Rights would serve as their model.

Over time, Parliament itself became more democratic. By the late 1600s, the House of Lords held less power. The House of Commons held more. Members of the House of Lords still inherited their positions. But House of Commons members were elected by the people.

Revolution in America

George III became king of England in 1760. When he came to the throne, England had colonies in North America. George asked for the loyalty of his subjects in the New World. They seemed happy to give that loyalty.

But George III had wars to pay for, too. In 1763 the French and Indian War ended in America. The Americans and British had defeated the French and some Indian tribes. That war had cost a lot of money. Someone had to pay the bills. So King George demanded high taxes from his subjects in the colonies.

The French and Indian War was the last battle between France and England for control of the North American continent.

"High taxes, but no rights!" the American colonists complained. They had seen that people had won new rights in England. They read the words of Locke, Rousseau, and Voltaire. The Americans wanted rights and freedom, too.

"No taxation without **representation**!" was their cry. If they paid taxes to King George, they wanted a say in his government.

And some Americans wanted more than representation. There were men like Samuel Adams, who didn't want representation at all. They wanted freedom!

Americans were willing to fight for that freedom. **Patriots** like Thomas Jefferson spoke out for liberty. Jefferson used his pen to fight for **independence**. He wrote that Parliament had no right to control the colonies. And he said that unfair acts by the king meant the colonists owed him no loyalty. The colonies asked Jefferson to write a **declaration** of independence.

On July 4, 1776, the Declaration of Independence was approved. King George sent troops to the colonies. The colonists had to fight the English for their independence. General George Washington led the fight. Washington would later become the first president of the new United States of America.

Other lands watched as Americans won their freedom. They witnessed the birth of a new nation. That nation had promised its people freedom of speech, of religion, and of the press. It promised a voice in government. It promised trial by jury. And it spoke of equality.

The American Revolution gave hope to people in other lands. It made them confident that one day they would also have freedom.

WORDS FROM THE PAST:
The Declaration of Independence

The following passages are from Thomas Jefferson's *Declaration of Independence*.

We hold these truths to be self-evident, that all men are created equal, that they are endowed by their Creator with certain unalienable Rights, that among these are Life, Liberty and the pursuit of Happiness.

That to secure these rights, Governments are instituted among Men, deriving their just powers from the consent of the governed.

That whenever any form of Government becomes destructive of these ends, it is the Right of the People to alter or to abolish it, and to institute new Government . . .

We, therefore, the Representatives of the United States of America . . . do . . . declare, That these United Colonies are, and of Right ought to be Free and Independent States. . . .

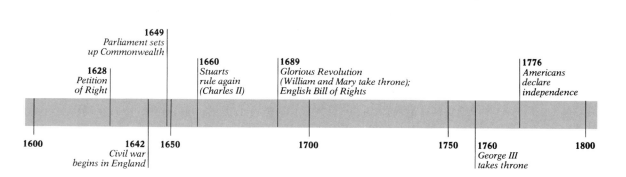

Chapter Review

Chapter Summary

- Ideas of freedom, equality, and fairness of rule came out of the Age of Reason.

- English Parliament helped limit the powers of the monarch.

- There are two houses of Parliament: the House of Lords and the House of Commons.

- Some rulers did not like asking Parliament to allow them to raise taxes.

- During England's civil war, Oliver Cromwell supported Parliament in overthrowing the king.

- After the war, Cromwell headed the English Commonwealth for nine years.

- With the return to Stuart kings came the Glorious Revolution. It was a bloodless takeover of the throne by Mary, of the Stuart line, and her husband, William of Orange.

- The Glorious Revolution brought still more power for Parliament and a Bill of Rights for the English people.

- English colonists in America had thoughts of freedom, too, and they were angered by King George's high taxes.

- In 1776 the American colonists declared their independence. They fought a war and won their freedom.

Chapter Quiz

A. Checking Your Facts

petition commonwealth council representation declaration

Complete each sentence below. Use the correct word from the box. Rewrite the sentences on a separate sheet of paper.

1. King Edward I invited merchants, knights, and landowners, as well as nobles, to the Great _____ .

2. In 1628 Parliament presented King Charles with a _____ of Right.

3. The republic, known as the _____ of England, lasted from 1649 until 1660.

4. "No taxation without _____ ," cried the Americans.

5. Thomas Jefferson wrote a _____ of independence.

B. Think About It!

Write answers to the following questions on a separate sheet of paper.

1. Compare the new ideas of the Age of Reason—ideas of freedom, equality, and fairness of rule—to the idea of the divine right of kings. Which ideas appeal to you most?

2. How did the Glorious Revolution put England on the road to democracy?

3. What led to revolution in America? Who were some of the leaders of the American Revolution?

Chapter 19
Revolution in France

An angry mob stormed the Bastille in Paris on July 14, 1789. Why do you think the mob attacked the Bastille?

Chapter Learning Objectives

- Explain how the Age of Reason and the American Revolution led to revolution in France.
- Identify the Three Estates.
- Name two French writers in the 1700s who had new ideas.
- Explain how the storming of the Bastille led to a bloody rebellion.
- Describe how the rest of Europe reacted to the French Revolution.

Words to Know

arsenal   a place where guns and ammunition are stored

betraying   giving help to the enemy; being unfaithful to; for example, *betraying* one's own country

colonial   having settlements in far-off lands; for example, Great Britain was a *colonial* power because it ruled colonies in many parts of the world

dictator   a ruler who has total power

dungeons   dark, underground rooms used as prisons

fortress   a building with strong walls for defense against an enemy

fraternity   brotherhood

guillotine   an instrument used for cutting off a person's head; it has two posts crossed by a heavy blade

motto   a word or phrase that expresses goals, ideas, or ideals

oath   a serious promise, often pledged in the name of God

riot   a violent disturbance created by a crowd of people

symbol   an object that stands for an idea; for example, the dove is a *symbol* of peace

turmoil   a condition of great confusion

The Age of Reason in France

France, in the early 1700s, had a government that was still locked into the Middle Ages. French kings ruled by "divine right." They considered their thrones a right given to them by God. No matter how unfair the rule, French people had to accept it. King Louis XIV is said to have declared, "I am the State."

Nobles led lives of luxury. They lived in fine palaces paid for by taxes collected from the lower and middle classes. While the nobles lived splendidly, the peasants often went without enough to eat.

What happened to the kings in England who thought they could rule by divine right?

But by the 1780s, Frenchmen were listening to new ideas. They read the works of Rousseau and Voltaire. "Look at England," the writers said. "The people there are free. Look at America, at their successful fight for freedom. We, too, deserve some rights!" Political conditions did not yet show it. But the Age of Reason had come to France.

The French had helped the Americans in their war for independence from British rule. French nobles were happy to see the British defeated by anyone. French peasants liked the idea of a fight against tyranny. The Frenchman, Lafayette, went to America and joined the colonists' battle. George Washington gave Lafayette command of a division, and the two fought side by side.

When the Americans won the war, the French began thinking about freedom for themselves.

King Louis XVI

The Estates-General

By 1788 trouble was brewing in France. The peasants and the middle class were unhappy. The government was in trouble, too. The king was out of money. Fancy living and too many wars had resulted in an empty treasury.

In 1789 King Louis XVI called a meeting of the Estates-General. This was a government body something like Parliament. The Estates-General had not met for 175 years. Now there was to be a meeting at Versailles. This was the name of the fine palace just outside of Paris where King Louis lived with his queen, Marie Antoinette. King Louis wanted the Estates-General to grant him more money in new taxes.

Three groups of people made up the Estates-General. Each group was called an *estate*. The First Estate included wealthy clergymen. They arrived at King Louis's meeting dressed in fine clothing and riding in beautiful carriages.

Members of the Second Estate were the nobles. Many were wealthy and came from large country manors. Some of the noblemen, however, had lost most of their wealth. They had only their titles left.

The First and Second Estates represented only a tiny part of the French population. Most of the people were represented by the Third Estate. The Third Estate included a middle class made up of merchants and city workers. And the Third Estate also included the peasants of France.

Each of the three estates had *one* vote in meetings. This was hardly fair since the Third Estate represented 98 percent of the population. The First and Second Estates could band together. And they could outvote the Third Estate every time they wanted to. Members of the Third Estate were ready for change.

At the 1789 meeting in Versailles, the Third Estate asked for more votes. King Louis XVI refused.

The Tennis Court Meeting

The Third Estate rebelled. The members called their own meeting. They declared themselves the National Assembly of France. The king refused to give them a government meeting hall. So the Third Estate held its own meeting at a nearby tennis court.

At the meeting, members of the Third Estate took the Tennis Court **Oath**. They swore that they would give France a constitution. At this point, Louis XVI gave in. He said that he would accept the National Assembly. He said that he would divide votes more fairly among the Three Estates.

Marie Antoinette was told that the French people no longer had bread to eat. In reply, she was rumored to have said, "Then let them eat cake!"

Marie Antoinette

In the meantime, the king was organizing his troops. When he gathered an army near an assembly meeting, people began to worry. Was the king planning to stop the National Assembly by force? The people grew angry. Force, they said, would be met by force! France was now approaching the boiling point.

The Storming of the Bastille

To the people of Paris, the Bastille was a terrible **symbol**. It stood for the tyranny of their king and for the injustices they faced. The Bastille was a gloomy **fortress** built in 1370. It was used as a prison. All that was needed to throw a Frenchman into prison was the say-so of the king.

The Bastille was a dark, mysterious place. People were locked away there for disagreeing with the king or for failing to pay taxes. There were stories of men rotting away in the Bastille's dark **dungeons** and of terrible tortures. Actually, under earlier kings the prison had done away with dungeons and tortures. But the horror stories remained. Most Frenchmen hated and feared the Bastille.

French people celebrate Bastille Day much as Americans celebrate the Fourth of July.

On July 14, 1789, a **riot** broke out in Paris. The people had become alarmed by the king's gathering troops. They decided it was time to make a stand for freedom. They would attack that symbol of the king's unjust powers—the hated Bastille.

Early in the day, a mob of rioters broke into an **arsenal**. They took muskets and cannons. Then they attacked. "Down with the Bastille!" the excited rebels shouted. There was no stopping the mob. They murdered the governor of the prison. They carried his head on a stick through the streets.

The rebels then took the keys to the prison as their prize. They unlocked the doors to find only seven prisoners inside! But the Bastille had fallen, and the Revolution had begun.

On this same day, the king returned to his palace at Versailles after a day of hunting. Communication was slow in the eighteenth century. So he knew nothing of the riots and murders. It had been poor hunting that day. No deer had been killed. And so King Louis wrote only one word in his diary on July 14, 1789. He wrote *Rien*, a French word meaning *nothing*.

The day that King Louis wrote "nothing" was a day that France would always remember!

What methods of communication do we have today that didn't exist in 1789?

History Practice

Write answers to the following questions on a separate sheet of paper.

1. What did King Louis XIV mean when he declared, "I am the State"?

2. What affect did the Age of Reason and the American Revolution have on the French?

3. What groups made up each of the Three Estates that met in Versailles in 1789?

The French Revolution

Revolutionaries throughout France were excited by the storming of the Bastille. They began their own riots for freedom. In October a group of women set out from Paris. They tried to attack the royal family in the palace at Versailles. The king's guards had to keep order.

Peasants rose up against feudal lords. Many noblemen did not feel safe in France. They fled the country.

During the next two years, 1789–1791, the National Assembly wrote the new constitution it had promised. New laws were made doing away with the feudal system. The nobles lost most of their rights and privileges. The king lost much of his power. And the old system of taxes was ended.

On August 26, 1789, the National Assembly wrote the Declaration of the Rights of Man. It was based on the English Bill of Rights and the American Declaration of Independence.

"Liberty, Equality, and Fraternity!"

Rulers throughout Europe saw what was happening in France. They were frightened. They worried that ideas of revolution could spread to their lands. So rulers of Austria and Prussia sent armies into France to try to crush the Revolution.

Louis XVI left France bankrupt through his wild spending.

The leaders of the French Revolution were outraged. They thought that their own king had called for the outside armies. They accused Louis XVI of **betraying** France. They forced him out of office. And they held elections for a new law-making body called the *National Convention*.

In 1792 the National Convention declared France a republic. The **motto** of the new republic was "Liberty, Equality, and **Fraternity**!"

The Reign of Terror

Leaders of the new republic became fearful of their enemies. Their main goal was to seek out those enemies and do away with them. The revolution became bloodier.

Revolutionaries found King Louis XVI guilty of betraying his country. In 1793 Louis XVI and Marie Antoinette were executed. Throughout 1793 and 1794,

The Guillotine: Execution of Robespierre

the new leaders of France arrested and executed many people. Anyone suspected of being against the Republic was attacked. It was a time known as the *Reign of Terror.* "Off with their heads!" became the cry of that stage of the French Revolution.

A Frenchman had invented the **guillotine**, a machine for quickly cutting off heads! Hundreds of suspected enemies of the revolution were beheaded. Carts rolled through the streets of Paris, carrying victims to the guillotine.

A man named Robespierre was one of the most violent leaders of the Revolution. Robespierre believed the Republic would never be safe as long as one enemy lived. Later, the people turned on Robespierre himself. After sentencing so many others to death, Robespierre lost his own head to the French guillotine.

The country was in a **turmoil**. The leaders of the Revolution could not control the people or organize the government. The fighting and bloodshed went on and on.

Do you think Robespierre got what he deserved?

Napoleon Bonaparte

The Revolution had created a strong, new army. That army drove Austrian and Prussian forces out of France. One of the officers in the French army was a young man named Napoleon Bonaparte.

Meanwhile, the National Convention of France had been growing steadily weaker. In October 1795 it came under attack by an army of 30,000 national guardsmen. The guardsmen wanted to get rid of the National Convention and bring back the monarchy. The Convention called on General Napoleon Bonaparte to put down the uprising. Napoleon, a general at age 26, proved his military worth. On October 5, 1795, he brought in a battery of cannons. The uprising was ended "with a whiff of grapeshot," he said.

The Directory soon replaced the National Convention in the leadership of France. As Napoleon won battles and gained power, the Directory began to worry. Was Napoleon trying to become the sole ruler of all of France?

That is exactly what Napoleon did. He pushed out the Directory. And in 1799 he made himself **dictator** of France. One of the first things Napoleon did as ruler was to set up the Napoleonic Code. This was a new constitution that contained a single set of laws for all of France and its territories. The Napoleonic Code remains to this day as the basis of French law.

France soon discovered that Napoleon was a good politician as well as a good soldier. Napoleon put himself directly in charge of the army. He brought a quick end to the fighting within France. He set up a police force responsible only to him. He invited back the nobles who had fled France during the Revolution. "You will be safe," Napoleon told them, "if you are loyal to me."

Napoleon Bonaparte

France Under Napoleon

Napoleon put an end to the French Republic that the revolution had won. In 1804 Napoleon had himself crowned emperor. He then crowned his wife, Josephine, empress. He let his ambition and desire for power spread war across Europe. But he did make some good changes in the French government.

Napoleon's empire

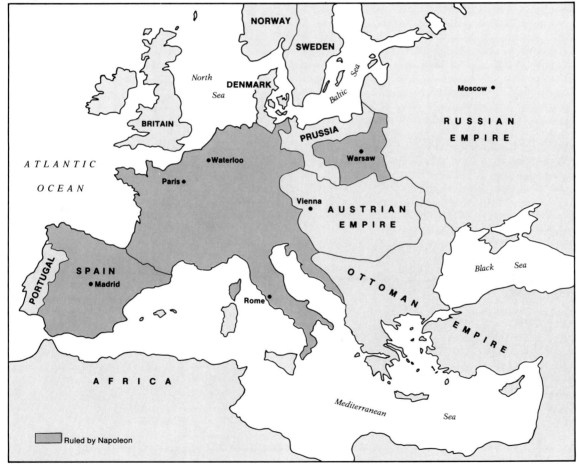

Map Skills

Name four cities in lands ruled by Napoleon. In which empire is Vienna?

Napoleon changed unfair tax laws. He required all people, rich and poor, to pay taxes under the same laws. The rich received no favors. Napoleon also strengthened and reorganized the French schools.

But everything, including education, religion, and the press, was subject to strict government control. And the French government *was* Napoleon!

Napoleon had a strong, wealthy France behind him now. He had the loyalty of the people. He now set out to conquer a European empire. He led France into war with Great Britain and most of the rest of Europe. Napoleon was a clever general. He won battle after battle. By 1812 Napoleon controlled most of Europe. Only Britain could not be conquered by Napoleon's armies.

For 15 years, the history of Europe was the history of Napoleon's conquests.

Napoleon's retreat from Moscow

LEARN MORE ABOUT IT: Napoleon's Mistake

In 1812, Napoleon declared war on Russia. He attacked with an army of nearly 600,000 men. He won a major victory over the Russians at the battle of Borodino. But the Russian armies were clever. They fled eastward, leading Napoleon's men on a chase deep into the heart of Russia. As the Russians retreated, they destroyed everything of value in Napoleon's path.

When Napoleon and his army reached Moscow, they found a deserted city. Most of the people had fled. Those who stayed behind set fire to the city. The French soon found themselves occupying a city of ruins.

Then winter came. It was an icy Russian winter. Napoleon's army had almost run out of food. They were starving. They were freezing. There was only one thing to do. Napoleon gave the orders to head for home. The Russians attacked again and again as Napoleon's weakened forces struggled toward France. The French suffered terrible losses during the retreat from Russia. Over 500,000 men either were killed, or died of illness or starvation. Others deserted or were captured. Many simply froze to death. The attack on Russia was Napoleon's mistake.

The End for Napoleon

Other countries took heart when they heard of France's defeat in Russia. Napoleon could be beaten! These countries joined together. Prussia, Sweden, and Spain joined with Great Britain and Russia to march as allies against Napoleon.

The French saw that their emperor was beaten. So the French Senate turned against him. They called for a new king to rule France. On April 11, 1814, Napoleon gave up his throne. Louis XVIII was crowned King of France. Napoleon was exiled. The king sent him to the island of Elba off the coast of Italy.

Napoleon was not a man who gave up easily. In less than a year, he escaped from Elba and returned to France. There he found supporters and actually ruled France again for 100 days. But Napoleon's dream of ruling Europe was about to come to an end.

The Battle of Waterloo

The allies joined forces as soon as they heard of Napoleon's return. With about 75,000 troops, Napoleon marched into Belgium to meet the allied forces. The Duke of Wellington had about 67,000 troops from England, Belgium, Hanover, and the Netherlands.

The fighting began on June 18, 1815. The battle between the French and the allies was just about even for a few hours. Then Prussian troops arrived to back up the allies. That tipped the scale. After one last, fierce attack by France's famous *Old Guard,* the French had to retreat.

Again Napoleon was sent away as a prisoner. The English sent him to far-off Saint Helena. This was a tiny island off the west coast of Africa. It was there on May 5, 1821, that Napoleon died.

France After Napoleon

A royal line of kings ruled in France once more. And then again, there was a revolution. For the next 55 years, France saw change after change; three revolutions in all. There was a Second Republic, a Second Empire, and then, in 1870, a Third Republic.

Under the Third Republic, France built a **colonial** empire. French colonies around the world strengthened trade and industry. France's Third Republic lasted until World War II when Germany took over France.

After World War II a Fourth Republic was set up and then a Fifth. Social revolution continued. Women struggled to take their place in society, to hold property, and to take jobs. Minority groups looked for work, for fair pay, and for good housing. The French still worked toward "Liberty, Equality, and Fraternity."

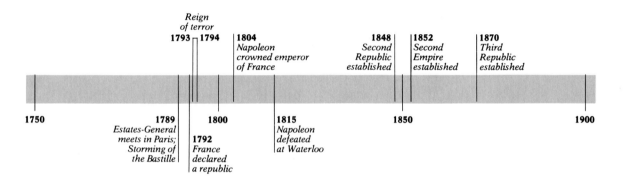

Reign
of terror
1793 ⌐ 1794

1804
Napoleon
crowned emperor
of France

1848
Second
Republic
established

1852
Second
Empire
established

1870
Third
Republic
established

1750

1789
Estates-General
meets in Paris;
Storming of
the Bastille

1792
France
declared
a republic

1800

1815
Napoleon
defeated
at Waterloo

1850

1900

Chapter Review

Chapter Summary

- The Age of Reason and the American War of Independence gave Frenchmen ideas of fighting for their own freedom.

- French kings, like Louis XVI, believed that they ruled by "divine right."

- The Third Estate of the French Estates-General represented all the common people.

- A National Assembly met in 1789 and decided that France should have a constitution.

- The French Revolution officially began on July 14, 1789, with the storming of the Bastille.

- A Reign of Terror from 1793 to 1794 led to turmoil and bloodshed.

- Napoleon Bonaparte stepped in to restore order in France.

- Napoleon's ambition led him to become emperor of France and to conquer much of Europe.

- Napoleon met final defeat at Waterloo in 1815.

- The French government underwent several other changes in a series of social and political revolutions.

Chapter Quiz

A. Checking Your Facts

symbol	guillotine	dungeons	oath	arsenal

Complete each sentence below. Use the correct word from the box. Rewrite the sentences on a separate sheet of paper.

1. Members of the Third Estate met at a tennis court and took an _____ .

2. There were stories of men rotting away in the Bastille's dark _____ .

3. The mob broke into an _____ and took muskets and cannons.

4. To the people of Paris, the Bastille was a _____ of the tyranny of their king.

5. The _____ was a machine for cutting off people's heads.

B. Think About It!

1. What three words made up the motto of the French Revolution? What do they mean?

2. King Louis XIV declared that he *was* the state. And after the revolution, the French government *was* Emperor Napoleon. What do you think was the difference, if any, between the ways these two men ruled France?

3. Which European countries tried to crush the French Revolution? Why do you think they feared revolution?

Unit Seven Review

Write answers to the following questions on a separate sheet of paper.

1. How did the English Parliament system begin? How did it operate?

2. How was Parliament different from the earlier Great Council?

3. What kinds of problems did Parliament have with Stuart kings?

4. How did Voltaire, Locke, and Rousseau influence England and America?

5. Where did the French National Assembly hold its first meeting? What did the Assembly decide?

6. Why did the Third Estate feel it was getting cheated?

7. Explain how the storming of the Bastille led to a bloody rebellion.

8. Compare the Three Estates with the British Parliament and its two houses.

9. How did Napoleon Bonaparte gain leadership in France? How was he defeated?

10. What were some of the useful things that Napoleon Bonaparte did for France?

Unit Eight

The Age of Imperialism

Chapter 20

The Industrial Revolution

These women worked in a pen factory. Why were they no longer working in their homes or in small workshops?

Chapter Learning Objectives

- Tell why the Industrial Revolution began in Great Britain.
- List five inventions of the 1700s.
- Explain how the Industrial Revolution encouraged imperialism.
- Describe how the Industrial Revolution both improved and worsened people's lives.
- Explain how the Industrial Revolution made countries more dependent on each other.

Words to Know

factories   buildings where goods are made by machinery

imperialism   the practice of conquering other lands, forming colonies in other lands, or controlling the government and wealth of weaker lands

imported   brought into one country from another

industry   business and manufacturing

investors   those who expect to make a profit by lending money to a business

labor unions   groups of workers who join together to protect their wages, working conditions, and job benefits

looms   machines for weaving thread or yarn into cloth

natural resources   materials that are provided by nature, such as forests, minerals, and water

raw materials   matter in its natural condition, not changed by some human process

shuttle   a device in weaving that carries thread back and forth between threads stretched up and down

textile   cloth or fabric made by weaving

transportation   the act of carrying from one place to another

---

The name *Industrial Revolution* is used to describe one of the biggest changes in history. It describes the time when people went from making goods by hand to making them with machines.

Before the 1700s most goods were made by hand. Individual workers crafted tools and jewelry, cloth and housewares. Any machines that were used were small, simple, and privately owned. Work was done in homes or in small workshops.

Before 1750 any changes in production methods came slowly. But after 1750, those changes were rapid. The changes in the ways goods were produced happened fast enough to be called a "revolution."

In today's world changes happen so fast that, according to the writer Alvin Toffler, we are living in a state of "future shock."

Great Britain Leads the Industrial Revolution

The most dramatic changes in industry began in Great Britain in about 1750. Scientists, it is true, had been inventing things during earlier years. But most of their work centered around theories and ideas. Now science and invention took a more practical turn. Inventors developed machines especially designed to increase the production of goods and to help people make a profit.

The Industrial Revolution began in Great Britain for a number of reasons. For one thing, Britain had a large supply of workers. Women, as well as men, were ready to leave their homes and join the industrial force.

Name some natural resources that are very important in the United States today.

Great Britain also had the **natural resources** needed for **industry**. Britain had a good supply of coal and iron. Coal could produce the energy to keep the new steam engines running. And coal was needed to produce iron. Iron could be used to improve machines and tools. And it could be used to build railroad tracks, bridges, and ships.

Britain had the **transportation** that industry needed. Products had to be marketed and moved. Steam locomotives and ocean-going steamships were developed in Britain.

Britain had **investors**. These were people with money to back the new businesses.

Britain had colonies to serve as ready markets for the goods. British colonies also supplied **raw materials**, like cotton, to the **factories** in London and other cities. And the British government was eager to support growing industry.

For all these reasons, Great Britain saw a burst of industrial development. In the late 1700s and 1800s, Britain became known as the "Workshop of the World."

The Textile Industry

Britain's **textile** industry produced cloth. This industry is a good example of what the early Industrial Revolution was all about.

In the earliest days, British merchants **imported** cloth from other lands. Because of the costs of shipping finished goods, cloth was very expensive.

Later, in the 1600s, Britain began importing raw cotton. The British spun their own threads and then wove their own cloth.

Farm families did the work. They set up spinning wheels and **looms** in their cottages. Both spinning wheel and loom were operated by hand. The families who worked this way were called *cottage weavers*.

Merchants would buy the finished cloth from the cottage weavers. The amounts of cloth produced were never very large. In order to meet their own needs, the weavers had to farm land, too. They could only make cloth in their spare time. There was never enough finished cloth for all the people who wanted to buy it. So English businessmen looked for ways to improve and increase the production of textiles.

New Inventions Move Textile Making Out of Cottages

In the 1700s some new machines were invented that changed the textile industry. Spinners and weavers left their cottages and went to work in new factories.

The first important invention in the textile-making revolution was the *flying shuttle*. In 1733 a man named John Kay invented a **shuttle**, a device on a loom. The shuttle made it possible to weave wider pieces of cloth. Now one worker could do the work of two.

Woman using a spinning jenny

Soon more cotton yarn was needed than could be produced. Businessmen offered prizes to the inventor of a machine to spin yarn. In 1764 James Hargreaves came up with just such a machine. He named it after his wife. The *spinning jenny* used the same ideas as the spinning wheel. But it could spin as many as 80 threads at one time.

The biggest change came in 1769. Then Richard Arkwright invented a machine called the *water frame*. Now even more cotton thread could be spun at once. The water frame ran by water power. It was big, so big that it could not fit into a cottage. It was also an expensive piece of machinery. The water frame required a special building of its own.

And so the textile business moved out of the English cottages. Mills and factories were built. Workers were no longer their own bosses. They became factory hands. They worked in large mills that often employed up to 600 people.

In 1779 Samuel Crompton combined the spinning jenny and the water frame into one machine. He called it the *mule*. The mule could spin much finer threads very rapidly.

Now the weavers had to keep step with the spinners. With so much thread being produced, the textile industry needed a better loom. In 1785 Edmund Cartwright invented a steam-powered loom.

Workers sometimes feared the new machines. Would the machines completely replace the workers? Would they lose their jobs? At one point, antimachine riots broke out. Mobs smashed machines, shouting, "Men, not machines!" Sometimes progress was a frightening thing. But the industrial revolution could not be stopped.

Within 50 years' time the textile industry had entirely changed. What had been a cottage industry had turned into a big business. And a way of life had changed, too, for thousands of textile workers.

Workers who destroyed machines in the early 1800s were called *Luddites*.

History Practice

Write answers to the following questions on a separate sheet of paper.

1. List four reasons why the Industrial Revolution began in Great Britain.

2. What was the first important invention in the textile-making revolution? Who invented it?

3. What machine did Richard Arkwright invent in 1769?

The Steam Machine

The new machines needed power. Water power was not strong enough to run heavy machines. During the 1600s inventors had begun experimenting with "fire engines," or steam engines. In 1698 Thomas Savery built the first commercial steam engine. Around 1712 Thomas Newcomen improved on Savery's engine. It was, however, far from perfect. It used too much coal.

The power unit called the *watt* was named in honor of the man who made steam power practical.

Early steam locomotive

Faraday's work gave the first clue to the existence of electrons.

In 1769 a Scottish engineer named James Watt invented an improved steam engine. For several years only the textile industry made use of Watt's engine. By 1850, however, it was being used throughout Britain. Then it spread throughout the rest of Europe.

The invention of the steam engine completely changed transportation. In 1804 a British engineer, Richard Trevithick, built the first steam locomotive. Steam locomotives came into general use in Britain in the late 1830s. And by 1850, Great Britain had 6,600 miles of railroad track. The United States, France, and Germany built their own rail systems during the next ten years.

An American, Robert Fulton, built the first successful steamboat in 1807. Within a few years, steamboats were being used on British rivers. By the mid-1800s, steam-powered ships were carrying raw materials and finished goods across the ocean.

Electricity and Petroleum

In 1831 an Englishman named Michael Faraday invented a machine called the *dynamo*. It generated an electric current by using magnets. Faraday's discovery led to the building of more powerful electric generators and electric motors. In time the use of electricity as a source of power would become widespread.

In the 1850s Americans discovered that petroleum, or unrefined oil, could be used for many things. It could be used to make kerosene, and kerosene could be used for heat and light. Oil could make machinery run more smoothly. Fortunately, there was a good supply of crude oil available in the United States.

Oil was to become one of the most valuable resources in the world. This would come about with the invention of the internal combustion engine and the diesel engine. Petroleum could be turned into gasoline and diesel fuel to run those engines. Oil would give nations new wealth and power.

Imperialism

The Industrial Revolution meant new inventions and new products. It also meant new needs. As the ability to produce goods increased, so did the need for more raw materials. Britain needed even more coal to fire the steam engines. It needed more cotton to spin into thread. And it needed more iron to make railroad tracks and machinery.

Imperialism seemed to be a solution to the problems of getting raw materials. Britain took over territories in Africa and Asia and formed colonies there. The colonies also served as markets for English goods. People living in the colonies bought finished products from Britain.

The Industrial Revolution Changes Life: The Workers

Did the Industrial Revolution improve the lives of the English people? Or did it make life harder? A look at life in England in the late 1700s and early 1800s gives a mixed picture.

In many ways life was better. Average incomes tripled between 1700 and 1815. Between 1815 and 1836, incomes increased 30 times over! People had better food to eat. They had more meat, more sugar and tea and coffee. Coal not only fueled the industrial machines, it also heated homes and cooked food.

Most factory workers were very poor and could not read or write.

For the merchants, bankers, shipowners, and factory owners, the Industrial Revolution meant wealth. The middle class now had a greater voice in the British government.

New inventions in communication let people learn what was going on in their world. In 1837 Samuel F. B. Morse invented the telegraph. He also invented a code to send telegrams—the Morse code. By 1866 a telegraph cable reached across the Atlantic.

But life did not improve for everyone. As the Industrial Revolution went on, life got harder for many city workers. People spent long days in dirty, dangerous factories, working for poor wages.

At first factory work had paid well. But soon the owners found they could hire women and children for less wages than men. Soon most of the factory workers were women and children, often very young children. Wages dropped.

Young boys working in a cotton mill

LEARN MORE ABOUT IT: Child Labor

Many of the children working in factories came from orphanages or very poor families. They were treated much like slaves. They often had to work from five in the morning until eight at night. Some factory owners treated the children quite well. Others beat the young workers for such crimes as falling asleep at their work or working too slowly.

In the 1800s there were new laws called Factory Acts. These laws took the very youngest children out of the factories. The laws also put limits on the number of hours children and women could work.

But there were no such things then as safety measures or protection against industrial accidents. It is easy to imagine what happened to many little children working on dangerous machines with no safety devices.

The Industrial Revolution Changes Life: The Cities

Britain's cities were becoming dark with ash from the new coal-burning factories. But these factories drew people to the cities. As a result, Great Britain's cities went through a population explosion. In 1801 about 78 percent of people in Britain lived on farms. By 1901 about 75 percent lived in cities.

Where were all these people going to make their homes? Housing had to be built quickly and cheaply. The results were poorly built slum buildings. Inside were small apartments where whole families often shared one room. Sewage and garbage could not be disposed of properly. These conditions led to the outbreak and spread of disease.

If factory work and living conditions in the cities were so awful, why do you think so many people moved to the cities?

London slums, 1870s

It would not be long before people began to protest against this kind of life. They protested against factories that employed young children and paid terrible wages. And they protested against having to work with dangerous machines that had no safety devices.

The Industrial Revolution taught workers that they had to band together. They formed **labor unions** to demand better, fairer conditions. Of course factory owners were not in favor of the workers' unions. Until 1825 unions in Great Britain were against the law.

The Industrial Revolution Spreads

Industrialization began in Great Britain. But during the 1800s, it spread to other parts of the world. France, Germany, the United States, and then Russia all began to industrialize. Then came Japan.

An American visited a British textile mill in 1810. Within a few years he built America's first textile factory in Waltham, Massachusetts.

Industrialization has forced nations of the world to depend on each other. Countries have had to work out trade agreements. The more industrialized countries build the factories and produce the goods. They often depend on other nations for raw materials. Less developed countries need finished products. Many of these countries profit from their natural resources.

The United States, Germany, Japan, and England depend on Saudi Arabia, Mexico, Indonesia, and Nigeria for crude oil. They get uranium from nations in Africa. Chile and Peru export copper.

The results of the Industrial Revolution are all around us. They can be seen in British coal mines, in Japanese electronics factories, in cities, and on farms. The Industrial Revolution has changed the way people live and where they live. It has changed the way they depend on each other.

At one time, some people thought that the Industrial Revolution would come to an end. They thought that all the great changes and developments had already happened. In the late 1800s, it was actually suggested that the United States Patent Office be closed. Surely, some people thought, everything possible had already been invented. We know now that the revolution is far from over. New developments continue every day.

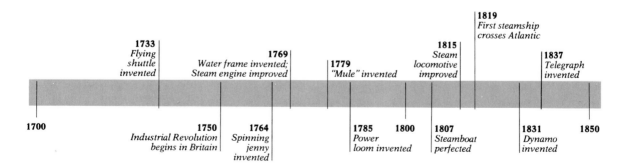

Chapter Review

Chapter Summary

- During the Industrial Revolution, people went from making goods by hand to making goods by machine.

- Great Britain led the Industrial Revolution with rapid changes beginning around 1750.

- Britain's textile industry moved out of country cottages and into city factories.

- The invention of steam power revolutionized manufacturing and transportation.

- The need for raw materials caused Europeans to seek new colonies.

- Industrialization caused a rapid growth in city populations.

- Life for many improved. A strong, wealthy middle class grew.

- Life for many became harder. Working conditions were often unsafe and unhealthy, with men, women, and children working long hours.

- More and more countries industrialized over the years. Nations became dependent on each other for raw materials and finished products.

Chapter Quiz

A. Checking Your Facts

Choose the correct word to make each of the sentences below a true statement. Rewrite the sentences on a separate sheet of paper.

1. Great Britain had the (neutral/natural) resources needed for industry.

2. The first important invention in the textile making revolution was the (flying/space) shuttle.

3. The spinning jenny was invented by James (Arkwright/ Hargreaves).

4. In 1785 Edmund (Cartwright/Arkwright) invented a steam-powered loom.

5. The first commercial steam engine was built by Thomas Savery in (1769/1698).

B. Think About It!

Write answers to the following questions on a separate sheet of paper.

1. The Industrial Revolution made life better for people in England during the 1700s and 1800s. Give three reasons why you agree or disagree with this statement.

2. How did the Industrial Revolution make countries more dependent on each other? Do you think this was good or bad?

3. It was wrong to allow children to work in the factories. Give two reasons why you agree or disagree with this statement.

Chapter 21

The Struggle for Independence in Latin America

Some Indians in Peru still live much like their Inca ancestors. Why do you think they raise llamas?

Chapter Learning Objectives

- Explain how Central and South America came to be called "Latin America."
- Tell why the Creoles and mestizos were ready to fight for independence.
- Name six Latin American revolutionaries.
- Describe the governments of the new independent Latin American nations.

Words to Know

burros   small donkeys, usually used as pack animals

descendants   people who come from certain ancestors

discrimination   treating a person or people unfairly because of their race or religion

dominate   to be most important, most powerful, strongest

haciendas   large Spanish-style ranches or country homes

influence   the power to affect other people or things

liberator   one who frees a group of people

mural   a large picture painted on a wall

viceroy   the governor of a country or province, who rules as the representative of his king

Colonization

For 300 years Spaniards built colonies in the New World. From about 1500 until about 1800, they settled in Mexico, Central America, and South America. Some Portuguese settled in the eastern part of South America. And the French also founded a few settlements. But most of the lands fell to the Spanish. All the lands in this area are called *Latin America*. That is because the Spanish, Portuguese, and French languages came from Latin.

Wherever the Spanish settled they took power. They thought they were better than the Indians. Unlike the hard-working English settlers in North America, most Spanish settlers came from wealthy families. They felt "above" doing hard work themselves. So they made the Indians work for them. They also brought Africans to the New World to work as slaves on farms and in mines.

Can you think of another language that came from Latin?

Many wealthy Spaniards lived on **haciendas**. These were large cattle ranches with rich farmlands. Work on the haciendas was done by Indian field hands or by African slaves.

Latin America Is Late to Industrialize

Spain and Portugal controlled all trade in their colonies. The colonies were not allowed to trade among themselves or with other nations. They were kept dependent on the mother country. And any effort to develop industry in the New World was crushed. Latin America had to sell all its raw materials to Spain and Portugal. And it had to buy all its finished products from them, too.

This kind of control kept industry from developing in Latin America. Eventually the people of Latin America rose up against their foreign rulers. The 1800s saw waves of revolution sweep through Latin America.

Social Classes in the Colonies

The people who had been born in Spain felt superior to the other Latin Americans. They did not adopt any native customs. Instead, the Spaniards tried to make the new land as much like Spain as possible.

The Creoles were people of Spanish blood who were born and raised in Latin America. Many Creoles resented the haughty attitude of the Spanish-born people. The Creoles would play a large part in the soon-to-come struggles for independence.

Most of the Spaniards and Portuguese who settled in Latin America did not bring their families. Many were soldiers and fortune-seekers. They did not plan to stay any longer than it took to get rich. Some fathered the children of native women. Over time there came to be a large class of people of mixed race. They were called *mestizos*.

Many of the mestizos were angered by their lack of social standing. They hated the **discrimination** they felt from their Spanish rulers. The mestizos were ready for freedom from European rule.

The Indians and the African slaves were certainly ready for a change of government. Year after year, they worked hard and remained poor. They had nothing for themselves under European rule—no land, no wealth, no power, no hope.

The poor people of Latin America were now ready to fight for freedom. They saw North America's colonies win freedom from the English. They saw the French rise up against tyranny. Now they needed leaders to call them together and organize revolts.

Is there discrimination against any group of people in the United States today?

The eastern part of Hispaniola is called the Dominican Republic.

Toussaint L'Ouverture

Haiti covers the western third of the island of Hispaniola in the Carribean Sea. It was the first Latin American country to fight for freedom. Haiti was a French colony. When news of revolution in France reached Haiti, the people of the colony got excited. They began to think about freedom, too.

In 1791 the slaves rebelled against their French masters. A black revolutionist named Toussaint L'Ouverture became a leader in Haiti's fight for freedom. Toussaint, a son of slaves, was a slave himself until he was 50. He led the slave revolt until 1793, when France freed all the slaves. In 1801 Toussaint became governor of Haiti. The very next year, however, Napoleon sent a French army to Haiti. He planned to reestablish slavery in the country. War broke out again. The French threw Toussaint into prison, where he died in 1803. But by 1804, the French army was defeated, and French rule in Haiti ended. Haiti declared its independence.

Wars of revolution continued. Other Latin American countries demanded freedom.

Toussaint L'Ouverture

Hidalgo and Morelos

Miguel Hidalgo and José Morelos led Mexico's revolt against Spain. Both men were Catholic priests. They organized the Indians in a revolution.

On September 6, 1810, in the town of Dolores, Miguel Hidalgo rang his church bells. He shouted the *grito de Dolores,* or "cry of Dolores": "Long live independence! Down with bad government!"

Both Hidalgo and Morelos lost their lives fighting for Mexico's independence. But by 1821, the fight was won. Now Mexico celebrates September 16th as its independence day. And the town of Dolores is now called Dolores Hidalgo.

Simón Bolívar

Why do you think Simón Bolívar is compared to George Washington?

Perhaps the best-known Latin American **liberator** was Simón Bolívar. Today he is called "The Liberator" and the "George Washington of South America."

Bolívar spent much of his life fighting for the independence of South American nations. He was a Creole, born in Venezuela. His parents were wealthy Spaniards. To keep his wealth and social position, Bolívar might have sided with Spain. But he believed in freedom from European rule. He spent all his money backing revolutions.

Bolívar died alone and poor. It was not until his death that he became honored as South America's liberator.

Starting in 1810, Simón Bolívar helped to organize an army. He then led the army to a series of victories against the Spanish. He liberated one country after another. At one time he ruled the newly formed Republic of Gran Colombia. This was made up of Colombia, Venezuela, Ecuador, Panama, and Peru. Then Upper Peru became a separate state. In 1825 it was named Bolivia, in Bolívar's honor. Then, one by one, each country withdrew from the union. By 1828 Bolívar ruled only Colombia. His own people did not appreciate him. After a failed attempt on his life, he resigned as president in 1830.

Bernardo O'Higgins

Chile owes its liberation to the son of an Irishman. Bernardo O'Higgins's father had been a **viceroy** of Peru. Bernardo O'Higgins led a revolution that began in 1810. After winning Chile's independence from Spain in 1818, O'Higgins acted as the country's dictator. He planned to bring about reform in Chile. He taxed the wealthy landowners to pay for new schools and roads. And he tried to break up their big estates. But a revolt by the landowners in 1823 sent O'Higgins into exile.

History Practice

Write answers to the following questions on a separate sheet of paper.

1. Why did Central and South America come to be called "Latin" America?

2. Who were the Creoles? Who were the mestizos?

3. Why were the Creoles and mestizos ready to fight for independence?

Dom Pedro

Dom Pedro led Brazil to independence without bloodshed. He was a Portuguese born in Rio de Janeiro. He inherited the Brazilian kingdom when it was still under Portuguese rule. When he asked for independence, the Portuguese ordered him to come to Portugal. But he refused.

"I remain!" he stated. And on September 7, 1822, he declared Brazil an independent country. He took the throne of the newly independent nation as Pedro I.

GREAT NAMES IN HISTORY:
José de San Martín

Bernardo O'Higgins was helped in his struggle against Spain by another great leader, José de San Martín. San Martín was born in Argentina, but was educated in Spain. While in Spain, he fought with the Spanish army against Napoleon. When he returned to Argentina, the fight for independence had already begun in South America.

In 1812 San Martín took command of a rebel army. For the next several years he fought to free his country from Spain's rule. In 1816 Argentina declared its independence. Then San Martín decided to help the rest of South America become free. He planned a daring surprise attack against the Spanish army in Chile. In 1817 he joined forces with Bernardo O'Higgins. Together, they led their army across the Andes Mountains. It was a difficult and dangerous march. Blizzards struck without warning. The men had to plow through deep snow-drifts. Slowly they made their way across the icy mountain passes. Many men died along the way. Finally the brave leaders and their army came down from the mountains in Chile. There they attacked the Spanish army. The Spaniards were completely taken by surprise, and they were easily defeated.

San Martín then went on to help win independence for Peru in 1821. When he finally returned to Argentina, a fierce struggle for political power was going on. San Martín felt bad about this and would have nothing to do with it. He went back to Europe and for the rest of his life lived in France.

Governments of the New Nations

The Latin American countries' struggles for independence did not necessarily mean freedom for the people. Most of the countries did not become democracies. So life did not change much for poor Indians.

Dictators ruled most of the new nations. These dictators were powerful men with strong armies behind them. Any changes in government usually came only by military takeovers.

Latin American Cultures

Latin American culture is really more than one culture. It is a mixture of several different peoples: Indian, Spanish, Portuguese, African, and French.

Some of the Indians still live much like their ancestors. They wear woven shawls and take their goods to market along mountain roads on **burros** and llamas. They play music on handmade wooden instruments and weave baskets of cane and reed. Indian women still spin and weave colorful cloth. There is often a note of sadness to the Indians' art. A **mural** in Mexico City shows the Indians suffering at the hands of Spanish conquistadors.

The Spanish and Portuguese brought their languages and religion to Latin America. Most of the people of Latin America speak Spanish. Portuguese is the main language of Brazil. And the different Indian tribes speak their own native languages. Roman Catholicism is the main religion.

Spanish architecture is common in Latin America. Many homes, churches, and public buildings have a Spanish flavor. But much Latin American music reflects the music of Africa. The Africans brought their songs and dances with them when they came to Latin America as slaves.

Typical Spanish colonial architecture, Mexico City

Latin American nations become independent

UNITED STATES

MEXICO 1821

Gulf of Mexico

BAHAMAS 1973

CUBA 1898

HAITI 1804

DOMINICAN REPUBLIC 1844

PUERTO RICO (U.S.)

ATLANTIC OCEAN

ANTIGUA & BARBUDA 1981

BELIZE 1981

HONDURAS 1838

JAMAICA 1962

Caribbean Sea

BARBADOS 1966

GRENADA 1974

GUATEMALA 1821

EL SALVADOR 1821

NICARAGUA 1838

COSTA RICA 1838

PANAMA 1903

TRINIDAD & TOBAGO 1962

GUYANA 1966

SURINAME 1975

FR GUIANA

VENEZUELA 1830

COLOMBIA 1811

ECUADOR 1830

PERU 1821

BRAZIL 1822

PACIFIC OCEAN

BOLIVIA 1825

CHILE 1818

PARAGUAY 1811

ARGENTINA 1816

URUGUAY 1814

Map Skills

Which is the largest country in Latin America? In what year did it become independent? Which Latin American country shares a border with the United States?

Different races and cultures **dominate** different areas of Latin America. In some countries, most of the people are Indians. The art, music, dress, and customs in Guatemala, Bolivia, and Peru are Indian. And in some countries, like Haiti, the people are mostly **descendants** of Africans.

Latin America gets its name from the colonization and **influence** of Latin peoples—the Spanish, the Portuguese, and the French. But the Indians and the Africans also played a large part in making the land what it is today.

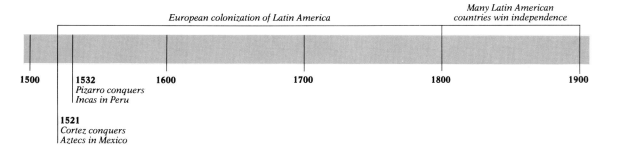

European colonization of Latin America

Many Latin American countries win independence

1500

1532
Pizarro conquers Incas in Peru

1600

1700

1800

1900

1521
Cortez conquers Aztecs in Mexico

Chapter Review

Chapter Summary

- Most areas of Latin America were settled by the Spanish and the Portuguese.

- The European settlers made workers of the Indians and brought slaves to Latin America from Africa.

- Mother countries did not allow industry to develop in Latin America.

- The various populations of Latin America, between 1500 and 1900, consisted of Europeans, Creoles, mestizos, Indians, and African slaves.

- The 1800s brought revolutions for independence to Latin America.

- By the end of the 1800s, there were many independent Latin American countries.

- The governments of the independent countries were often ruled by dictators.

- Latin American culture is a blend of Spanish, Portuguese, French, Indian, and African cultures.

Chapter Quiz

A. Checking Your Facts

Choose the correct word or words to make each sentence a true statement. Rewrite the sentences on a separate sheet of paper.

1. People born in Spain felt (inferior/superior) to the other Latin Americans.

2. People of mixed race were called (mestizos/Creoles).

3. Haiti covers the (eastern/western) third of the island of Hispaniola.

4. Simón (San Martín/Bolívar) is called the "George Washington of South America."

5. The people of Haiti are mostly descendants of (Africans/Indians).

B. Think About It!

Write answers to the following questions on a separate sheet of paper.

1. In what ways were the Europeans who settled in Latin America different from the colonists in North America?

2. Why do you think the United States would have been disappointed with many of the governments that developed in the independent Latin American nations?

3. What effect do you think the American and French revolutions had on Latin America?

Chapter 22

The United States Becomes an Imperialist Power

The United States began building the Panama Canal in 1906. Why did Americans want a canal across Panama?

Chapter Learning Objectives

- Tell how the United States gained the Louisiana Territory.
- List the problems the United States faced in establishing its northern and southern borders.
- Tell how the United States acquired Alaska and Hawaii.
- Explain the effects of the Spanish-American War.

Words to Know

reaper   a machine for cutting down and gathering grain crops

sympathy   feeling sorry for another's suffering

territory   the land ruled by a nation or state

victor   the winner of a battle, war, struggle, or contest

Imperialism and the Monroe Doctrine

Smaller nations are often threatened by larger and stronger nations. The new, independent countries in Latin America struggled to survive. The United States wanted these countries to remain independent.

In 1823 James Monroe, president of the United States, spoke before his congress. He said that the United States would not allow Europe to set up new colonies in North or South America. Nor would it allow any existing colonies to take over more land. The president's statement against European imperialism is called the Monroe Doctrine.

A Growing United States: The Louisiana Purchase

The United States grew rapidly during the early 1800s. Settlers moved west, taking lands from the Indians.

In 1803 Thomas Jefferson was president of the United States. He arranged for the United States to buy a large piece of land from France. This treaty was called the *Louisiana Purchase*. The United States paid about $15 million for 828,000 square miles of land. This land, the Louisiana **Territory**, almost doubled the size of the United States.

Do you think Jefferson got a good deal when he bought the Louisiana Territory for $15 million?

The Louisiana Purchase

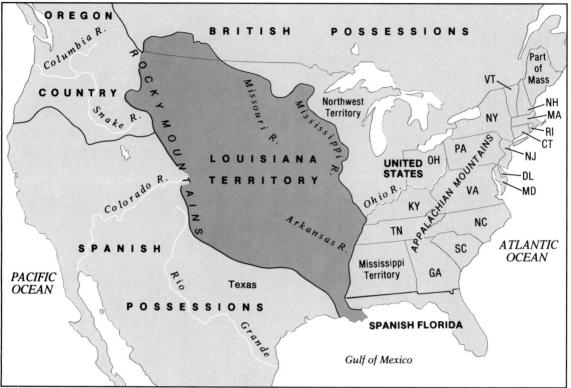

Map Skills
Which river formed the eastern border of the Louisiana Territory? Name two rivers inside the Louisiana Territory. Which mountain range bordered the Louisiana Territory on the west?

American pioneers streamed into the new land. They settled first in what would become the states of Louisiana, Arkansas, and Missouri.

United States Borders

The United States needed to set up clear northern and southern borders. England still controlled Canada, to the north. War broke out between England and the United States in 1812. But the border had never been in question. Other problems had led to the war. England had been interfering with United States trade. A peace treaty was signed in December of 1814. The border remained the same as it had been before. In the southern United States, however, border disagreements *were* the cause of war.

What is now the state of Texas once belonged to the Republic of Mexico. But many settlers from the United States moved into Texas.

The Mexicans worried about the large numbers of settlers from the North. They said that no more settlers could come in from the United States. So the settlers rebelled. In November 1835 they declared themselves free from Mexico. Then the battles began.

General Santa Anna made himself dictator of Mexico in 1834. Americans in Texas did not want to live under his rule.

WORDS FROM THE PAST:
"Remember the Alamo!"

The Battle of the Alamo was one of the most famous battles in the Texas war of independence. The Alamo was an old Spanish mission in San Antonio that the Texans were using as their fort.

On February 23, 1836, 5,000 Mexican soldiers stormed the fort. Inside the Alamo were 187 Texans, among them Davy Crockett and James Bowie. They managed to hold the fort for 12 days. In the end, every American defending the Alamo was killed. But their brave fight gave spirit to the Texans' struggle and helped to win the war.

"Remember the Alamo!" became the battle cry of the United States forces. By April 1836 the Mexican army was defeated. The Mexican general Santa Anna signed a peace treaty.

The Battle of the Alamo

War with Mexico

In 1845 Texas became the 28th state to join the United States. The Mexican government had never actually agreed to Texas's independence. So the declaration of statehood led to war in 1846 between the United States and Mexico.

Mexico lost the war in 1848. The United States gained vast new territory that had belonged to Mexico. This included California, Nevada, Utah, Arizona, and parts of New Mexico and Colorado. Now Mexico accused the Americans of imperialism. The United States was charged with taking over foreign lands and ruling them.

Do you think Mexico was right in accusing the Americans of imperialism? Why or why not?

America's Civil War

Like European history, American history is scarred with many wars. Between 1861 and 1865, Americans fought a bloody civil war between the northern and southern states.

While slavery was an issue, it was not the cause of the war. After Abraham Lincoln became president, the southern states broke away from the United States. They formed a separate nation called the Confederate States of America. Lincoln could not allow the South to break up the union. He felt he had no choice but to go to war.

The North had many more people than the South. And the North had more manufacturing and industry. It was able to produce more guns and cannons. The South was still mainly agricultural. Its main crops were cotton and tobacco. And the southern plantations depended on slave labor.

Northerners expected the war to be over soon. And they were sure they would be the winners. But they were in for a surprise. The very first battle of the war, at Bull Run on April 21, 1861, was easily won by the South! And the Confederate army went on to win one battle after another. The army was led by brilliant generals such as Robert E. Lee and Stonewall Jackson.

Then Ulysses S. Grant took command of the northern armies. The tides of battle turned. The North finally began to get the upper hand. In 1863 Lincoln signed the *Emancipation Proclamation*, outlawing slavery. Blacks were invited to join the northern forces. By the end of the war, about 200,000 African Americans had fought for the North.

By 1865 much of the South lay in ruins. And the southern armies had become much weaker. Little by little, the North had cut off all of the South's supply routes. Lee's army was trapped in Virginia by Grant's army. Lee decided it was hopeless to keep on fighting.

Before the war, Lincoln called the United States "a house divided . . . half slave and half free."

He surrendered to Grant on April 9, 1865, at Appomattox Court House.

The bloodiest war in American history was over. More than 600,000 people had been killed. Many cities and farms had been destroyed. But the North had won the war. And all of the states remained united.

History Practice

Write answers to the following questions on a separate sheet of paper.

1. Why did war break out between England and the United States in 1812?

2. Why did the United States and Mexico go to war in 1846?

3. What was the main cause of the American Civil War?

Industry in the United States

Many changes occurred in the United States during the early 1800s. The introduction of the steam locomotive led to great improvements in overland transportation. And Samuel Morse's telegraph, first demonstrated in 1837, led to greatly improved communication. In 1834 Cyrus McCormick invented a mechanical **reaper**. This machine allowed farmers to harvest grain much more quickly than before. And beginning in the early 1800s, some businesses began building factories. Inside the factories were machines that enabled workers to produce goods more rapidly.

After the Civil War, changes occurred faster. More and more factories were built. And machines began to replace hand labor as the main means of manufacturing. At this time, a new nationwide network of railroads was being built. In 1869 the transcontinental railroad was completed. This linked up the eastern and western parts of the country. And it helped speed up the settlement of the West.

The railroad system helped businesses to distribute their goods more quickly. And there were more and more goods available. Inventors developed new products. And businesses were able to make the products in large quantities. The United States now had its own industrial revolution.

Many big businesses grew up during this period. They included coal mining, petroleum, steel, and industrial machinery. New England, New York, and Pennsylvania became important industrial centers in the North. The United States was on its way to becoming an industrial giant.

Further Expansion: Alaska and Hawaii

"A foolish purchase!" "Who wants a hunk of frozen land?" That is what many Americans said about the territory known as Alaska. In 1867 Secretary of State William Seward had persuaded the United States to buy Alaska from Russia. It cost just over $7 milion. But in 1897, gold was discovered there. It was only then that Americans began to realize the value of the purchase.

Today oil is the most important resource in Alaska.

Americans' interest in Hawaii began in 1820. That year a group of Protestant missionaries from New England arrived there. In 1835 the first sugar plantation began operating. It was owned by an American company. Commercial development of the pineapple began in the mid-1800s. Also, around this time, hundreds of American whaling ships began to visit Hawaii regularly. In 1887 the United States signed a treaty with Hawaii. It gave the United States the right to use Pearl Harbor as a naval base. United States interests were now well-established on the islands.

Honolulu in the 1800s.

Liliuokalani made two trips to the United States after she lost her throne.

In 1893 the Hawaiians staged a revolution against Liliuokalani, queen of Hawaii. Americans, who by that time owned most of Hawaii's industry, encouraged and led the revolt. Queen Liliuokalani left her throne. In 1900 Hawaii became a territory of the United States.

The United States used the Monroe Doctrine to keep European interests out of the Americas. Meanwhile the United States gained more and more territory for itself.

The Spanish-American War

A war broke out between the United States and Spain in 1898. This resulted in the United States gaining still more territory.

The United States wanted Spain out of the Caribbean area. Many Americans felt **sympathy** for the Cubans who lived under harsh Spanish rule. And some Americans saw a chance for the United States to gain more power.

Relations between the United States and Spain were tense. Then, in February of 1898, the U.S. battleship *Maine* exploded in the harbor at Havana, Cuba. Many Americans blamed Spain. By April the Spanish-American War had begun.

By August of that same year, the war was over. The United States was the **victor**. In December, Spain and the United States sent representatives to Paris to sign a treaty. The Treaty of Paris gave the United States possession of Puerto Rico, the Philippines, and the Pacific Island of Guam. Spain gave Cuba its freedom.

U.S. Power

By the early 1900s, the United States was the strongest country on the American continents. It held control over lands gained in the Spanish-American War. During that war, the U.S. Navy sent a battleship from San Francisco to Cuba. It had to sail all the way around the tip of South America. This is a distance of 13,000 miles. If there had been a canal across Central America, the trip would have been only 4,600 miles.

U.S. president Theodore Roosevelt wanted to build such a canal across Panama. But Colombia ruled Panama. And Colombia would not grant the United States the land it needed for the canal. So America encouraged Panama to declare its independence from Colombia.

Panama's rebellion in November of 1903 was a success. The United States gained the right to build the canal. Panama sold the United States a "canal zone" ten miles wide. The Panama Canal and the Canal Zone belonged to the United States. But in 1977, the United States and Panama signed a treaty. In keeping with the treaty, Panama regained control of the Canal Zone in 1979. And in 1999, Panama is to gain control of the canal itself.

But with the canal built, the United States grew as an economic, military, and industrial power. And the United States took its place as a major force in the history of the modern world.

It took thousands of workers ten years to build the Panama Canal. It was finally completed in 1914.

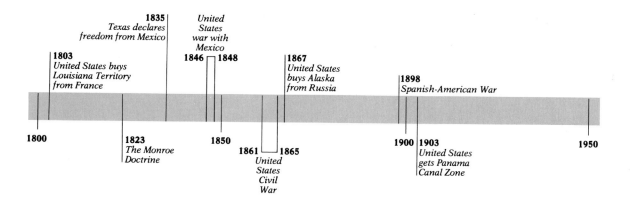

1800

1803
United States buys
Louisiana Territory
from France

1823
The Monroe
Doctrine

1835
Texas declares
freedom from Mexico

1846 ⌐ 1848

1850

1861 ⌐ 1865
United
States
Civil
War

United
States
war with
Mexico

1867
United States
buys Alaska
from Russia

1898
Spanish-American War

1900

1903
United States
gets Panama
Canal Zone

1950

Chapter Review

Chapter Summary

- The Monroe Doctrine said that the United States would not allow Europeans to set up colonies in the Americas.

- The United States expanded by adding the Louisiana Territory, Alaska, and Hawaii.

- War with Mexico established the southern border of the United States.

- The United States was torn apart by a bloody civil war from 1861 to 1865.

- The United States became a more industrialized nation after the Civil War.

- The Spanish-American War gave the United States Puerto Rico, the Philippines, and Guam.

- The United States became an imperialistic nation itself.

Chapter Quiz

A. Checking Your Facts

Choose the correct word to make each sentence a true statement. Rewrite the sentences on a separate sheet of paper.

1. The (Monroe/Jefferson) Doctrine in 1823 was a strong statement against European imperialism.

2. In 1836 Americans fought the (Spanish/Mexicans) at the Alamo.

3. On April 21, 1861, the Battle of Bull Run was easily won by the (North/South).

4. More than (600,000/6,000,000) people were killed in the American Civil War.

5. A mechanical reaper was invented in 1834 by Cyrus (Morse/ McCormick).

B. Think About It!

Write answers to the following questions on a separate sheet of paper.

1. The Monroe Doctrine was a clear statement against European imperialism. Why do you think the United States wanted to keep European interests out of the Americas?

2. What do you think might have happened to the United States if the South had won the Civil War?

3. Why might some countries object to the way the United States got the Panama Canal?

Chapter 23

Imperialism and the Far East

In 1900, American troops helped to put down the Boxer Rebellion. Why did the United States send troops to China?

Chapter Learning Objectives
- Describe the Open-Door Policy.
- Tell how Sun Yat-sen put an end to Manchu rule in China.
- Tell how Commodore Matthew C. Perry opened the doors of trade to Japan.
- List the ways in which Japan modernized after a powerful emperor took over in 1867.
- Explain how Japan's industrialization led to Japanese imperialism.

Words to Know

addicted   having a strong habit that is hard to give up

impressed   affected thoughts and feelings

interference   meddling in another's affairs without being asked

international   having to do with many nations

modern   of the present time, up-to-date

policies   rules; methods of action or conduct

smuggled   moved something into or out of a country secretly because it is against the law

sought   looked for, searched for

The Manchus Establish the Ch'ing Dynasty in China

Manchuria is a region in the northeastern part of China. At one time, it did not belong to China. In 1644 the Manchus—the people of Manchuria—invaded northern China. They overthrew the Ming dynasty that was then in power. Then they conquered the rest of China. The Manchus set up their own dynasty called the Ch'ing dynasty. The Manchus would remain in power for more than 250 years. And the Ch'ing dynasty would be the last of the Chinese dynasties.

The Manchus were a proud people—too proud, perhaps. They thought they were better than the other Chinese people. They passed a law saying that a Manchu could not marry a Chinese. They forced Chinese men to wear a Manchu hairstyle. This was a long braid down the back of the head. The British later called the long braid a *queue*.

Queue **comes from a Latin word meaning** *tail*.

Chinese men with hair braided in queue

Do you think the Manchu rulers were wise to look down on all other people? Why or why not?

The Manchus not only looked down on other Chinese, they looked down on the rest of the world. Until the mid-1800s, foreign trade was allowed through only one Chinese city—Canton. When European nations and America asked for more trade with China, the Manchu rulers always refused.

During the first 150 years of Manchu rule, China enjoyed prosperity. Agriculture increased, and the handicraft industry did, too. The population expanded rapidly. But by the late 1700s, the times had changed. The population had increased faster than the food supply. Life became harder for most people.

China under the Ch'ing Dynasty

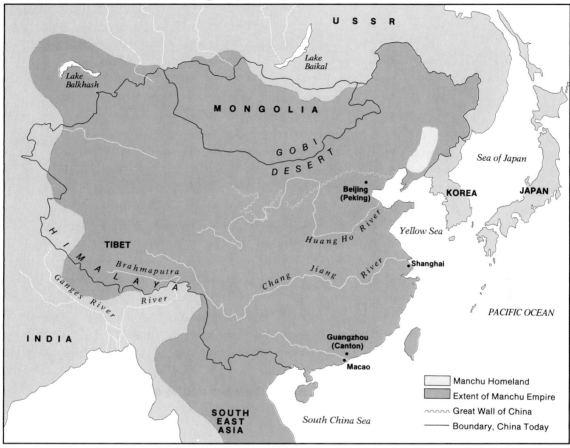

Map Skill
Name the large desert on the China-Mongolia border. Name the river that empties into the Yellow Sea near the city of Shanghai.

China also suffered because of the Manchus' isolationist **policies**. Once China had been a leader in science and medicine. But by the 1800s, the Chinese had fallen behind the Europeans in all areas of science and invention. From this point on, the Manchus would rule a troubled China.

The Opium Wars

Europeans wanted tea and silk from China. And they wanted a new source of raw materials.

"But there is nothing we want from you in return," The Manchus told the Europeans. "Why should we allow trade?"

Then the Europeans found something the Chinese did want. They found opium.

Opium is a dangerous drug made from the seeds of a poppy. The poppies grew in India. European merchants began to bring opium to China during the early 1800s. Many Chinese became **addicted** to the drug. So China passed a law making opium trade illegal. But the demand for opium was still there. Now the Europeans **smuggled** the drug into China, making large profits.

In 1839 a Manchu official seized 20,000 chests of opium from British merchants in Canton. He had the opium burned. The British were angry. Valuable property had been destroyed. Great Britain went to war with China, demanding better trading rights. China had little chance against Britain's armies. In 1842 the Chinese surrendered. They signed the Treaty of Nan-ching.

This was the first of what the Chinese called the "Unequal Treaties." China not only had to pay for the lost opium but for the cost of the war. China had to open five ports to British trade. And China gave the island of Hong Kong to Great Britain. Also, the new treaties totally protected British merchants from Chinese law. No Englishman could be tried for any crime in a Chinese court—even if the crime were committed in China. The Chinese felt helpless.

In today's world, drugs are still a problem. And people still make large profits smuggling drugs.

Do you think the major powers today would be more likely to go to war to protect the drug trade or to destroy it? Why?

Chinese Rebellion

The Manchus had trouble with foreigners and trouble with their own people. Chinese farmers were not happy under Manchu rule. They said that the rulers were greedy and unfair. Most Chinese farmers were very poor. Finally the peasants rebelled. They called their rebellion *Taiping*, meaning *Great Peace*. The Taiping Rebellion lasted from 1851 to 1864. Millions of lives were lost. When it was over, the Manchus still ruled China.

The peasants might have won their fight. They might have overthrown the Manchu government. But foreign **interference** worked against them. Foreign governments wanted to keep the Manchus in power. They worried that they might lose their trade rights if the Manchus were overthrown. So the British supported the Manchus throughout the Taiping Rebellion. They sent military help, and the peasants were defeated.

War with Japan

Next the Manchus faced war with Japan. China had had claims on Korea for hundreds of years. When a rebellion broke out in Korea in 1894, the Chinese sent troops in to crush it. Japan had interests in Korea, too. So it sent in its own troops. The rebellion was put down. But neither Japan nor China would withdraw troops. Instead, the two countries began fighting each other.

By April of 1895, the Japanese had defeated the Chinese. China had to give up much of its claim on Korea. China also had to give the island of Taiwan to the Japanese. By 1910 Japan would take complete control of Korea.

LEARN MORE ABOUT IT: The Boxer Rebellion

For 60 years, foreigners had been interfering in China. As the outsiders gained more and more power, the Chinese became angry.

In 1898 the Manchu empress T'zu Hsi ruled the Ch'ing dynasty. She was very old-fashioned. She wanted to stop any change in China. Perhaps she remembered China's glorious past. If she had her way, she would keep China the way it was.

Then something happened in 1900, during the empress's reign. A group of Chinese rebelled against all foreigners in China. The revolt was called the Boxer Rebellion. And the empress T'zu Hsi secretly supported the rebels.

The Boxers were members of a secret society. Westerners called them *Boxers* because they practiced Chinese exercises that resembled shadow-boxing. The Boxers attempted to kill all foreigners in China. They were put down by an **international** army that included soldiers from the United States.

China was forced to make payments to the foreign countries to make up for the rebellion. The United States used much of the money it received to educate Chinese students. Because of this the United States won China's favor.

The Chinese-Japanese war left China weak. From then on Manchu rulers commanded little respect. The Manchus feared that European nations might step in and divide China into colonies. The United States suggested an Open-Door Policy. This meant that all countries would have equal rights to trade in China. The Manchus agreed to this policy. The Chinese had once kept everyone out. Now they opened their ports to the world.

History Practice

Write answers to the following questions on a separate sheet of paper.

1. What was the Manchu dynasty called?

2. Who benefited from the "Unequal Treaties"? In what ways did they benefit?

3. Why did the Chinese peasants rebel against the Manchus from 1851 to 1864?

Sun Yat-sen and the Chinese Nationalists

The Ch'ing dynasty was nearly at its end. It would be the last dynasty to rule China. Rebellions had weakened the government. The war with Japan had cost China both land and power. Many foreign countries had interests in China now. And the weak Manchus were unable to protect China against the foreigners. China needed a new government if it were to survive.

In 1911 a Chinese doctor named Sun Yat-sen was in Denver, Colorado. He had been traveling throughout Japan, Europe, and the United Sates. He was trying to raise money to help overthrow the Manchu government. When he heard about sparks of revolution in China, he returned there. He led the revolution and overthrew the Manchu empire. On January 1, 1912, he became the first president of China's new republic. The last Manchu emperor, Pu-Yi, gave up the throne on February 12, 1912. He was only six years old at the time.

Sun's term as president was short, less than two months. Then a strong, northern Chinese group took over. They put a dictator in charge and exiled Sun Yat-sen.

In China, Sun Yat-sen is called "the father of the Revolution."

But Sun's followers remained. They organized the *Kuomintang,* or Nationalist party. For ten years the Chinese people suffered under harsh rulers who fought each other for power.

Then Sun Yat-sen returned and set up a rival government in Canton. By 1922 the republic had failed and civil war was widespread. With the support of the Soviet Union and Chinese communists, Sun and his Nationalist party trained an army. They set out to bring China together under a Nationalist government.

Sun Yat-sen died in 1925, but his work was finished by Chiang Kai-shek. By 1928 Chiang was able to set up a Nationalist government in China.

More days of war and revolution were ahead. But China had left its great dynasties behind and moved into the **modern** world.

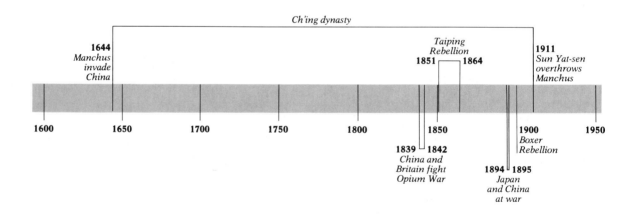

Japan Opens Its Doors

Since 1600 Japan had been an isolated nation. The whole country was under the rule of the Tokugawa family. All foreign trade and travel were forbidden. Japan did not allow foreign products to enter its ports. Nor did it send any products to other lands. Japan would not accept visitors from other countries.

In fact, if a foreign seaman were shipwrecked on Japan's shores, he was in for trouble. He could be arrested or even killed.

In 1853 an American naval officer, Commodore Matthew C. Perry, changed all that. Commodore Perry sailed four U.S. warships into Tokyo Bay. He brought a letter from U.S. president Franklin Pierce. The letter asked the Japanese to change their policies. It asked for better treatment of any shipwrecked American sailors. It asked that American whaling ships be allowed to buy supplies at Japanese ports. It asked that Japan agree to trade with the United States.

The Japanese were **impressed** by Perry and his United States ships. They had never seen such large vessels or such mighty guns. Perry was a stern man. He met the Japanese with dignity. He refused to speak to anyone except the highest officials. Perry left his requests for the Japanese to consider.

Commodore Perry's procession through the streets of Yokohama

The next year Commodore Perry returned to Japan. This time he brought even more ships. The ruling shogun spoke with Perry. Then the Japanese ruler signed a treaty with the United States. Japanese ports would be open to United States ships. It was the beginning of a new Japan.

A Modern Japan

In 1858 Townsend Harris, a U.S. diplomat, signed a more extensive treaty with Japan. That same year Japan signed trade treaties with Great Britain, France, the Netherlands, and Russia. Japan was no longer an isolated nation.

Why do you think some Japanese considered the treaties to be "unequal"?

Then came years of change. Japan was torn between its old ways and the new. Some Japanese wanted to drive the foreigners out of Japan again. They said the treaties Japan had signed were "unequal treaties." Others wanted to accept the western world and learn what they could. They realized that their feudal system of government was outdated. The rule of the shoguns with their samurai warriors had to end.

In 1867 a young emperor came to power. He and his followers began to modernize Japan. Their motto was, "Knowledge shall be **sought** throughout the world." The emperor adopted *Meiji* as his title, which means *enlightened rule*. He was to rule Japan until 1912. These years are known as the Meiji period. The Japanese traveled to other nations. They wanted to learn what they could about industry, education, transportation, and banking. They built thousands of schools. And they invited foreigners to teach in Japan.

In 1889 Japan's first constitution was written. The emperor, whom the Japanese considered divine, still held the power. But he accepted advice from elected representatives.

By the 1890s Japan was keeping step with the modern world. Japan had done away with the samurai and now had a modern army and navy. Japan had steel mills and shipyards and electrical power plants. In just over 25 years, Japan had made amazing progress. It had gone from an isolated, feudal nation to become one of the world's industrial powers.

Japanese Imperialism

As industry grew, Japan needed more raw materials. Like many strong nations, Japan decided to set up overseas colonies to supply those raw materials. But gaining such colonies meant war.

From 1894 to 1895, Japan was at war with China. China and Japan had conflicting claims in Korea. Japan, with its new, modern military, easily defeated China.

In 1904 Russia tried to stake claims in Korea. Japan declared war. The Russo-Japanese War was costly to both sides. But in 1905 the war was over. Again the Japanese were the victors. Japan took over some lands in China that had been controlled by Russia. And in 1910, Japan took complete control of Korea. Japan's victory over Russia surprised the world. For the first time, an Asian nation had proved to be stronger than a European nation. And this was to be only the first chapter in the story of Japanese imperialism.

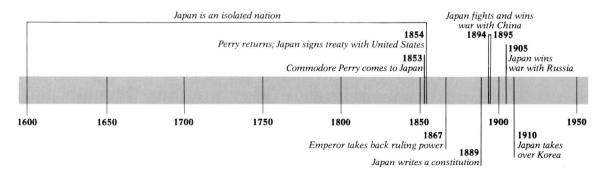

Chapter Review

Chapter Summary

- The Manchus conquered China in 1644 and established the Ch'ing dynasty.

- The Manchus tried to limit foreign trade in China.

- China and Britain fought a war after China destroyed an illegal British opium cargo.

- Chinese peasants rebelled in the Taiping Rebellion in 1851. But they were put down by the Manchus and British by 1864.

- The United States persuaded China to have an "open-door policy" toward foreign trade.

- In 1900 the Boxers tried to drive foreigners out of China. But the Boxer Rebellion was crushed by foreign armies.

- The Manchus were overthrown in 1911 by Chinese Nationalists led by Dr. Sun Yat-sen. That was the end of dynasty rule in China.

- In 1853 Commodore Perry sailed into Tokyo Bay and negotiated trade treaties with Japan.

- In 1867 a young emperor took over the rule of Japan from the shoguns. Japan's feudal days were over.

- Japan became a powerful industrial nation in just over 25 years.

- When new industry led to a need for raw materials, Japan became imperialistic.

- Japan won new lands in wars with China in 1894 to 1895 and with Russia in 1904 to 1905.

Chapter Quiz

A. Checking Your Facts

impressed	interference	smuggled	international	addicted

Complete each sentence below. Use the correct word from the box. Rewrite the sentences on a separate sheet of paper.

1. Many Chinese became _____ to opium.

2. Europeans _____ the drug into China.

3. Foreign _____ worked against the peasants who were fighting the Manchus.

4. The _____ army included soldiers from the United States.

5. The Japanese were _____ by Commodore Perry.

B. Think About It!

Write answers to the following questions on a separate sheet of paper.

1. Why do you think the Chinese feared European imperialism?

2. In what ways did Japan modernize after a powerful emperor took over in 1867?

3. How do you think Japan's industrialization led to Japanese imperialism?

Chapter 24

Imperialism and India

This railroad station near Calcutta was built in the 1800s. Who do you think built the railroads in India?

Chapter Learning Objectives

- Tell how the British East India Company came to rule India.
- Tell how the Sepoy Rebellion began and how it led to direct British rule.
- List five good things Britain did for India.
- Explain why many Indians were unhappy with British rule.
- Identify Mahatma Gandhi, and tell what was different about his way of revolution.

Words to Know

agents   people who have the authority to act for some other person or company

cartridge   a small metal or cardboard tube that holds gunpowder and a bullet

civil disobedience   the refusal to obey rules, orders, or laws

fast   to go without food

imposed   forced one's ideas or wishes on another

indirectly   in a roundabout way

loincloth   a small cloth worn about the hips and lower part of the stomach

nonviolent   without using force, without causing injury

resistance   the act of opposing, working against

superiority   a feeling of being better than others

The Fall of the Mogul Empire

Aurangzeb, the last powerful Mogul emperor, died in 1707. The Moguls had ruled India for almost 200 years. Aurangzeb, a Moslem, had been a harsh ruler. He had angered the Hindus by destroying many of their temples. He had tried to force non-Moslems to convert to Islam.

After the death of Aurangzeb, the Mogul Empire began to break up. Once again, India was divided into small kingdoms. The rajas of the different kingdoms quarreled. The Mogul rulers no longer had any real power.

As the Moguls weakened, stronger countries saw their chance. Europeans would take advantage of the unsteady government in India.

The British East India Company

Trading between Europe and India had been going on for a long time. In 1498 the Portuguese explorer Vasco da Gama reached India by sailing around Africa. From that time on, European merchants made regular voyages to India. Dutch, Portuguese, French, and English traders fought each other for control of Indian trade.

In 1600 a private business called the British East India Company was formed. Its purpose was to trade with India. It set up trading posts along India's coastline at Bombay, Calcutta, and Madras. At around this time, the Dutch East India Company was formed. It began operating out of Java, in Indonesia.

The Europeans gained little in India as long as the Mogul Empire was strong. But by the mid-1700s, there was no longer a strong central government in India. The British East India Company became very involved in what went on in that country. It took sides in Indian civil wars. And it supported rulers who gave it favorable trade rights.

When the French began the French East India Company, the British went to war with them. In 1757 an Englishman named Robert Clive led the British to victory against the French. Both Clive's army and the French army used Indian soldiers to fight their war. The Indian soldiers were called *sepoys*. The British drove the French out of India. And the British East India Company became a powerful force in India.

The East India Company Rules

Soon **agents** of the East India company became stronger than the local rajas. By 1850 the British agents controlled more than half of the land in India. The British put their own men into all the important positions. Englishmen led sepoy armies. They became wealthy landholders.

The British **imposed** their own ways on Indian society. They built Christian churches and spoke out against the Hindu caste system. Many of the Indians did not like the English ways. And they did not like the East India Company, either.

For almost 100 years, Britain **indirectly** ruled India through its East India Company. India was not officially a British colony. But the British held all the power.

LEARN MORE ABOUT IT: The Sepoy Rebellion

To protect their own power, the East India agents from Britain built up armies of sepoys. Most of the British army officers never tried to understand Indian customs and culture. They insisted that the Indians accept British ways.

The sepoys grumbled about this. Then in 1857, the British started using a new kind of bullet in India. To open the **cartridge**, a soldier had to bite off its end. The new cartridges were greased with the fat from cows and pigs. The Moslem religion forbids its followers to eat pork. Hindus are not allowed to eat the meat of a cow. So the sepoys refused to bite the bullets. When British officers ordered them to bite open the cartridges, the sepoys rebelled.

The British put down the Sepoy Rebellion in 1858. But many lives were lost. Britain saw that the East India Company could no longer be trusted with control of India.

Have you ever heard someone say he had to "bite the bullet"? That means he was forced to do something he didn't want to do.

The Sepoy Rebellion

British Rule

In 1858 the British Parliament took over the rule of India. India became a colony of Great Britain. It was now called "British India," or the "British Raj."

A viceroy ran the colony. He was appointed by the British monarch. In 1877 the British held a splendid ceremony in India. On this occasion Queen Victoria was named empress of India.

The British profited from their Indian colony. They called India the "Jewel of the British Empire." In turn, the British government tried to treat Indians more fairly than the East India Company had.

The British tried to solve the problems of poverty that had always troubled India. They helped farmers dig irrigation canals. They set up hospitals in cities and in some villages. They built railroads and factories and roads and schools. The British tried to do away with the harsh caste system that kept many people so poor.

But many Indians were unhappy. Some were poorer than ever. India's raw materials were all going to British industry. Manufactured goods were brought in from Britain, killing off India's own industries. Machine-made cloth poured in from Britain. This resulted in Indian spinners and weavers being put out of work. And all of India's top jobs went to the British.

It was clear to the Indians that the British looked down on them. The British did not allow Indians in their restaurants or hotels. To the people of India, it seemed that British imperialism encouraged British feelings of **superiority**.

Name another country you have read about in which the ruling class looked down on the rest of the people.

Ideas of Independence

The British chose some Indian students to send off to school in Great Britain. They planned to give the students "English" ideas and training. But the plan backfired. Once the students from India learned about English democracy, they wanted independence for their own people.

In 1885 a group called the Indian National Congress was founded. It was made up of educated Indians. They said they were meeting to improve relations with Britain. But in truth, they discussed revolution. In the early 1900s, there were some violent uprisings. The British always crushed them. To improve the situation, the British allowed a few Indians to be included in the government. A few years later, the British increased the number of Indians in the government. But protests continued.

Why do you think protests continued even though Indians were included in the government?

Then on April 13, 1919, British troops fired on an unarmed crowd in Amritsar. Nearly 400 Indians were killed. And at least 1,200 were wounded. The Amritsar Massacre marked a turning point in British-Indian relations. From then on, Indians knew what they could expect from the British. They were determined to keep on fighting for independence. But no real progress toward independence came until leadership went to a man called Gandhi.

History Practice

Write answers to the following questions on a separate sheet of paper.

1. When was the British East India Company formed, and what was its purpose?

2. Why did the sepoys refuse to bite the bullets greased with animal fat?

3. In which year did the British Parliament take over rule of India?

Mahatma Gandhi

Mohandas K. Gandhi was born in 1869. He was a Hindu. His family belonged to the merchant caste. Gandhi studied law in London. He worked as a lawyer in South Africa for 21 years. At that time, South Africa was ruled by Great Britain. Gandhi worked for the rights of Indians who were being discriminated against. In 1915 Gandhi returned to India. There he began to work for independence from Britain. In 1920 he became leader of the Indian National Congress.

Gandhi had new ideas. He said that the way to freedom was not through violence or bloodshed. Gandhi taught **nonviolent resistance** and **civil disobedience**.

Calmly and peacefully, Gandhi led Indians to refuse to obey the British government. "Conquer by love," he taught. His followers called him *Mahatma* Gandhi. Mahatma means *Great Soul*.

"We cannot win against British guns," Gandhi said. "The British only know how to fight against guns. We will show them a new kind of resistance." Gandhi said that civil disobedience was a weapon stronger than guns. He told Indians to refuse to work in British mines, shops, and factories.

Gandhi led a revolution for independence. It was, for the most part, a revolution of the poor. Although he was a Hindu, Gandhi did not believe in the caste system. He lived among the poorest Indians, the untouchables, for many years. He lived simply, often wearing only a linen **loincloth**.

Years later, a man named Martin Luther King, Jr., would follow Gandhi's ideas. He would practice nonviolent resistance in the struggle for civil rights in the United States.

Mahatma Gandhi and followers on his "march to the sea"

India and Pakistan

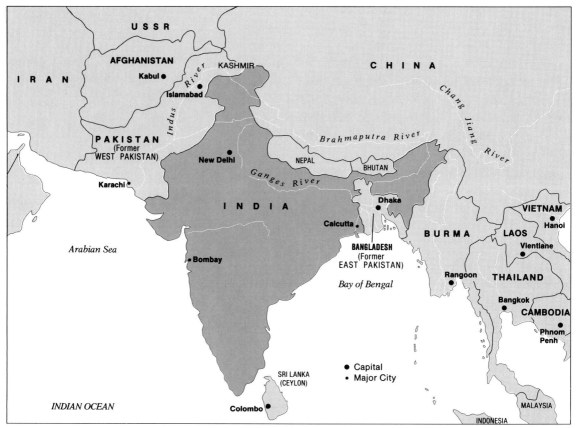

Map Skills
Name three cities in India. Name two cities in Pakistan. What is the name of the large island off the coast of India?

In one act of resistance, Gandhi led thousands of Indian women to the train tracks. There they lay down, stopping the British trains. When the British put an unfair tax on salt, Gandhi peacefully led a march 200 miles to the sea to get salt from the ocean.

Gandhi was often arrested for his activities. He spent a total of seven years in jail. But in time, the British began to listen to Gandhi and his followers.

Gandhi Fasts for Peace

The British knew that the Indian people no longer wanted them in their country. They knew it was just a matter of time before they would be forced to leave. So they offered independence to India. But the Moslems demanded a separate nation. Their protests led to bloody rioting between Moslems and Hindus. As a result, India was divided into two nations. Pakistan would be a Moslem nation, and India would be Hindu.

Mahatma Gandhi saw his country gain independence in 1947. Unfortunately, more fighting between Hindus and Moslems came with independence. There was terrible loss of life. Entire villages were wiped out. Gandhi insisted that the fighting stop. He went on a **fast**, refusing to eat until the bloodshed ended. He almost starved to death. At last, Hindu and Moslem leaders promised to stop the fighting. They did not want their leader to die.

Gandhi's fast ended on June 30, 1948. Shortly after that, Gandhi was shot down by a Hindu gunman. Both Hindus and Moslems mourned their great leader.

Moslems and Hindus had fought each other throughout much of India's history.

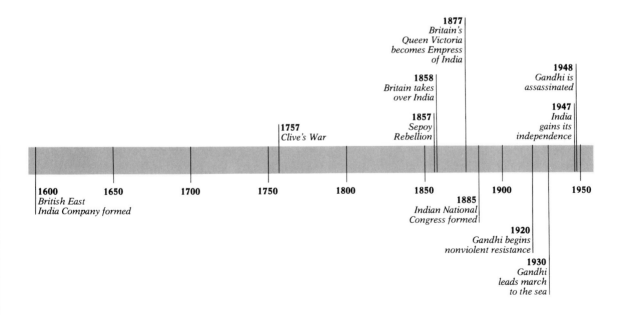

1757
Clive's War

1857
Sepoy Rebellion

1858
Britain takes over India

1877
Britain's Queen Victoria becomes Empress of India

1947
India gains its independence

1948
Gandhi is assassinated

1600
British East India Company formed

1650

1700

1750

1800

1850

1885
Indian National Congress formed

1900

1950

1920
Gandhi begins nonviolent resistance

1930
Gandhi leads march to the sea

Chapter 25

Imperialism and Africa

Zulu warriors fought against European rule of southern Africa during the 1800s. What finally happened to the Zulu kingdom?

Chapter Learning Objectives

- Name the early kingdoms of western Africa.
- Tell how Mali became a wealthy kingdom.
- Explain why Europe had little contact with Africa south of the Sahara Desert before the 1400s.
- List the European nations that took part in the slave trade.
- Explain why Europeans wanted colonies in Africa.

Words to Know

caravans   groups of people traveling together, often through a desert

conference   a meeting of people to discuss something

dominance   the act of ruling, controlling, being most powerful

inferior   not as good as someone or something else

prejudice   dislike of a people just because they are of a different race or religion, or are from another country

racism   the idea that one race is better than another

staff   a pole used for support in walking or to hold a flag

Early Kingdoms

One of the world's earliest civilizations was that of the ancient Egyptians, in Northern Africa. The Egyptian pharaohs built great pyramids and temples. In time, other nations founded colonies in northern Africa. The Phoenicians built the city of Carthage. Then the Romans came and built their own cities. Still later came the Arab conquerors. Their armies swept across northern Africa, bringing the Moslem religion with them.

But what about the rest of the continent of Africa? What about the land south of the Sahara Desert?

Along the Nile River, just south of Egypt, is a country called Sudan. During the time of ancient Egypt, this land was called Nubia. A civilization arose there about 2000 B.C. The people of Nubia, or Kush, as it was also called, were black. In about 1500 B.C., Egypt conquered Kush. For the next 500 years, Kush was ruled by the Egyptians. And the Kushites were greatly influenced by them. Kush became an important center of art, learning, and trade. But by about 1000 B.C., the Egyptians had lost much of their power. The Kushites were able to drive out the Egyptians.

Many Egyptian pyramids and temples are still standing, thousands of years after they were built.

Ancient kingdoms of Africa

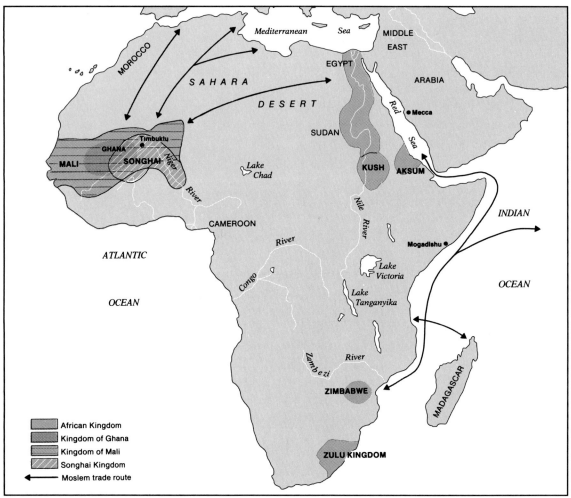

Map Skills
Name a large island off the coast of eastern Africa. Name three lakes in Africa. Name four rivers in Africa.

At about this time, Kushites began mining iron. They used the iron to make tools and weapons. The Kushites kept growing stronger. In about 750 B.C., they conquered Egypt and ruled there until about 670 B.C.

The civilization of Kush lasted until about A.D. 350. Kush was then conquered by the neighboring kingdom of Aksum. By then both Kush and Aksum had come under the influence of the Roman Empire and Christianity. Nubia was to remain Christian until the 1300s when Arabs conquered the region. The Nubians then converted to the Moslem religion.

Kush was an important trading center.

In western Africa, just on the southern side of the Sahara Desert, is a vast area of grasslands. The land was populated by tribes of black Africans.

By about A.D. 1000, Arab traders from northern Africa began to cross the Sahara in **caravans**. The trade caravans brought goods that the people of western Africa needed. They brought tools and clothing. And they brought the thing that the people needed most—salt. The climate south of the Sahara is very hot and dry. People needed salt to stay healthy. They needed salt to preserve their food. Salt was so important that the people were willing to trade gold for it. Luckily there was plenty of gold available in western Africa.

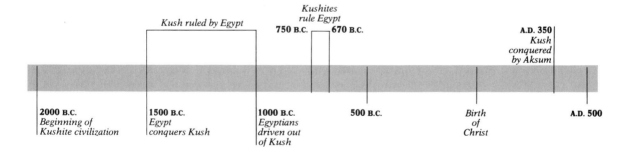

WHICH CAME FIRST?

Use the time line to choose the event, year, or period of time that came first. Write your answers on a separate sheet of paper.

1. Egyptians driven out of Kush *or* Egypt conquers Kush?

2. 670 B.C. *or* 750 B.C.?

3. Kush conquered by Aksum *or* Egyptians driven out of Kush?

4. A.D. 500 *or* 500 B.C.?

5. Kushites rule Egypt *or* Kush ruled by Egypt?

The Kingdom of Ghana

During the A.D. 300s, a kingdom called Ghana grew up in western Africa. The kingdom began to prosper about A.D. 1000. This is when the Arabs from northern Africa became interested in trade with Ghana. They had learned that Ghana was rich in gold. But trade turned out to be a mixed blessing. The Arab trading caravans brought not only goods but religion to Ghana, too. In time, Ghana's rulers became Moslems. But most of the people living in Ghana did not convert. They still practiced their own, ancient worship of many gods.

Moslem rulers tried to force the people to practice Islam. This weakened the kingdom. The Mandingo people of a kingdom called Mali took over Ghana near the end of the thirteenth century. By 1300 the kingdom of Ghana was gone, replaced by Mali.

Mansa Musa, the Mali King

From 1312 to 1337, the Mali kingdom was ruled by a man named Mansa Musa. *Mansa* means *king*. Mansa Musa was a good king. He built Mali's wealth by encouraging and then taxing caravan trade. Mansa Musa was a Moslem. And he invited Arab scholars to come to Mali to teach. The city of Timbuktu became a center of Moslem learning.

Mansa Musa became famous when he made his pilgrimage to the holy city of Mecca, in Arabia. He decided to show the rest of the world just how wealthy his kingdom was. He took a splendid caravan with him on his pilgrimage to Mecca. Across the grasslands and deserts he went, along with thousands of his people. Mansa Musa took 500 slaves with him. Each slave carried a solid gold **staff**. He also took 100 camels, each loaded with bags of gold dust. Everywhere he went, the Mali ruler gave out gold and other gifts. Stories quickly spread about the fabulous wealth of the kingdom of Mali.

Do you think Mansa Musa was a good king? Why or why not?

The Kingdom of Songhai

When Mansa Musa died, Mali weakened. A kingdom called Songhai took over control of Mali during the 1400s. One of the Songhai rulers was a king named Askia Mohammed. Askia ruled from 1493 to 1528. This was a time of growth in Songhai power. The city of Timbuktu reached its height as an important center of trade and of learning. Songhai remained strong until the late 1500s. Then the Moroccan king, Mohamed al-Mansur, The Victorious, attacked. The Moroccans had guns. The Songhai warriors fought with spears. Songhai was defeated.

History Practice

Write answers to the following questions on a separate sheet of paper.

1. What did the people of western Africa need that they were able to get from Arab traders? What did the Arabs get in return?

2. Which people took over Ghana near the end of the thirteenth century?

3. Name the ruler of the Mali Kingdom from 1312 to 1337. What was his religion?

Other Peoples of Africa

At about the time of Christ, a great migration began in Africa. Black peoples of what is now Nigeria and Cameroon moved southward into the forests of central Africa. The population had been growing, and the people needed more land. Migration continued over the next 1,000 years. The people spoke Bantu languages. They settled in many parts of central, eastern, and southern Africa.

By about A.D. 1100, trading cities dotted the eastern African coast. A city called Mogadishu was one of the largest. The people living in coastal towns had frequent contact with Arab traders. They became Moslems, and they followed many Arabic customs. They spoke Swahili. The language is still used in much of central and southern Africa.

Swahili is a Bantu language that uses many Arabic words.

A number of kingdoms arose in southern Africa. One of these was the kingdom of Zimbabwe. Another was the kingdom of the Zulus. The Zulus moved into southern Africa in the 1600s. They were powerful warriors. During the 1800s they had a strong military under a ruthless ruler named Shaka. Shaka led his armies to conquer other tribes. Meanwhile, southern

Africa was being settled by the Dutch and the British. The Zulus fought against European rule. In 1879 the British defeated the Zulu kingdom.

The Europeans in Africa

Africa was not an easy land to explore. The Sahara Desert kept many European traders from traveling south by land. But during the Renaissance, interest in travel grew. Seamen sailed better ships. In the 1400s the Europeans began to arrive in Africa by sea routes.

The Portuguese were the first to sail the waters along Africa's coast. Prince Henry the Navigator sent ships along the west coast. He was searching for a trade route to India. Portuguese sailors soon learned of the gold in western Africa. They called a section of the African coastline the *Gold Coast*.

In 1497 the Portuguese sea captian, Vasco da Gama, discovered the sea route around Africa. Soon Portugal set up trading posts along Africa's coasts. In 1571 Angola, in southwestern Africa, became a Portuguese colony.

Then the Portuguese found something in Africa that was a better money-maker than gold. They found that they could get rich by buying and selling human beings.

Slavery

There had been slaves in Africa for a long time. When tribes conquered other tribes, they often made slaves of their captives. But African slavery was very different from the kind of slavery the Europeans practiced. The Africans treated their slaves like human beings. Children of African slaves were free. The Europeans treated their slaves like goods to be traded and sold, not like people.

YOU ARE THERE:
A jungle clearing in western Africa, A.D. 1550

You are trying to hide. You press your body close to the earth. You hope the tall grass will make you invisible. The white men are near now. You can hear the sounds of their heavy boots on the ground. You feel a twitch in your bare feet. You want to jump up and run. But you know it is safer to stay hidden.

The white men have sailed to your land from a place called Portugal. You know that if they find you, they will capture you like an animal. The chief of your tribe will not stop them. The men gave the chief presents and promised him favors. If he gave them trouble, they would take him, just like they had taken his father and his uncle. They would put him aboard a giant ship. And he would sail away, never to return.

The tall blades of grass rustle in the dry wind. One of the white men is saying something but you cannot understand him. You stay very still. You're afraid to breathe. The sounds of boots are coming closer. . . .

The Portuguese were the first European slave traders. By the early 1500s, the Portuguese were capturing Africans and packing them onto crowded ships. Many Africans died on the terrible voyages. Those who survived had to work as slaves in mines and on plantations in the West Indies. Soon the Spanish were also shipping slaves to the Americas.

By the mid-1600s, the French, English, and Dutch had joined in the profitable slave trade. Some Africans helped supply the Europeans with slaves.

The lower deck of a slave ship

Tribes fought each other to capture people to supply the slave traders. The fighting between tribes weakened Africa.

The slave markets wanted only the healthiest, strongest young Africans. Over time about 10 million men and women were taken out of Africa to be sold as slaves. The loss of some of its finest people also weakened Africa. Africa was in no position to defend itself against European imperialism.

Fortunately, people finally recognized that slavery was wrong. By the 1800s many countries made slave trading illegal. In 1834 Britain outlawed slavery in its colonies. Other European countries soon did the same. The United States abolished slavery in 1865. By 1888 slavery was illegal throughout the Americas.

European Imperialism

The slave trade finally came to an end. But Africa had not seen the end of European **dominance** and European **prejudice**. In the 1800s there had been an industrial revolution in Europe. Now Europeans needed raw materials and new markets for finished products. European nations wanted new colonies. And the continent of Africa had lots of land.

The Industrial Revolution led to imperialism. But there was also another reason that led the Europeans into Africa. That was **racism**. Some Europeans simply thought they were better than the dark-skinned peoples of the world. Some thought it was their "duty" to bring their own culture to the black Africans. So the Europeans took over Africa. European explorers moved away from the coastline and into the very heart of the continent.

Europe Divides Up Africa

In 1884 European nations held a **conference** in Berlin, Germany. The United States and Turkey sent representatives, too. No one invited African representatives. The conference set up rules for forming colonies in Africa. When the conference ended, one of the greatest land grabs in history began. By 1914 Europeans had taken over almost all the land in Africa.

The Europeans formed some of their colonies very easily. They made agreements with local tribal chiefs. They gave the chiefs presents and promised chances for trade. Some of the tribal leaders simply gave away their kingdoms.

European missionaries helped set up colonies. They had come to convert the Africans to Christianity. Often they were very unwelcome. But again, the Europeans felt it was their duty to show Africans a "better way."

Soon there were only two independent countries left in all of Africa. Ethiopia, in the northeast, was the larger one. The little country of Liberia, on the west coast, was the other. It had been founded in 1822 by blacks from the United States. It had declared its independence in 1847.

Life in Colonial Africa

It is easy to see the wrongs and injustices of European imperialism in Africa. African culture was damaged. The Europeans did not understand tribal differences and tribal customs. They did not even try to understand.

The Europeans forced the Africans to learn new ways. They tried to make the Africans feel **inferior**. They forced the Africans to accept European government, religion, and languages. They drew up colonial boundaries without giving any thought to splitting up tribes.

Some of the things the Europeans did in Africa helped the natives. But most of those things were done for the sake of the Europeans. Railway systems, roads, and schools were built and the continent of Africa was opened up to the rest of the world.

In the years ahead, new ideas would come to Africa. These would be ideas of freedom, of self-government, and, in some cases, of revolution.

The Europeans tied the African economy to world needs rather than local needs.

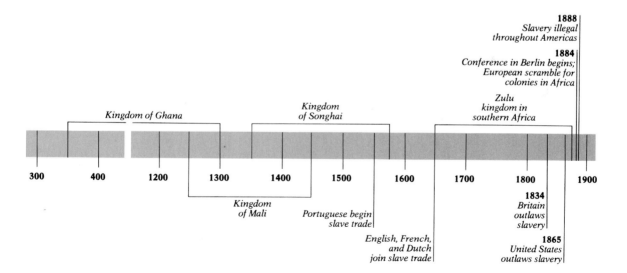

Chapter Review

Chapter Summary

- The ancient African civilization of Kush was greatly influenced by the Egyptians.

- There were rich kingdoms called Ghana, Mali, and Songhai in western Africa.

- Europeans began arriving in Africa by sea in the 1400s.

- The Portuguese found that they could make money by taking Africans abroad and selling them as slaves.

- The British, French, and Dutch soon joined the slave trade.

- The Industrial Revolution and racial prejudices played a part in European colonization of Africa.

- In 1884 a conference in Berlin laid down ground rules for colonizing Africa.

- By 1914 almost the entire continent of Africa had fallen under European imperialism.

Chapter Quiz

A. Checking Your Facts

Choose the correct word or words to make each sentence a true statement. Rewrite the sentences on a separate sheet of paper.

1. Along the Nile River, just south of Egypt, is a country called (Sudan/Mali).

2. In about (670 B.C./750 B.C.) the Kushites conquered Egypt.

3. Nubia remained Christian until the 1300s when (Arabs/ Kushites) conquered the region.

4. The Mandingo people of (Songhai/Mali) took over Ghana near the end of the thirteenth century.

5. Everywhere he went (Askia Mohammed/Mansa Musa) gave out gold and other gifts.

B. Think About It!

Write answers to the following questions on a separate sheet of paper.

1. Why do you think Europe had little contact with Africa south of the Sahara Desert before the 1400s?

2. What were the differences between early African slavery and the European slave trade?

3. Why do you think Europeans wanted colonies in Africa? Why were Europeans able to set up African colonies so easily in the nineteenth century?

Unit Eight Review

Write answers to the following questions on a separate sheet of paper.

1. Why was Great Britain called the "Workshop of the World"?

2. What is an industrial revolution?

3. Name six men who fought for independence in Latin America.

4. Latin American culture comes from a blend of which peoples?

5. How did the United States gain the Louisiana Territory?

6. What is imperialism?

7. What was the Open-Door Policy?

8. List five things the British did for India. Tell whether each was good or bad for India.

9. Which two religious groups fought each other throughout much of India's history? How was India divided between these groups after it gained independence?

10. Name the European nations that took part in the slave trade. Give two examples showing how Europeans practiced racism in the African colonies.

Nationalism and the Spread of War and Revolution

Chapter 26

The Unification of Italy and of Germany

Napoleon invaded the Italian peninsula in 1796. He did away with old boundary lines. How did this give rise to a spirit of nationalism?

Chapter Learning Objectives

- Define nationalism and explain why it develops.
- Tell how the spirit of nationalism led to the unification of Italy.
- Name three men who helped unify Italy.
- Explain why Prussia was the strongest state in Germany.
- Tell how Bismarck united Germany under a Prussian kaiser.

Words to Know

anthem   the official song of a country

chancellor   the head of government, or prime minister, in some European countries

confederation   a group of independent states joined together for a purpose

diplomat   a person in government whose job is dealing with other countries

legislature   a group of persons who make the laws of a nation or state

militarism   a national policy of maintaining a powerful army and constant readiness for war

prime minister   the chief official of the government in some countries

societies   groups of people joined together for a common purpose

unification   bringing together into one whole

volunteers   those who offer to do something of their own free will

---

Nationalism is a feeling of strong loyalty to one's country and culture. Such a feeling often develops among people who speak the same language and follow similar customs. Nationalism leads people to honor their flag and to sing a national **anthem**. It leads people to risk their very lives to support their nation.

"The Star-Spangled Banner" is the national anthem of the United States.

The spirit of nationalism helped the French fight off countries that were against their revolution. It gave the colonies in the Americas the strength to break away from the European imperialists.

In the nineteenth century, the spirit of nationalism led to the **unification** of Italy and of Germany. In both places people were feeling the bonds of language and customs and culture. They decided it was time to unite as single nations.

Italy before unification

Nationalism in Italy

During the early Roman times, Italy had been a united country. It was the center of the Roman Empire. But late in the fifth century A.D., the Roman Empire fell. Italy was divided into many small kingdoms. For more than a thousand years, different nations and monarchs fought for control of the Italian territories. French troops, Spanish troops, German troops—all marched through Italy. Then in 1796, Napoleon Bonaparte invaded the Italian peninsula and took power.

Italy after unification

Map Skills
Italy is bordered by which two seas? Name the small kingdoms and states that joined together to form the nation of Italy.

Napoleon granted Venetia to Austria. Venetia was the kingdom that included the city of Venice. Napoleon put the rest of the small kingdoms under his own rule. In 1804 he crowned himself ruler of the new kingdom. The crown he wore bore these words: "God gave it [the Italian peninsula] to me; woe to him who dares touch it."

Napleon's actions gave rise to the spirit of nationalism. This spirit would one day carry Italy to independence. Napoleon did away with old boundary lines and joined the little kingdoms together. By doing this, he gave Italians a chance to look at themselves as members of one group. The idea that all of them were Italians began to grow.

Secret Societies

As feelings of nationalism grew, Italians began to think about unity. They dreamed about one independent Italy. But by 1815, Italy was once again divided into many kingdoms and states. Most of these were either ruled by Austria or by the pope. Those who wanted to unify Italy had some barriers to overcome.

Austria tried to crush any ideas of unity. Austria wanted Italy to remain weak and divided. The pope also tried to crush any ideas of unity. He feared nationalism as a threat to his own power.

But the people wanted to be free. They wanted to join together as one nation. So secret revolutionary **societies** sprang up. During the mid-1800s, three men became leaders of the movement toward a unified Italy. Italians called these men "The Soul," "The Brain," and "The Sword."

"The Soul"

The Soul of Italy was a man named Giuseppe Mazzini. In 1830 he joined a group that was working to unify Italy. That same year he was exiled because of his political activities. He would remain in exile for 18 years. In 1832 Mazzini organized a secret society known as "Young Italy." The society's goal was to free the Italian peninsula from Austrian rule. Young Italy wanted to join the country together under one government.

In 1848 revolutions broke out in many European countries. Mazzini returned to Italy to stir up a revolution there. The ruler of the kingdom of Sardinia favored the revolutionaries. He tried to help their cause by declaring war on Austria. But Austrian and French armies helped put down the Italian revolt. Not only did the revolution fail, but Sardinia was also defeated. Mazzini had to go into exile once again.

The Austrians forced the Sardinian king from his throne. His son, Victor Emmanuel II, became king of Sardinia in 1849.

"The Brain"

The new king of Sardinia was also in favor of Italian unity. He named Camillo di Cavour as his **prime minister**. This act moved Italy closer to freedom. Camillo di Cavour would soon be known as "The Brain," the clever leader of the unification movement.

Cavour was a **diplomat**, a master of foreign affairs. He recognized Austria as an enemy to unification. In 1858 he arranged a defense agreement between Sardinia and France. The next year Austria declared war on Sardinia. But French and Italian soldiers pushed the Austrians almost as far east as Venice. Sardinia gained the nearby regions of Lombardy. Then in 1860, people from Modena, Parma, and Tuscany showed their respect for Sardinia's accomplishments. They united with Sardinia and turned against Austria.

"The Sword"

Giuseppe Garibaldi was a revolutionary most of his life. When he was 26, he joined the secret society, Young Italy. Garibaldi was a soldier in the battle for freedom. His attempts to lead Italy to independence won him the nickname of "The Sword."

Giuseppe Garibaldi

Have you ever been a volunteer? What were you trying to accomplish?

Failed rebellions forced Garibaldi to flee Italy or face death. He returned in 1848 to fight under Mazzini. When this revolution failed, he went into exile again.

In 1859 Garibaldi was back in Italy. He joined the fight for freedom led by King Victor Emmanuel of Sardinia. Garibaldi led an army of 1,000 **volunteers** to Sicily. His men were called "Red Shirts" because they wore red shirts as uniforms.

When Garibaldi and his army reached Sicily, many Sicilians joined them. Sicily was soon free. Then Garibaldi, The Sword, led his army north on the Italian mainland. He headed for Naples. Cavour, The Brain, sent an army south. By the end of 1860, the two armies had freed most of Italy. In 1861 Victor Emmanuel II became ruler of an almost completely united Italy.

Unification, at Last

Only Rome and the northern kingdom of Venetia were still not free. The pope ruled Rome, and Austria ruled Venetia. In 1866 the Italians helped Prussia defeat Austria in war. In return for its support, Italy was given Venetia.

Then came Rome. Garibaldi tried to take Rome twice, but failed. He was defeated by French troops who came to aid the pope. In 1870 Italy got another chance at Rome. France was fighting a war against Prussia. France took its troops out of Rome to help fight the Prussians. It was Italy's time to move! The pope's own small army could not fight off the Italian troops. Rome finally became part of the united nation of Italy. And in 1871, Rome became the capital of Italy.

History Practice

Answer the following questions on a separate sheet of paper.

1. What is nationalism?

2. Name three men who helped unify Italy.

3. In what year did Rome become the capital of a unified Italy?

Nationalism in Germany

Just as he did in Italy, Napoleon lit the first flames of nationalism in Germany. Napoleon took over large parts of Germany in 1806. These lands were made up of many small kingdoms. Napoleon decided to join them together to rule them more easily. He called the group of kingdoms the **Confederation** of the Rhine. People living within the confederation began to have a sense of loyalty toward one another.

When Napoleon was defeated in 1815, a new German Confederation was formed. Thirty-nine states, including Austria and Prussia, were joined together. Since Austria was large, it considered itself the leader. But Prussia had a well-organized government and real strength—military strength.

Many Germans thought about unifying the states under a central government. But Austria was against German unity. Austrians thought they could remain more powerful with the German states divided. It was not until 1862 that Germany moved toward becoming one nation.

The 39 states agreed to be members of the confederation, but each one remained an independent state.

Otto von Bismarck

The king of Prussia, Wilhelm I, was having problems with his **legislature**. King Wilhelm wanted to add to his already mighty army. But the legislature would not give him the money that he needed. So King Wilhelm turned to a Prussian landowner and soldier to help him. In 1862 he appointed a new prime minister, Otto von Bismarck.

Otto von Bismarck had a strong sense of Prussian loyalty. Bismarck was not interested in democracy or individual rights. He believed that duty to one's country was most important.

WORDS FROM THE PAST:
Bismarck's Policy of "Blood and Iron"

Bismarck promised the Prussian king a firm hand over the legislature and the people. The new prime minister thought that could be accomplished with a strong army. "The importance of a state," Bismarck said, "is measured by the number of soliders it can put into the field of battle. . . . "

Why do you suppose Bismarck was called the "Iron Chancellor"?

Bismarck followed a policy of "blood and iron." In other words, it was a policy of war. "The great questions of our day," he said, "cannot be settled by speeches and majority votes, but by blood and iron."

Bismarck encouraged King Wilhelm to unite the German states under one rule—Prussian rule.

How was this to be done? Bismarck's answer was war!

The Unification of Germany

In 1864 Bismarck began a war with Denmark. After just seven months of fighting, Prussia seized two provinces from Denmark. In 1866 Prussia and Italy defeated Austria in the Seven Weeks' War. The German Confederation was dissolved.

Then Prussia formed the North German Confederation in 1867, without Austria. Most of the German states joined. The Confederation's seat of power was Prussia. And at its head was Wilhelm I. Austria and Hungary joined to form the Austro-Hungarian Empire.

Bismarck would not be satisfied until all the German states were united under Wilhelm's rule. He decided on the best way to join the states. He would rally them together against one common enemy. For that purpose, in 1870, Bismarck started a war with France. Prussia's mighty armies won easily. They took the provinces of Alsace and Lorraine as their prize.

At the end of the war, all German states joined with Prussia. They formed a united German Empire. On January 18, 1871, the new German Empire was officially declared. It was also called the *Second Reich*. King Wilhelm I of Prussia was crowned its emperor, or *kaiser*.

The German Nation

There were two main features of the new Germany. Each would have tremendous effects on the world in the years ahead.

First, Germany was not a democratic nation. Germans accepted rule by a single person. Bismarck became the **chancellor** of Germany. He was responsible only to Kaiser Wilhelm I. Neither the kaiser nor the chancellor had to answer to any legislature nor to any elected representatives. These two men alone had complete power in Germany.

The title *kaiser* came from the Latin word *Caesar*.

Kaiser Wilhelm I

Why do you think German nationalism seemed to lead mainly to militarism?

Second, Germany had a strong tradition of **militarism**. Bismarck's "blood and iron" policy had become the German way. German nationalism meant pride in a mighty military force.

Germans gave their soldiers respect and honor. It was a German man's privilege to belong to a great army. It was an honor to fight for the glory of the empire.

All of Germany was geared toward a strong military. Large businesses supported the army. Industrialists, like Friedrich Krupp of the Krupp Iron and Steel Works, devoted factories to making war machines. Krupp built guns and cannons. The whole nation stood behind the military effort. Germany was ready for war!

Krupp armament factory, Essen, Germany

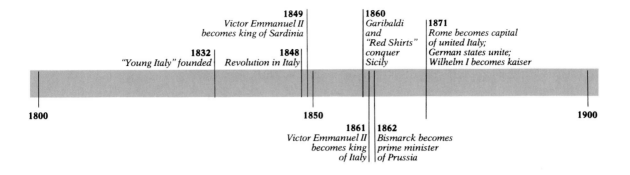

1849
*Victor Emmanuel II
becomes king of Sardinia*

1832
"Young Italy" founded

1848
Revolution in Italy

1860
*Garibaldi
and
"Red Shirts"
conquer
Sicily*

1871
*Rome becomes capital
of united Italy;
German states unite;
Wilhelm I becomes kaiser*

1800

1850

1900

1861
*Victor Emmanuel II
becomes king
of Italy*

1862
*Bismarck becomes
prime minister
of Prussia*

WHICH CAME FIRST?

Use the time line to choose the event, year, or period of time that came first. Write your answers on a separate sheet of paper.

1. Wilhelm I becomes kaiser *or* Bismarck becomes prime minister of Prussia?

2. Victor Emmanuel II becomes king of Sardinia *or* Victor Emmanuel II becomes king of Italy?

3. 1871 *or* 1861?

4. Garibaldi and "Red Shirts" conquer Sicily *or* "Young Italy" founded?

5. Revolution in Italy *or* Rome becomes capital of united Italy?

Chapter Review

Chapter Summary

- The spirit of nationalism led the people of Italy to unite under a central government.
- During the nineteenth century, the Italians worked toward independence and unification.
- In 1870 Italy was totally united.
- Sardinia's King Victor Emmanuel II became the king of Italy.
- During the nineteenth century many Germans wanted to see a unified Germany.
- Austria opposed the unification of Germany.
- The prime minister of Prussia, Otto von Bismarck, waged many wars in a movement toward unification.
- Bismarck won his wars, and in 1871 Germany was united.
- Prussia's Wilhelm I became the kaiser of the German Empire.
- Germany was not a democracy.
- Germany had a strong tradition of militarism.

Chapter Quiz

A. Checking Your Facts

Choose the correct word or words to make each sentence a true statement. Rewrite the sentences on a separate sheet of paper.

1. In 1796 Napoleon Bonaparte invaded the (Iberian/Italian) peninsula and took power.

2. (Mazzini/Garibaldi) organized a secret society known as "Young Italy."

3. In 1858 Camillo di Cavour arranged a defense agreement between (Sicily/Sardinia) and France.

4. In 1864 Bismarck began a war with (Denmark/Austria).

5. The (Second Reich/North German Confederation) was officially declared in 1867.

B. Think About It!

Write answers to the following questions on a separate sheet of paper.

1. How do you think Napoleon's actions led to a spirit of nationalism in Italy? Do you think that there is a spirit of nationalism in the United States today?

2. It is important to be loyal to your country. Explain why you agree or disagree with this statement.

3. Why do you think Giuseppe Garibaldi was called the "Sword of Italy"?

Chapter 27

World War I

Almost eight million soldiers died during World War I. Many of them were killed in the fighting in the trenches. What caused this war?

Chapter Learning Objectives

- Explain what is meant by a "balance of power."
- Name the two alliances made in 1914.
- Tell what event directly triggered World War I.
- Tell how the presence of U.S. soldiers and supplies affected the outcome of the war.
- Describe the terms of peace at the end of the war.

Words to Know

alliances   nations joined together for some purpose

armistice   an agreement to stop fighting; a truce before a formal peace treaty

casualties   soldiers who have been killed, wounded, captured, or are missing

fronts   the different places where the actual fighting is going on during a war

neutral   joining neither side in a war

sniper   a person who shoots from a hidden spot

submarines   warships that travel under the water

torpedoed   attacked with a large, exploding, cigar-shaped missile

trenches   long ditches dug in the ground to protect soldiers in battle

---

World War I began on July 28, 1914. No one nation wanted a war. But in truth, all the major powers in Europe had been gathering military strength for many years.

The nationalism of the 1800s led to stronger armies. People who were loyal to their own nations felt that military strength showed pride and power.

The imperialism of the 1800s also created a need for strong armies. Nations had their colonies to protect. Each nation feared that it might lose what it had without a strong military.

The Balance of Power

Relations between countries were strained in the early 1900s. By 1914 Europe had divided itself into two sides. Nations formed **alliances**. They promised to protect each other and to help each other in case of war.

Europe, 1914

Map Skills
In 1914, which countries were neutral in Europe? Name the Allied Powers. Name the Central Powers.

One group of nations was called the *Central Powers.* The nations of the Central Powers included Germany, Austria-Hungary, the Ottoman Empire (Turkey), and, for a short time, Italy. The other group of nations was called the *Allies.* On that side were Britain, France, and Russia.

Each alliance tried to keep the other from getting too strong. They wanted to keep a "balance of power" in Europe.

Rising Tensions

As the year 1914 began, there was tension throughout Europe. France and Germany had been bitter enemies for years. France had lost a war against Bismarck's armies in 1871. Ever since then, France wanted to get back the provinces of Alsace and Lorraine.

Russia faced an ongoing quarrel with Austria-Hungary. They disagreed about the territorial borders in the Balkans.

Nations watched each other as each built up its military forces. Airplanes, bigger warships, and machine guns made armies more capable of destruction. One country would build new arms. Then another would panic and race to keep up. No one wanted war, but everyone was getting ready.

Since the end of World War II, there has been a dangerous nuclear arms race between the United States and the Soviet Union.

The War Begins

It took a single incident in July of 1914 to explode the already tense situation in Europe. The Austrian Archduke Francis Ferdinand was assassinated. This is named as the incident that began the First World War.

Archduke Ferdinand was the next in line to the throne of Austria-Hungary. He and his wife, Sophie, were visiting Sarajevo, a city in the Austrian province of Bosnia. Many Serbs also lived in Bosnia. And some of them believed Bosnia should belong to Serbia.

Archduke Ferdinand and his wife were traveling by motor car on a road in Sarajevo. They were a fine-looking pair. The Archduke wore a white uniform, and his wife wore a matching white gown. Riding in an open car, they were clear targets. As the royal procession drove through the streets, two shots rang out. Archduke Ferdinand and his wife were both killed by a **sniper**.

The assassin, Gavrilo Princip, was a Serb. He was a member of a Serbian revolutionary group called the "Black Hand."

Austria-Hungary blamed the Serbian government for the assassination. On July 28, 1914, it declared war on Serbia. Now the alliances came into play. Germany stood behind Austria-Hungary. Russia came to the aid of Serbia. France came to Russia's aid. Soon England joined in to help its allies. World War I had begun.

The assassination of Archduke Francis Ferdinand

The Great War

World War I is sometimes called "The Great War." It was not really a "worldwide" war. Most of the fighting took place in Europe. And not every country in the world was fighting. However, more than 30 countries, including all the major powers, were involved. The Great War's effects were certainly felt worldwide.

At first the Central Powers seeemed to be winning. Germany and Austria-Hungary, joined by Turkey and Bulgaria, made gains. Italy had been allied with the Central Powers. But it remained **neutral** in the early part of the war. Then in 1915, Italy changed its alliance. It joined forces with the Allies.

Switzerland was one of the few European nations to remain neutral throughout the war. It would also stay neutral during World War II.

Trench Warfare

The Central Powers wanted to take France. They came within 25 miles of Paris. But the French and British held them off in a major battle, the Battle of the Marne. Then both sides dug in. The soldiers dug long **trenches**. Armies could hide in the trenches and shoot at each other.

The **fronts** were lined with networks of trenches. There were three fronts in Europe. The Western Front ran from Belgium to Switzerland. The Eastern Front ran from the Baltic Sea to the Black Sea. The Italian, or Southern Front ran between Italy and Austria-Hungary.

Some trenches were more than a mile long.

The battle trenches along the fronts became home for the soldiers. They ate in the trenches and slept in the trenches. And many soldiers died in the trenches.

Most of the battles of World War I were fought inside Europe. But there was also some fighting in Africa and in the Middle East. The powerful British navy kept control of most of the seas.

The United States Enters the War

Despite Britain's great navy, German **submarines** were terrorizing the oceans. They attacked enemy merchant ships without warning. Then in 1915, a British luxury liner, the *Lusitania*, was **torpedoed** and sunk. The death list of 1,198 persons included 128 Americans. In 1917 the submarines began attacking ships of neutral nations. Several American merchant ships were sunk.

In April 1917, U.S. President Woodrow Wilson made an announcement. He said that it was time to "make the world safe for democracy." The United States declared war on Germany and joined the Allies. The United States entered the battlefields at a good time.

Do you think the United States "made the world safe for democracy" by entering the war?

The sinking of the *Lusitania*

The Allies needed help. The United States sent fresh soldiers and supplies of arms to Europe. The scale in the balance of power was now tipped in favor of the Allies.

Then in November of 1917, a revolution took place in Russia. The new government signed a peace treaty with Germany and pulled out of the war.

You will read about the revolution in Russia in the next chapter.

LEARN MORE ABOUT IT: Wartime Inventions

The war brought many changes in the world. New inventions were perfected in a hurry to meet war needs. The Germans developed submarines to travel under the water like sharks. The submarines were also called "U-boats" (underwater boats). They moved unseen, seeking their prey.

Allied countries could not find a defense against the submarines for the first three years of the war. Eventually depth charges were used to destroy the submarines. Fast British ships known as *subchasers* carried the depth charges. These ships also used zigzag courses to avoid German submarines.

The submarines were very successful. Only 203 German submarines were destroyed during the whole war. But the German submarines sank 6,604 Allied ships.

For the first time, airplanes were used for war. At first they were just used for scouting, watching the enemy, and taking pictures. They were not used for fighting until later in the war.

Planes were improved rapidly. In 1914 an airplane could go 90 miles an hour. By 1917 they were flying at 175 miles an hour. They carried bombs and machine guns. Some pilots became famous as "war aces" for shooting down five or more enemy airplanes.

Germany used *zeppelins* in the air. Zeppelins were huge, cigar-shaped crafts, 600 feet long. They were inflated with hydrogen gas and used in bombing raids over England and France.

British engineers invented the tank, an armored vehicle with caterpillar tracks. The big tanks rumbled their way across the battlefields of Europe. And there were other new weapons, like poison gas and flame throwers. Each side tried to outdo the other with more powerful and more horrible weaponry.

The submarine was the most deadly military vessel of World War I.

World War I fighter planes

Answer the following questions on a separate sheet of paper.

1. What is meant by a "balance of power"?

2. The assassination of Archduke Ferdinand was the spark that set off World War I. But there were other reasons for the tense situation in Europe. Name three of them.

3. Why did the United States enter the war?

The German government finally agreed to the Allies' terms and Kaiser Wilhelm gave up his throne.

The End of the War

With new American soldiers and supplies, the Allies began to push back the Germans. The other Central Powers had given up. Germany stood alone, and German armies were losing ground.

Germany asked for an end to the war. On November 11, 1918, an **armistice** was declared. All fighting was to stop at 11:00 A.M. that day.

The Treaty of Versailles

After the war, leaders of the Allied nations and Germany met in Versailles, France. Their purpose was to write a peace treaty. The treaty, which was signed in 1919, made many demands on Germany.

Germany lost all of its colonies and had to return Alsace and Lorraine to France. Germany took all blame for the war, so it had to pay for many of the war's costs. And Germany promised to disarm. The nation was not supposed to rebuild its navy or air force. And it could maintain only a small army. This was quite a blow to a nation that had taken such pride in a powerful military.

Another big loser in the war was Turkey. In 1919 most of the Middle East and North Africa was still ruled by the Ottoman Turks. But the end of the war brought about the end of the Ottoman Empire. Most of the Arab lands that had been ruled by the Turks now fell under British control.

Europe after World War I

Map Skills
Name the new nations in Europe after World War I.

The League of Nations: A Peacekeeper

The Great War ended four years after it had begun. Those four years meant the loss of almost eight million soldiers. Millions of others died, too. They died of disease and of starvation, side effects of war. Russia suffered the most **casualties** in World War I.

The total cost of the war to all countries involved was more than $337,000,000,000. All of Europe was weakened.

People spoke of the Great War as "the war to end all wars."

Do you think the United States was right not to join the League of Nations? Why or why not?

When the war ended, leaders of the world's nations looked at the results. They decided there must be a better way to solve conflicts between nations. President Wilson proposed setting up a League of Nations. European leaders welcomed the idea. They knew that their people would support such a league. And Wilson was confident that the American people would support it as well.

So in 1920, the League of Nations was set up. Its headquarters were in Geneva, Switzerland—a neutral, peaceful country. Representatives of member nations could meet there to discuss their problems. It was the first organization designed to keep the peace of the entire world.

Many nations joined the League. Some, including the United States, did not. Wilson was greatly disappointed. Many people in the United States didn't like the idea of Wilson's League. A certain part of Wilson's plan caused major problems. That was Article Ten. It mentioned threats to any member nation of the League. It said that if any threats were made, the other members would aid the threatened nation.

Americans felt they had seen too much of war. They didn't want to have anything to do with Europe and its problems anymore. They thought Article Ten seemed to invite trouble.

President Wilson put up a strong fight. He made speeches all around the country. He did everything he could to try to convince Americans to join the League. But the Senate voted against it in March, 1920. Wilson died in 1924, a defeated man. He'd warned that another world war was not far off. He'd said that only the League of Nations could prevent it. But all his talk was in vain. America didn't want to hear him.

The League of Nations had no army to enforce its decisions. It was based on good will and the idea that nations wanted peace. The war years, 1914 to 1918, had left everyone fearful of war. Now the whole world was anxious to avoid war. People everywhere were hopeful that a war would never be fought again.

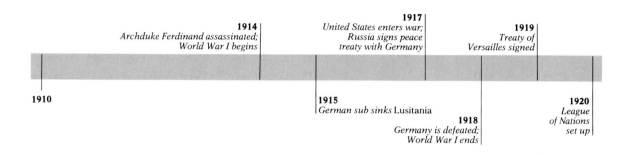

WHICH CAME FIRST?

Use the time line to choose the event, year, or period of time that came first. Write your answers on a separate sheet of paper.

1. United States enters war *or* German sub sinks *Lusitania*?
2. Germany is defeated *or* Russia signs peace treaty with Germany?
3. 1918 *or* 1914?
4. Archduke Ferdinand assassinated *or* Treaty of Versailles signed?
5. League of Nations set up *or* World War I ends?

Chapter Review

Chapter Summary

- World War I began in July 1914. An armistice was declared in November 1918.

- Before the war, tensions were building between two European alliances. One alliance, the Central Powers, included Germany and Austria-Hungary, and, for a time, Italy. The Allies included Britain, France, and Russia. When the war began, Italy was neutral. But in 1915 it joined the Allies.

- The two alliances hoped to keep a balance of power in Europe.

- The assassination of Austrian Archduke Francis Ferdinand triggered World War I.

- The United States joined the war on the side of the Allies in 1917.

- Russia withdrew from the war, signing a peace treaty with Germany in 1917.

- American forces and supplies helped the Allies win the war.

- The Treaty of Versailles, signed in 1919, set up terms for peace.

- Wartime developments included the submarine, improved airplanes, and more powerful weaponry.

- The League of Nations was set up after the war in the hope of maintaining world peace.

Chapter Quiz

A. Checking Your Facts

Complete each sentence below. Use the correct word from the box. Rewrite the sentences on a separate sheet of paper.

alliances	fronts	trenches	submarines	casualties

1. Soldiers lived, fought, and often died in the long _____ they had dug.

2. Three _____ extended across much of Europe.

3. Nations formed _____ to protect each other and help each other in case of war.

4. German _____ attacked enemy ships without warning.

5. Russia suffered the most _____ in World War I.

B. Think About It!

Write answers to the following questions on a separate sheet of paper.

1. Explain how each of the following led to World War I:
   (a) militarism (b) nationalism (c) imperialism

2. If not every country was involved in World War I, why do you think it was called a "world" war?

3. Why was the League of Nations set up in 1920?

Chapter 28

Revolution in Russia:
The Birth of the Soviet Union

In 1905, protests by Russian workers led to street fighting. What do you think the workers were protesting about?

Chapter Learning Objectives

- Explain why Peter the Great wanted to open a "window to the West."
- Explain how "Bloody Sunday" touched off a revolution in 1905.
- Describe how the common people of Russia felt about their country's involvement in World War I.
- Identify Karl Marx, the Bolsheviks, and Lenin.

Words to Know

censor   to examine communications before they are released and to remove any parts that are objected to

collective   run by a group; a *collective* farm

communism   a political system based on an absence of social class, common ownership of industries and farms, and a sharing of work and of goods produced

dialects   forms of a language used only in a certain place or among a certain group

geography   the natural surface features of the Earth, or any part of it

---

The **geography** of the Soviet Union is varied. The country takes in frozen wastelands, thick forests, and wide plains known as *steppes*. There are also sandy deserts and huge snow-capped mountains. And some of the longest rivers in the world are in the Soviet Union.

The people of the Soviet Union are just as varied as the geography. Some are tall and blond-haired, others are olive skinned and dark-haired. Altogether, Soviet people speak more than 200 different languages and **dialects**.

The Soviet Union is the largest country on Earth. But the country was not always so large, and it was not always strong. Russia did not become the powerful Soviet Union until after World War I.

The Soviet Union

Map Skills

Name four rivers in the Soviet Union. The Soviet Union borders which two oceans?

The Early History of Russia

Do you remember Genghis Khan? Why was he famous?

In A.D. 1237 a Mongol leader named Batu Khan invaded Russia with a huge army. Batu was a grandson of Genghis Khan. He destroyed one town after another. Russia became part of the Mongol empire.

The Mongols ruled for over 200 years. Then they grew weaker because of fighting among their leaders. Finally, in 1480 a group of Russian princes defeated the Mongols. Ivan III and his son, Basil III, led those princes. In 1547 Basil's son became the ruler, the first czar of all Russia. The first czar's name was Ivan IV. He became known as *Ivan the Terrible*.

Ivan IV changed Russian government. Earlier rulers, called Grand Dukes, had accepted advice and criticism from other nobles. Not Ivan IV. As czar he moved the head of the government to Moscow and made himself all-powerful. It is said that one nobleman who dared to disagree with Ivan IV was tossed to the hounds. And he was torn to shreds!

Ivan ruled by terror. With threats of cruel punishment, he frightened the Russian people into doing his bidding. Hundreds of people were murdered by Ivan and his special police force. Ivan even killed his oldest son with his own two hands.

Ivan fought many wars. He increased Russia's territory. But he worsened the daily lives of his people. Under Ivan the Terrible, the peasants were dreadfully poor. There was lots of land. But there were not enough people to keep the economy strong.

Ivan did grant the right to trade in Russia. This brought in money for the upper classes. But it did little to improve the lives of the common people. After Ivan, most Russian rulers would seem kindly in comparison.

During the 1600s, Russia added to its territory. It took over the Ukraine. And it extended its control of Siberia eastward to the Pacific Ocean. Slowly Russia increased its contact with the rest of the world. Czar Michael Romanov took the throne in 1613. He encouraged trade with Holland and England. He brought foreign engineers and doctors to Russia. Michael's son Alexis followed him. He, too, was open to European customs and cultures.

The word *czar* comes from the Latin word *Caesar*.

Ivan the Terrible

Peter the Great: A "Window to the West"

Toward the end of the seventeenth century, a czar named Peter ruled in Russia. Peter had big plans. He wanted to make Russia more powerful. His goal was to make Russia equal to the nations of western Europe. So Peter brought more Europeans into Russia. He brought engineers, artists, soldiers, and scientists to teach Russians the ways of Western Europe.

Still, Peter did not learn all he wanted to know. So he went on a journey. He traveled to the Netherlands to study shipbuilding. And he continued his studies in England where he visited factories, schools, and museums. He also visited France, Germany, and Austria.

When Czar Peter returned, he had many new ideas. He wanted to "westernize" his people. He ordered his subjects to wear European-style clothing instead of long, Oriental-type robes. He demanded that all

Peter the Great

Russian men cut off their beards to look more European. To set an example, Peter called his nobles together and cut off their beards himself. When people rebelled against Peter's no-beard orders, he demanded a tax from any man wearing a beard.

Fontanka Canal, St. Petersburg

Peter changed the old Russian calendar to make it match the European calendar. He gave women more freedom. He put the Russian church under complete control of his government.

Peter's desire to *westernize* Russia led him to his quest for a "window to the West." Peter wanted to open a Russian port on the ice-free Baltic Sea. But Sweden stood in his way, so in 1700 he attacked Sweden. The war lasted until 1721. A peace treaty gave Russia land along the eastern Baltic coast.

Meanwhile, in 1703 Peter began building the city of St. Petersburg. It was built along the Neva River, where the river flows into the Gulf of Finland. In 1712 Peter moved the nation's capital from Moscow to St. Petersburg. Today St. Petersburg is called Leningrad.

St. Petersburg would be Peter's European "window."

Peter brought new ideas, industrialization, and strength to Russia. That is why he was given the name *Peter the Great*. But he did little for common people. Russian peasants were still poor and completely at the mercy of their czar.

In 1762 Empress Catherine II ruled Russia. Catherine continued many of Peter's policies. She kept the "window to the West" open. She brought French culture to the nobles of Russia and improved their education. She was called *Catherine the Great*. But she, too, did little for the peasants. In 1773 Catherine's armies had to put down a peasant revolt.

In 1812 Russia's relations with the West took a turn for the worse. That year France's Napoleon Bonaparte invaded Russia. In Chapter 19 you read how this turned out to be Napoleon's big mistake. After taking Moscow, Napoleon's army began to run out of supplies as the weather turned bitter cold. Napoleon had to order a retreat. Less than half his men lived to reach France.

The great Russian author Tolstoy wrote about Napoleon's invasion of Russia in his famous novel, *War and Peace*.

"Bloody Sunday" and the 1905 Revolution

Russian peasants had lived under a feudal-type system for hundreds of years. Wealthy nobles owned all the farmlands. As industrialization came to Russia, factories sprang up in the cities. Thousands of peasants left the farms. They moved to the cities to work in those factories. Often the peasants found the factory owners as unfair and uncaring as the land-owning nobles had been.

YOU ARE THERE: St. Petersburg, January 22, 1905

The pale sun has just broken through the clouds. The snow on the street is frozen solid in some places. The sunlight glints on icy patches. Although the day is bitter cold, you and your friends from the factory are gathered in the square. You are part of a huge crowd of more than 200,000 workers from the other factories. The workers and their families have taken to the streets to ask for better working conditions. Even though they have jobs, they are hungry. You yourself have had nothing to eat in the past two days except a stale crust of bread.

The crowd begins to march slowly down the wide avenue toward the czar's Winter Palace. The leader of the march is a priest named Father Gapon. He is carrying a letter for the czar asking that the people be given higher wages and a voice in the government. The crowd begins to sing "God Save the Czar."

Suddenly you notice that the avenue up ahead is blocked by an army of the czar's soldiers on horseback. They begin heading toward you at a gallop. You stare in shock as the soldiers raise their rifles. The people are still singing as the first volley of shots rings out. There are screams, and men, women, and children fall to the ground. There are more shots. You feel something pound into your shoulder. You stagger to the side of the street and collapse into a snow bank. Now the soldiers charge into the crowd, slashing away with their swords. Angrily, you wonder how can the czar allow this to happen?

Czar Nicholas didn't trust his people. In fact, he feared them.

Hundreds of men, women, and children were shot and killed or wounded that day. January 22, 1905, became known as Russia's "Bloody Sunday."

Bloody Sunday was the end of any peaceful demand for change. Strikes, riots, and revolutionary battles broke out. In order to put a stop to the revolt, Nicholas II agreed to set up an elected Duma, or parliament. The Duma would have the power to rule on any proposals for new laws. Some people were satisfied with this change. Others felt that the Duma was not enough. But the Dumas lasted until 1917.

Many of the revolutionaries in Russia had read the works of Karl Marx. Marx was a German thinker of the 1800s. He had explained his ideas in the *Communist Manifesto,* which was published in 1848. He believed it was wrong for factory owners to make most of the money. He said the workers should share in the profits of their work. He encouraged workers to rise up against the middle class. Marx pictured a perfect world where there would be no classes and where government would be unnecessary. Marx's ideas were known as **communism**. Some of the revolutionaries in Russia wanted to see Marx's ideas become a reality in their country.

History Practice

Write answers to the following questions on a separate sheet of paper.

1. Why do you think Czar Ivan IV became known as "Ivan the Terrible"?

2. Why did Czar Peter want to open a "window to the West"? Why was he called "Peter the Great"?

3. Why was January 22, 1905, called "Bloody Sunday"?

World War I and the Overthrow of Czar Nicholas II

Russia entered World War I shortly after it began in 1914. The war brought severe food shortages to Russia. The poor people became even poorer. The common people of Russia were not interested in fighting Germany. But Czar Nicholas II had plunged Russia into the war.

In March 1917 the people of Russia demanded more food. The starving workers and peasants revolted. Czar Nicholas II was overthrown, and a new government took over. The czar and his family were put in prison. The government promised democracy in Russia. It did not, however, end Russia's involvement in World War I. The people were against the war. It was draining supplies, killing the men, and taking the food.

Lenin and the Bolshevik Revolution

Later that year, a man named Vladimir Ilyich Lenin returned to Russia from exile in Switzerland. Lenin had always hated the government of the czar. His brother had been hanged as a revolutionary. And Lenin himself had been exiled.

Lenin read Karl Marx. He became a communist revolutionary who believed in rebellion and in a classless society. On his return to Russia, Lenin became the leader of a communist group called the Bolsheviks. *Bolshevik* means "member of the majority." Lenin and the Bolsheviks promised to give the people what they wanted: "Peace, land, and bread."

Karl Marx

In November 1917 the Bolsheviks overthrew the government. Karl Marx had pictured a society with no need for government. But Lenin felt that a strict Communist party should be in charge. The country would need a planned economy. And the Communist party would draw up the plans. The country would be governed by councils called *soviets*. The soviets would be headed by Bolsheviks.

The Union of Soviet Socialist Republics (U.S.S.R.)

In July 1918 Czar Nicholas and his family were executed by the Bolsheviks.

In 1918 Moscow became the nation's capital once again. That year Russia was torn apart by a civil war. The Communists had taken power in the large cities of central Russia. But resistance developed in many other parts of the country. The "Whites," or anticommunists, had moved quickly to organize armies to fight the "Reds," or Communists. By 1920 most of the fighting was over. The Whites had been defeated.

In 1922 Russia became the Union of Soviet Socialist Republics. By then, Lenin had put the Communists firmly in charge. He had organized a strong police force. Every day the police arrested, jailed, and even killed enemies of communism. The police force often made their arrests at night, secretly. Many members of the clergy were arrested. Communists believed that religion was in the way. Religion misguided people, the Communists said.

Members of the nobility and of the middle class were labeled enemies of the state. They were arrested, jailed, and shot. The government took their businesses. Lenin and his secret police ruled by fear.

The Bolshevik Revolution was supposd to help the peasants. Now Lenin ordered farmers to turn their crops over to the government. Some farmers rebelled.

There was more fighting. Throughout the early 1920s, the Communists struggled to maintain power. For a brief period, the Communists let up on their hold over factories and farms in order to win support.

Then, in 1924 Lenin became ill and died. He is remembered as the "Father of the Revolution." After his death, the Communists began a new struggle for leadership of the government.

Joseph Stalin

Joseph Stalin was born in 1879 in what is now the Soviet republic of Georgia. He was educated in a religious school. His mother wanted him to become a priest. Then Joseph Stalin read the works of Karl Marx. "There is no God!" he announced at age 13.

Vladimir Ilyich Lenin

Joseph Stalin

Tractors on a collective farm near Rostov-on-Don, U.S.S.R.

When he grew up, he became a revolutionary and then a leader in the Communist party.

Stalin's real name was Dzhugashvili. But in 1913, he adopted the name *Stalin*, which means *man of iron* in Russian. Stalin took power after Lenin's death. He ruled the Soviet Union from 1924 until his death in 1953. He built up Russia's economy and industry. Stalin saw to the building of new factories and more heavy machinery. The peasants were forced to work on **collective** farms. He insisted that farmers use the new government machines. But he did not show the farmers how to operate them. Farm production went down. There were food shortages again.

Stalin made himself strong by destroying anyone who opposed him. Suspected enemies were shot or exiled to Siberia. People learned to be loyal to the Communist party and to Stalin.

Many people were unhappy living under such a tyrant. Stalin made life especially hard for Russian Jews. But throughout the country, there were food shortages for everyone. And certain goods, like clothing, were also hard to come by.

Russian newspapers and radio programs told nothing of the country's problems. Sources of news said only what Stalin wanted them to say. And Stalin would **censor** any news that came in from the rest of the world. Stalin did not allow Russians to travel outside the Soviet Union. For this reason, the Soviet Union was said to be surrounded by an "iron curtain."

Stalin had statues of himself put up all over Russia. He insisted that the statues be built to make him look taller and more handsome than he really was. Stalin actually rewrote Russian history. He tried to make it sound as if the Russian people had actually chosen him to be their leader.

Russia has a long history of being ruled by tyrants. Ivan the Terrible, Peter the Great, and many other czars were ruthless dictators. But many people think that Stalin was the most destructive and tyrannical dictator of all.

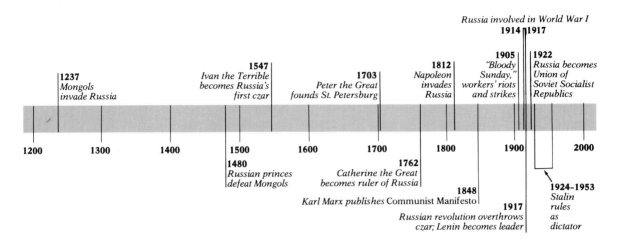

1237 Mongols invade Russia

1547 Ivan the Terrible becomes Russia's first czar

1480 Russian princes defeat Mongols

1703 Peter the Great founds St. Petersburg

1762 Catherine the Great becomes ruler of Russia

Karl Marx publishes Communist Manifesto **1848**

1812 Napoleon invades Russia

Russian revolution overthrows czar; Lenin becomes leader **1917**

1905 "Bloody Sunday," workers' riots and strikes

Russia involved in World War I **1914** **1917**

1922 Russia becomes Union of Soviet Socialist Republics

1924–1953 Stalin rules as dictator

1200 1300 1400 1500 1600 1700 1800 1900 2000

WHICH CAME FIRST?

Use the time line to choose the event, year, or period of time that came first. Write your answers on a separate sheet of paper.

1. "Bloody Sunday," workers' riots and strikes *or* Russian revolution overthrows czar?

2. Russian princes defeat Mongols *or* Mongols invade Russia?

3. 1547 *or* 1500?

4. Peter the Great founds St. Petersburg *or* Ivan the Terrible becomes Russia's first czar?

5. Napoleon invades Russia *or* Catherine the Great becomes ruler of Russia?

Chapter Review

Chapter Summary

- The Soviet Union takes in a huge area; it is home to many types of people.

- Russian czars came to power after 200 years of Mongol rule.

- Ivan the Terrible, who ruled by terror, was the first czar.

- Peter the Great gained land for Russia and opened a "window" to the rest of Europe. He westernized his country.

- Catherine the Great continued Peter's policies. The nobles of Russia were well educated and cultured, while the peasants grew poorer and poorer.

- Bloody Sunday, in 1905, began a revolt of the Russian workers.

- Czar Nicholas II led Russia into World War I in 1914. The war caused food shortages and was unpopular.

- In 1917 Nicholas II was overthrown. Later that year the Bolsheviks seized control of the government.

- The Bolsheviks, who followed the communist ideas of the German philosopher Karl Marx, supported Lenin as head of Russia's government.

- In 1922 Russia became known as the Union of Soviet Socialist Republics.

- Joseph Stalin followed Lenin as leader of the Communist party and of the Soviet Union.

Chapter Quiz

A. Checking Your Facts

Choose the correct word or words to make each sentence a true statement. Rewrite the sentences on a separate sheet of paper.

1. Russia did not become the Soviet Union until after (World War II/World War I).

2. (Batu Khan/Genghis Khan) invaded Russia with a huge army in 1237.

3. St. Petersburg was built along the Neva River, where the river flows into the Gulf of (Alaska/Finland).

4. The Bolsheviks overthrew the Russian government in (1905/1917).

5. Joseph Stalin was born in 1879 in what is now the Soviet republic of (Georgia/Armenia).

B. Think About It!

Write answers to the following questions on a separate sheet of paper.

1. What was life like for peasants, workers, and common people throughout most of Russia's history?

2. Why do you think Lenin and others believed that communism would be good for Russia? How did Lenin's ideas of communism differ from Marx's?

3. Joseph Stalin was not a good leader for the Soviet Union. Explain why you agree or disagree with this statement.

Chapter 29
World War II

On August <u>6</u>, 1945, an atomic bomb fell on Hiroshima, Japan. In seconds more than 90,000 people were killed. Why did the U.S. drop the bomb?

Chapter Learning Objectives

- Name three dangerous dictators who came to power before World War II.
- Explain how Germany helped to bring about World War II.
- Identify the Allied powers and the Axis powers.
- Explain how the United States became involved in the war.
- Describe how the war finally ended in Europe and in Japan.

Words to Know

anti-Semitism   prejudice against Jews

concentration camps   prison camps for people thought to be dangerous to a ruling group

depressions   periods of low business activity and high unemployment

fascists   dictators and their followers who take away rights of the people and glorify war

genocide   an attempt to kill all the people of a certain race or religious group

Holocaust   the killing of millions of Jews by Germany's Nazis

pact   an agreement

scapegoat   a person or group blamed for the mistakes and problems of others

---

After World War I the League of Nations hoped to keep the peace. World War I had been costly in lives and in money. No one was anxious for another war. Yet only 20 years after World War I ended, another war began.

The 20 years between World War I and World War II were troubled years. In the early 1930s, nations struggled through **depressions**. Businesses went broke. Millions of workers were out of jobs. Farmers could not sell crops to unemployed people. Banks closed. Poverty spread throughout the world. Historians would call the 1930s the "Great Depression."

There were other troubles, too. In India, people were fighting for freedom from British rule. Civil wars were raging in China and Spain. And Japan was attacking China as part of its plan to build a large empire.

The Rise of Dictators

The years between World War I and World War II brought new governments to several nations. They were governments ruled by dictators. The Great Depression created a perfect climate for the rise of dictators. Hungry, hopeless people wanted to see changes. They were ready to turn to a strong leader who promised a better future. Most of the dictators, however, were evil men who wanted power and control.

Italians said that Mussolini "made the trains run on time."

A man named Benito Mussolini took control of Italy in 1922. His followers were called **Fascists**. Mussolini won favor with his people by building roads and factories. He improved his country's economy and industry, but insisted on absolute rule. Anyone who refused to obey Mussolini was jailed or killed.

Mussolini wanted Italy to become a great empire. He wanted to win colonies, to make war, and to take new lands by force. In 1935 Mussolini sent troops into Ethiopia, a free African country. The League of Nations protested. But it could not stop Mussolini's drive into Africa.

Benito Mussolini

Hideki Tojo

In Japan, General Hideki Tojo arose as a dictator. He wanted to build an empire in Asia. Under the leadership of Tojo and other generals, Japanese forces invaded the Chinese province of Manchuria in 1931. When the League of Nations protested, Japan left the League. By 1932 Japan had claimed Manchuria. Japan invaded China again in 1937, taking over miles of coastal lands. By 1938 Japan controlled all of China's major ports and industrial centers.

Tojo was the son of a general. The military was his only interest.

During the 1930s Japanese military officers began taking over their own government. Anyone who got in their way or protested was either jailed or assassinated. By 1940 Tojo had become Minister of War. And in 1941 he became Premier. Japan still had an emperor. But the emperor had no real power.

Hitler

The country that was most willing to accept a dictator and to follow him without question was Germany. Germany had suffered greatly after World War I. German pride had been crushed. A country whose nationalistic spirit was based on military greatness had been beaten in war. German armies had been reduced to almost nothing. And the Treaty of Versailles had forbidden the rebuilding of the German military.

The Depression hit hard, and Germany still had war debts to pay. Germans were out of work and hungry. They were angry and ready for revenge.

This situation in Germany led people to accept Adolf Hitler as their leader in 1933. Hitler was the head of the National Socialist, or *Nazi*, party. Hitler and the Nazis seemed to have an answer to Germany's problems. Hitler appealed to the Germans' wounded pride. He told them that they were a "super race" who should rule the world. He promised to return Germany to a position of power and glory.

Adolf Hitler

They would remember the armored cars moving in next, followed by the Nazi foot soldiers.

The German *Blitzkrieg* then fell upon Holland, Luxembourg, and Belgium. Next came France.

France had been Germany's bitter enemy since losing a war to Bismarck in 1871.

When the Germans attacked France, they had some help from Italy. France's armies were unable to stop Hitler. With Germans at the gates of Paris and with Nazi planes overhead, the French surrendered. In June 1940 the French admitted their defeat. It is said that Hitler received the news of France's surrender with great joy. He was so happy, in fact, that he danced a little "victory jig."

WORDS FROM THE PAST:
Winston Churchill's speech to the
House of Commons, June 4, 1940

Sir Winston Churchill had become prime minister of Great Britain on May 10, 1940. That was the same day that Germany invaded Belgium, Luxembourg, and Holland. Soon after that, Belgium surrendered to Germany. It looked as if it would only be a matter of days until France fell to the Nazis. People in Britain began to worry about what would happen to their own country.

On June 4 Churchill gave a speech to the British House of Commons. He wanted to raise the spirits of the British people. He said that even though all of Europe might fall, ". . . we shall not flag or fail. We shall go on to the end . . . we shall fight in the seas and oceans . . . we shall fight on the beaches, we shall fight on the landing-grounds, we shall fight in the fields and in the streets, we shall fight in the hills; we shall never surrender . . ."

The Battle of Britain

With the fall of France, only Britain remained in Hitler's way. Hitler decided not to attack the island of Great Britain by sea. Britain's navy was too powerful. Hitler would launch an air attack instead.

The Battle of Britain was the first major air war in history. Beginning in July 1940, thousands of German planes attacked Britain. They bombed cities and airfields. But the British would not be defeated.

British civilians worked out air raid plans to protect their neighborhoods. Citizens even strung piano wire from balloons to catch Nazi planes. The British Royal Air Force (RAF) fought back. They were skilled young pilots. With speedy Spitfire planes and with newly developed radar, they fought off the German planes.

England's spirit remained strong in spite of the constant bombing.

Bombing damage in London

From September 1940 until May 1941, German planes bombed London almost every night. These attacks became known as the *London Blitz.* By May 1941 it was clear that the German bombing attacks had failed. Germany had lost more than 2600 planes. It was Germany's first defeat in World War II.

World War II in Europe

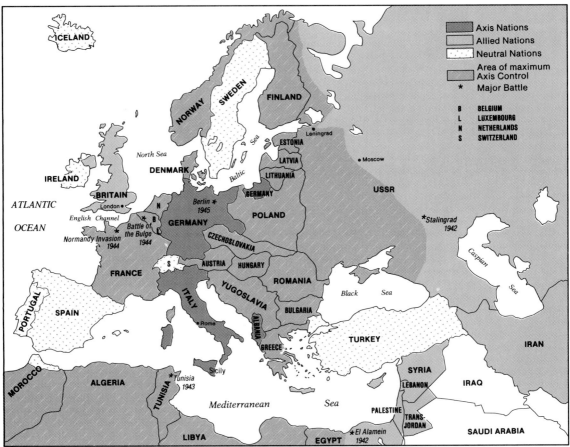

Map Skills

Which nations managed to remain neutral in World War II? Name three cities in the U.S.S.R. that were just at the edge of the area of Axis control.

Hitler Moves East

Unable to take Britain, Hitler's armies moved eastward. The Germans took Romania and its oil fields. Then Italy invaded Greece. Greece's armies fought bravely against the Italians. But when Hitler joined the Italians, Greece had to surrender.

Next the Axis nations took Hungary, Bulgaria, and Yugoslavia. Most of Europe had now fallen under Hitler. His next goal would be the conquest of the Soviet Union.

Hitler Turns on the Soviet Union

Like Napoleon Bonaparte, Hitler chose June 22 as the day to attack Russia. Napoleon had attacked on June 22, 1812. Now Hitler attacked on June 22, 1941, with three million German soldiers. He expected Russia to fall in a matter of weeks.

But the Russians surprised the world by fighting back with amazing strength and determination. Soldiers and civilians alike stood up against the Germans. But the Germans advanced toward Moscow. Just as in the fight against Napoleon, Russians burned whatever they could not move. They destroyed food supplies, machinery, and factories. The Germans approached Moscow, but they were unable to take the city.

Like Napoleon, Hitler did not count on the fierce Russian weather. Hitler's soldiers did not even have winter clothing. And the winter of 1941–1942 turned out to be the worst in years. Nazi soldiers froze on the icy Russian plains. It was beginning to look as if Hitler might have made a mistake by invading Russia.

Hitler made the same mistake in 1941 that Napoleon did in 1812.

History Practice

Write answers to the following questions on a separate sheet of paper.

1. Name the three Axis powers and the dictators who ruled them.

2. What action by Germany started World War II?

3. What is the meaning of *blitzkrieg*?

The Holocaust

Hitler forced his own ideas on the people he conquered. They were evil ideas of a "super race." White, Christian Europeans would be treated fairly well. But people who did not fit that mold were considered inferior. They were used as slave laborers or thrown into concentration camps.

Some Europeans fought the Nazi ideas. They formed resistance groups and waged secret, undercover wars. They wrecked telephone and telegraph lines to stop German communication. They blew up bridges and derailed trains. They killed Nazi officers. They helped Allied prisoners escape.

The Nazis answered the resistance by murdering hundreds of innocent men, women, and children. Nazi terror was aimed most directly at Europe's Jews. First Hitler forced Jews out of their jobs. He took their businesses and their property. Then Jews were made to live in special areas.

In 1941 Hitler's plans reached their evil peak. He announced his "final solution" to the "Jewish problem." That solution was **genocide**.

Jewish victims of Nazi persecution, Warsaw Ghetto

Hitler sent millions of Jews to concentration camps. Worse than any prison, these concentration camps were really death camps. There Jews were starved, lined up and shot, or gassed. Men were killed. Women were killed. Children were killed. Giant furnaces sent plumes of dark smoke into the sky as the prisoners' bodies were burned.

Over six million Jews died in Nazi concentration camps. Hitler's efforts to destroy all Jews is called the **Holocaust**. The Nazis also murdered millions of others—Russians, Poles, Gypsies, Slavs—all "inferior" enemies of Hitler.

The Nazi death camps are one of history's greatest horrors. "How could the world have let this happen?" question the ghosts of Hitler's victims. Survivors of the Holocaust tell of wishing for death in a world too evil to bear.

Healthy prisoners were sometimes hired out as slaves for private businesses. Often they were worked and starved to death.

Why do you think the
United States remained
neutral until December
1941?

The United States Declares War

The United States was a neutral nation from 1939 until 1941. It was not directly involved in the war.

The United States did, however, send aid to Germany's enemies. The United States sent food, arms, and raw materials to England and Russia. But it took a direct blow from Japan to bring the United States into World War II.

Japan was trying to create its empire in Asia. Japan felt that the United States stood in the way of control of the Pacific Ocean. On December 7, 1941, Japanese planes bombed the Pearl Harbor naval base in Hawaii. The attack took the United States by surprise. Almost one-half of the U.S. naval fleet was destroyed. Nearly 2,500 U.S. soldiers, sailors, and civilians died in the surprise attack.

In Japan, Emperor Hirohito declared war on the United States.

In America, President Franklin D. Roosevelt asked Congress to declare war on Japan. After a vote in Congress, Roosevelt addressed the nation. "We are now in this war," he declared. "We are in it all the way."

Three days later, Germany and Italy honored their pact with Japan. They declared war on the United States.

By the end of 1941, the war really had become a world war. The Axis countries stood on one side. The Allied countries, which now included the United States, stood on the other.

The Tide of War Turns Toward the Allies

In 1942 Russian and German armies were locked in battle. The battlefront stretched about 2,000 miles across Russia, from the Arctic to the Black Sea.

In the north, Leningrad (formerly St. Petersburg) was under siege by the Nazis. The siege began in August 1941, and would last until January 1944. About a million Russians died during the siege, most of them from starvation.

In September 1942, the German Sixth Army attacked Stalingrad (now called Volgograd). For five months, Russian soldiers fought the Germans. The battle raged back and forth from one block to the next. Finally, on January 31, 1943, the German Sixth Army surrendered. Only 90,000 of the original force of 350,000 German soldiers were still alive.

The Battle of Stalingrad marked a major turning point in the war. Now the Russian army went on the offensive. The Russians began to take back cities that had been captured by the Germans.

Meanwhile, fighting had been going on in northern Africa. Hitler had taken over most of Europe. Now he could be attacked only from Britain, the Soviet Union, or from North Africa. North Africa became important.

General Erwin Rommell, known as the clever "Desert Fox," led the Germans in Africa. Early in 1943, America's General Dwight D. Eisenhower set a trap for the Desert Fox and defeated the Germans. In May of 1943, German and Italian forces in Africa surrendered.

The Allies invaded Italy next. It was, according to President Roosevelt, the "beginning of the end" for the Axis countries. The Allies accepted the Italian surrender in 1943. And Rome was freed on June 4, 1944.

In one raid, 600 German planes bombed Stalingrad.

D-Day: American troops wading ashore at Normandy

The Invasion of Europe

Hitler still felt sure of his strength in Europe. But the Allies were preparing an invasion. By 1944 they were ready to attack France.

German forces protected the Normandy coast facing Great Britain. The Allies planned to invade Normandy. The day of the invasion was called "D-Day."

D-Day came at 2 A.M. on June 6, 1944. General Eisenhower was in charge of the attack. The first wave of troops crossed the English Channel. By 6:30 A.M. more than 150,000 Allied soldiers waded ashore on the beaches of Normandy. Within five days, the Allies had taken 80 miles of the coast.

The Allies began their sweep through France. In August they freed Paris. By October the Nazis were driven from all of France, as well as from Belgium and Luxembourg.

Hitler had defenses built all along the Atlantic shores. "No power on earth can drive us out," he boasted.

Germany Surrenders

The Germans were soundly defeated in December 1944 in the Battle of the Bulge. According to Winston Churchill, it was the greatest American victory of the war.

At last the Allies invaded Germany, early in 1945. Germany's capital, Berlin, fell on May 2. On May 7, 1945, Germany surrendered. The war in Europe was over.

Deaths of Two Dictators

What of the leaders of the fallen powers?

In Italy, Fascist leader Benito Mussolini met an ugly end. Mussolini tried to escape from Italy, to run from the antifascists. When he was captured, he begged for his life.

But Mussolini was executed—shot without a trial. His body was hung upside down outside a gas station in Milan, Italy. Italians shouted at the dictator's body, kicking it and throwing stones at it. A man who had lived by cruelty and terror met a cruel end.

Germany's Hitler died two days later. On April 30, 1945, reports came that the dictator had killed himself. He had been hiding in a bomb shelter beneath the flaming, shattered city of Berlin. Unable to face defeat, Hitler shot his new bride, Eva Braun, and then shot himself.

Hitler's madness had caused nearly six years of terrible war.

The War with Japan

The war had ended in Europe, but not in the Pacific. After Pearl Harbor, the Japanese had taken the Philippines, most of Southeast Asia, and islands in the Pacific.

General Douglas MacArthur led the U.S. forces against the Japanese in the Pacific. Although his campaigns were successful, the Japanese would not give up. Most of Japan's navy and air force had been destroyed by August of 1945. But there was no surrender. The Japanese felt it was their duty and their honor to fight to the very end.

The Japanese turned to desperate measures. *Kamikaze* pilots became human bombs. They did this by strapping themselves into planes filled with explosives. Then they flew their planes into American warships.

It was time for the terrors of war to end. But unfortunately, the greatest terror was still to come.

The Atom Bomb

Scientists had discovered how to split the atom to create great energy. Nations at war decided to use this energy as a weapon. They planned to build an atomic bomb. Throughout World War II, the Allies and the Axis nations had been racing to create such a bomb. Working on the project in America were scientists such as Enrico Fermi and J. Robert Oppenheimer. They, with the help of many others, finally built the powerful weapon.

U.S. President Harry S Truman made the difficult decision. The atomic bomb would be the quickest way to end the war.

Japan was warned. But the Japanese refused to surrender. So on August 6, 1945, an American plane dropped the atomic bomb on Hiroshima, Japan. In seconds, more than 90,000 people were killed, and Hiroshima was gone.

Still, Japan did not surrender. So three days later, a second A-bomb was dropped on Nagasaki's 250,000 people.

Mushroom cloud from atomic bombing of Nagasaki

At last, on September 2, 1945, the Japanese surrendered. It was their first military defeat in 2,000 years. General Tojo was arrested and convicted as a war criminal. He was hanged on December 23, 1948.

The Costs of War

World War II was over at last. It was the most expensive war in history. The figures were shocking.

- Over a trillion dollars had been spent for arms and war machinery.
- Fifty-five million lives were lost. (This includes civilian and military losses.)
- Germany lost almost three million soldiers.
- Japan lost more than two million soldiers.
- Italy lost about 160,000 soldiers.
- Russia lost about 7,500,000 soldiers.
- Britain lost about 270,000 soldiers.
- The United States lost more than 400,000 soldiers.
- France lost about 200,000 soldiers.

The world was left with questions to answer. How could people have so easily accepted the horrors of the Nazi concentration camps? And what about the atom bomb? What was to become of a world that possessed such a terrible and powerful weapon?

The United Nations

The League of Nations had tried to keep the peace after World War I. But the League had failed. So how could future wars be prevented? Since the beginning of World War II, many national leaders were thinking about it. In June of 1941, representatives of nine countries met in London to talk about it. There those officials signed a pledge to work for a free world. This pledge was called the *Inter-Allied Declaration*.

By early 1942, the idea of a "United Nations" gained wide support. In January, representatives from 26 nations met in Washington, D.C. There they signed a pact calling for world peace and freedom for all people. The agreement also called for eventual disarmament and economic cooperation. The pact they signed was called the *Declaration by United Nations.*

At that time, of course, there was still a world war going on. But by 1944 it was clear that the Allies would win the war. So Allied representatives began planning the new organization. In February, 1945, a date was set for a United Nations meeting in San Francisco. As scheduled, the meeting was held on April 25.

At that first meeting of the United Nations, a constitution was established. Representatives from 50 nations signed the *United Nations Charter.* The delegates also set up a Security Council with permanent members from five countries. They were the United States, the Soviet Union, Great Britain, France, and China. Each member had veto power over any decision the Security Council made. Just one veto would keep a decision from going into effect.

On October 24, 1945, the United Nations became official. The new organization had a big job ahead of it. Its aim was to protect world peace and to safeguard human rights throughout the world.

Whenever a world problem comes up, the United Nations meets to work for a peaceful settlement. Delegates from every member nation attend meetings of the United Nation's General Assembly. They try to solve problems without war. Other branches of the United Nations work on problems of education, trade, labor, health, and economics.

The weapons of the world have grown to unbelievable destructive power. The purpose of the United Nations has become more and more important. The United Nations has one victory as its major goal— the victory over war.

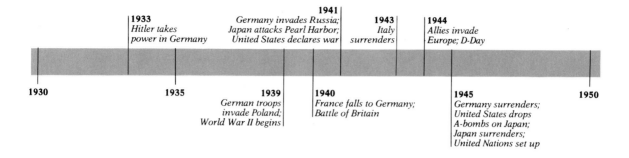

1933
*Hitler takes
power in Germany*

1941
*Germany invades Russia;
Japan attacks Pearl Harbor;
United States declares war*

1943
*Italy
surrenders*

1944
*Allies invade
Europe; D-Day*

1930

1935

1939
*German troops
invade Poland;
World War II begins*

1940
*France falls to Germany;
Battle of Britain*

1945
*Germany surrenders;
United States drops
A-bombs on Japan;
Japan surrenders;
United Nations set up*

1950

WHICH CAME FIRST?

Use the time line to choose the event, year, or period of time that came first. Write your answers on a separate sheet of paper.

1. France falls to Germany *or* Hitler takes power in Germany?

2. Germany invades Russia *or* German troops invade Poland?

3. 1945 *or* 1939?

4. Allies invade Europe *or* Italy surrenders?

5. World War II begins *or* Japan attacks Pearl Harbor?

Chapter Review

Chapter Summary

- Three strong dictators took power before World War II. They were Mussolini of Italy, General Tojo of Japan, and Hitler of Germany. Each wanted to build an empire.

- Hitler convinced the German people that they were members of a "super race" meant to rule the world.

- Germany, Italy, and Japan joined together as the Axis nations. The nations who would fight against them were called the Allied nations. The Allies included Britain, France, Russia, and the United States, as well as many smaller nations.

- Hitler's armies swept through Europe with a style of lightning warfare known as a *Blitzkrieg.*

- Germans took France but were unable to defeat Great Britain. Hitler tried to take the Soviet Union but failed.

- Hitler hated the Jews and tried to destroy them. In the Holocaust he imprisoned Jews in concentration camps where millions were murdered.

- The United States joined World War II in December 1941, after the Japanese bombed Pearl Harbor.

- The Invasion of Normandy on D-Day, June 6, 1944, began the Allied sweep to regain Europe.

- Germany surrendered on May 7, 1945.

- War with Japan ended on September 2, 1945, after the United States dropped atomic bombs on Hiroshima and Nagasaki. It was the first use of atomic power in war.

- Nations of the world set up the United Nations as a peace-keeping organization.

Chapter Quiz

A. Checking Your Facts

Choose the correct word to make each sentence a true statement. Rewrite the sentences on a separate sheet of paper.

1. In the 1930s a civil war was raging in (France/Spain).

2. Germany was forbidden to rebuild its armed forces by the Treaty of (Versailles/Vienna).

3. Hitler told the German people that they should be the (scapegoats/masters) of the world.

4. In Japan, Emperor (Tojo/Hirohito) declared war on the United States.

5. The United States dropped a second atom bomb on the Japanese city of (Nagasaki/Kamikaze).

B. Think About It!

Write answers to the following questions on a separate sheet of paper.

1. Why do you think the German people were eager to follow Hitler? If you had been living in Germany at that time, how would you have felt about Hitler?

2. How was the World War II experience different for the people of Britain and for the people of the United States?

3. How do you think the dropping of the atom bomb on Japan in 1945 changed the world? Why did the atom bomb make the United Nations so necessary?

Unit Nine Review

Write answers to the following questions on a separate sheet of paper.

1. Why was Camillo di Cavour called "The Brain"?

2. Who ruled the newly unified Italy? Who ruled the newly unified Germany?

3. What does the phrase "blood and iron" mean?

4. Why do you think the United States refused to join the League of Nations?

5. How did the Russian people feel about Russia's involvement in World War I?

6. What happened to religion in the Soviet Union under the Communists? To agriculture? To the middle class?

7. How did the Great Depression contribute to the rise of dictators?

8. What kind of world did Hitler hope to build?

9. What was the Holocaust?

10. Describe how World War II finally ended in Japan.

Unit Ten

The Postwar World

Chapter 30

Changes Around the World

In 1961 the East German Communists built the Berlin Wall between East Berlin and West Berlin. What was its purpose?

Chapter Learning Objectives

- Describe how Germany was divided after World War II.
- Explain why the "cold war" began.
- List three changes in the Soviet Union for which Mikhail Gorbachev is responsible.
- Tell how Mao Tse-tung and the Communists took over China.
- Explain why the United States became involved in the conflict in Vietnam.

Words to Know

apartheid   the separation of races based mainly on skin color

brainwashed   trained to have a whole new set of ideas and beliefs

capitalist   having business and industry privately owned and operated for profit

commune   a group of people working or living closely together, often sharing property and tasks

corrupt   dishonest, evil, selfish

curfews   times after which certain people cannot be on the streets

domino   a small, rectangular piece of wood or plastic used in a game; one side of the piece is either blank or marked with dots

guerilla   one of a group of fighters who are not part of a regular army, and who usually make surprise raids behind enemy lines

majority   a greater number, more than half

minority   a smaller number, less than half

oppressed   kept down by harsh rule

pollution   waste materials in the air or water

recognize   to accept the government of a country and deal with it in business and trade

refugees   those who flee their country or home

sanctions   actions taken by one nation against another for breaking international law; for example, a shipping blockade

satellites   countries that depend on and are controlled by a more powerful country

Europe After World War II

Europe was weakened by World War II. European countries were no longer the powerful nations they had been. It was time for these nations to rebuild. Many nations, including Italy and France, set up democratic governments. Charles de Gaulle served as the first president of postwar France.

Why do you think the
United States was so
interested in helping
the European nations
rebuild?

U.S. president Harry S Truman called for a plan to
help put Europe back on its feet. The Marshall Plan,
named for U.S. secretary of state George C. Marshall,
provided money for European recovery. From 1947
until 1951, the United States gave thirteen billion
dollars' worth of food, raw materials for industry, and
machinery to European nations.

War-torn nations welcomed the aid. But the Soviet
Union and its communist **satellites** refused to accept
the Marshall Plan. This refusal was just one act that
would divide the world into two camps.

The Eastern European countries did not turn to
democracy. They became communist satellites of the
Soviet Union. They had been freed from the Germans
by the Soviet Union at the end of the war. But they
remained under Soviet control.

Germany in Ruins

What of the defeated empire? Germany was a
shambles after World War II. Cities and farms had
been bombed. The economy was ruined.

The winning nations divided Germany into four
sections. Great Britain, France, the United States, and
the Soviet Union each took control of a section. Each
country put troops inside its zone to keep order.

After a few years the United States, France, and
Britain tried to bring Germany together as one
republic. But the Soviet Union refused. So the
democratic nations combined their regions to form
West Germany. The Soviet-controlled zone became
known as East Germany.

The city of Berlin is located in East Germany. It was
divided into East Berlin, a communist section, and
West Berlin, under democratic West German control.
In 1961 the Communists built the Berlin Wall to
separate the city's two sections. They also wanted to
keep East Berliners from escaping to the West.

Just two years after the wall was built, 16,456 people had escaped into West Berlin.

The division of Germany after World War II

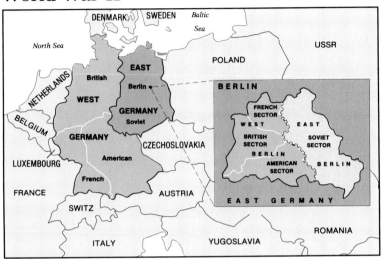

Map Skills
Name the four sections of Germany after World War II. Name the three parts of West Berlin.

Germany Today

Today Germany is still two separate countries. East Germany, called the German Democratic Republic, is a communist country. The people have had little individual freedom. But in 1989 a movement for democratic reform was sweeping across much of Eastern Europe. And the East German government declared that all East Germans who wanted to move to the West would be free to do so.

West Germany, called the Federal Republic of Germany, is a democracy with a parliament and elected representatives. World War II put an end to the old German tradition of militarism. The ideas of people like Bismarck and Hitler no longer push Germans to be conquerors. West Germany maintains an army. But it makes no moves of aggression.

You will read more about Eastern European reform later in this chapter.

Industry has grown rapidly in Germany since World War II. Many people, especially skilled workers and professional people, fled East Germany to live in West Germany. Today West Germans have one of the highest standards of living in the world.

The United States After World War II

The United States, unlike Europe, was not shattered by World War II. No battlefields tore apart U.S. lands. Wide oceans kept the United States separate and safe. The United States also had the power of the atomic bomb. At the end of World War II, the United States was the strongest nation in the world.

Except for its involvement in World War I, the United States had mostly kept to its own business. It followed a policy of isolationism. World War II connected the United States with the rest of the world. In 1945 the United States became one of the first countries to join the United Nations. The world was changing. Countries were becoming more and more dependent on each other. The United States could no longer stand alone, minding its own business.

The Cold War Begins

During the world wars, the United States and the Soviet Union were allies. After World War II, the two countries became the most powerful nations on earth. In fact, they are known as *superpowers*. Each had different ideas about what an ideal society should be like. Soviet peoples lived under communism, while Americans lived in a free democracy. Disputes and tensions between the two nations grew. The "cold war" had begun.

The cold war was not an outright conflict. It didn't involve actual battles or bombings. The cold war was a war of ideas.

Both the Soviet Union and the United States had their own allies in the cold war. The United States and its allies said that communism is bad. They pointed out that people in communist countries usually have little freedom. The communist nations criticized the United States for being a **capitalist** nation. They pointed out that some people in the United States are very rich and some are very poor. They said that because of this, the United States is a very unfair society.

Americans worried about a communist takeover of the whole world. President Truman announced that America would give aid to any country fighting communism. He made a plan for military and economic suport. This plan became known as the Truman Doctrine. Both Greece and Turkey were given aid under this plan.

Communism often grows strong in poor countries. Financial aid under the Marshall Plan helped to keep European nations strong enough to resist communist ideas.

Do you think the communist criticism of the United States is fair? Why or why not?

In 1948, communist Yugoslavia broke away from Soviet control. The Marshall Plan helped make this possible.

NATO

In 1950 sides were clearly drawn in the cold war. The United States led the setting up of the North Atlantic Treaty Organization (NATO). Members of NATO included the United States, Britain, France, Italy, Canada, and several smaller nations. In 1954 West Germany became a member.

NATO began as a defense against communism. Member nations promised to help each other. They said that an attack against any one of them would be taken as an attack against all.

In 1955 the Soviet Union created its own alliance to balance the NATO alliance. It was called the Warsaw Pact. It included the Soviet Union and its communist allies in Eastern Europe.

The Arms Race

The Soviet Union and the United States have tried to stay in step with each other. Each superpower fears that the other will become more powerful.

One measure of power is the buildup of weapons. When the United States exploded the atom bomb in 1945, it made America fearsome and powerful. Other nations wanted that power, too. In 1949 the Soviet Union exploded its first atomic bomb. By 1952 Great Britain also had the atomic secret. Then the United States pulled ahead again in the race for destructive power. In 1954 the U.S. tested a hydrogen bomb. It was thousands of times more powerful than the atomic bomb that had fallen on Hiroshima. Soon Great Britain, France, and the Soviet Union had hydrogen bombs, too.

Has the nuclear arms race made Americans safer?

Now the People's Republic of China has the bomb. So does India. The world has given itself something to fear. As nations struggled to keep pace in the cold war, the stakes became higher. Each superpower now has enough nuclear weapons to destroy the world many times over.

The Soviet Union After World War II

After World War II, Joseph Stalin worked to rebuild Soviet industry. He set up labor camps, forcing workers to build, build, and build some more. Between 1945 and 1965, Soviet industry boomed. But life was not easy for the Russian worker. Stalin had caused shortages of food and clothing with his emphasis on heavy industry.

After Stalin's death in 1953, there was a struggle for power. Then a new leader, Nikita Khrushchev, rose to the top of the Communist party.

Khrushchev accused Stalin of the arrests and deaths of many citizens. Khrushchev promised that now the country would be led by the Party rather than by a single dictator.

Under Khrushchev life became better for the people of the Soviet Union. Khrushchev halted some of the activities of the secret police. The government allowed somewhat greater freedom of speech. The work week was shortened to 40 hours. And Khrushchev tried to raise the standard of living for ordinary people. His economic plan included a greater production of consumer goods. But progress was very slow.

Nikita Khrushchev

The Spread of Communism

The Soviet Union helped spread communism to other parts of the world. China, Mongolia, North Korea, as well as some nations in Southeast Asia and in Africa, have turned to communism. And Cuba, only 90 miles from the United States, became a communist dictatorship under Fidel Castro.

In 1962 the Soviets tried to build missile bases in Cuba. To stop Soviet ships, U.S. president John F. Kennedy set up a blockade around Cuba. The cold war nearly turned hot at that point. The Cuban missile crisis brought the world to the edge of another big war. But Khrushchev agreed to take the missiles out of Cuba, and the situation cooled.

In 1963 Khrushchev's farm program collapsed. Russia had to buy a huge quantity of grain from the West. That year Soviet industrialization slowed down. Then Khrushchev came under heavy criticism for the way he had handled the Cuban situation. In 1964 he was forced to retire. Leonid Brezhnev and Alexei Kosygin replaced him as leaders of the Communist party. Now life became worse for the people of the Soviet Union. Once again, people had to be very careful about what they said.

When Khrushchev backed down, the whole world breathed a big sigh of relief.

History Practice

Write answers to the following questions on a separate sheet of paper.

1. What was the Marshall Plan?

2. How was Germany divided after World War II?

3. What was the cold war? How did it begin?

LEARN MORE ABOUT IT: Peace Talks

Both the United States and the Soviet Union realized that another world war would bring disaster. Between the quarrels and the peaks of tension, they met to try to solve their problems.

In 1963 the United States and the Soviet Union set up a "hot line." This was a special direct communications link between Moscow and Washington, D.C. It enabled the leaders of both countries to contact each other instantly. The purpose was to prevent an international crisis from turning the cold war into a hot war.

In 1972 the two powers held Strategic Arms Limitation Talks (SALT). They agreed to set some limits on nuclear arms. They understood that world peace was at stake.

A second SALT agreement was later proposed. SALT II was a treaty putting strict limits on the building of nuclear weapons. But the U.S. Congress did not approve SALT II. It was angered by the Soviet invasion of Afghanistan.

In 1987 Soviet leader Mikhail Gorbachev and U.S. president Ronald Reagan signed the INF (Intermediate Nuclear Forces) treaty. For the first time, both sides agreed to get rid of an entire class of nuclear weapons. Both countries now hope to reach agreement on START (Strategic Arms Reduction Treaty). This would cut in half the number of nuclear weapons on both sides.

Richard Nixon and Leonid Brezhnev signing the SALT agreement

Mikhail Gorbachev and Glasnost

Under Gorbachev there has been a real lessening of tensions between the superpowers. Both countries agreed to try to end regional conflicts in various parts of the world. In 1989 Gorbachev brought Soviet troops home from Afghanistan. And he agreed to stop supplying military aid to the Sandinista government in Nicaragua. He pressured Fidel Castro to bring home the Cuban troops from Angola. They had been involved there in a civil war. And he persuaded Vietnam to withdraw its forces from Cambodia.

Gorbachev put into action his policy of *Glasnost* or "openness." Suddenly Soviet citizens had more freedom of speech than ever before.

A new branch of the government was set up with members directly elected by the people. Soviet citizens could choose whomever they wanted to represent them in the government. The newly elected people did not even have to be members of the Communist party. For the first time, the communist leaders had to listen to the opinions and complaints of the Soviet people.

If you were a Soviet citizen, how would you feel about Gorbachev's policy of *Glasnost*?

The policy of *Glasnost* led many of the republics within the Soviet Union to demand the right to manage their own affairs. The Baltic states of Estonia, Latvia, and Lithuania even went so far as to seek outright independence from Moscow.

One unfortunate result of *Glasnost* has been an increase in tensions between different national groups within the Soviet Union. In many places, long-standing resentments boiled over into outbreaks of violence. For example, a fight broke out between Armenians and Azerbaijanis as to who owned a particular territory in the Caucasus Mountains. Many people were killed as a result.

Gorbachev knew that the Soviet economy was in big trouble. And he knew that he would have to make major changes in order to see any improvement. So he proposed a policy of *Perestroika*, or "restructuring." Factories and businesses around the country would no longer be controlled by Moscow. Each would be responsible for running its own operations. And individual Soviet citizens would be allowed to engage in small-scale private business.

Gorbachev also welcomed U.S. corporations to set up joint operations in the Soviet Union. A number of U.S. companies have already signed agreements with the Soviets. In Moscow the largest MacDonald's in the world opened for business.

Many people in both the Soviet Union and the United States were declaring that the cold war was over. But in spite of all the changes taking place, there were questions in the minds of every Russian. Would Gorbachev's plans be successful? And what would happen if Gorbachev were to fall from power?

Soviet Satellites

The Soviet Union was not the only country going through changes. As a result of Gorbachev's policy of *Glasnost*, some of the Soviet satellites began to move away from strict communist control.

Back in 1956 Hungary had tried to cut its ties with the Soviets. It wanted to set up its own communist government. But Soviet troops marched into Hungary, crushing the movement for independence.

Then in 1968 there was trouble in Czechoslovakia. The Soviet government felt that the Czechoslovakian Communist party was losing control of the country. The Russians were afraid that too much freedom of speech would turn the people away from communism. So in August of that year, Soviet tanks rumbled through the streets of Prague. Soon new people were running the government—people chosen by the Russians.

In the 1970s workers rioted in Poland. They were demanding higher pay and better working conditions. They wanted a union, something unheard of under communist governments. In 1980 the Polish government allowed the workers to form the union. The new workers' union was called Solidarity. Its leader is named Lech Walesa.

In 1982 the government began to fear that Solidarity went against communist ideals. That year, the Communists arrested Solidarity's leaders and declared the union illegal. Many insisted that the Soviet Union backed the breakup of the workers' union in Poland.

Mikhail Gorbachev

Lech Walesa

Throughout the 1980s, economic conditions in Poland continued to worsen. By 1989, the Polish leaders were ready to try a different approach. Encouraged by the radical changes taking place in the Soviet Union, they made Solidarity legal again. Solidarity then formed a political party and was voted into office to run the government. For the first time in more than 40 years, Poland would have a government led by non-Communists.

Poland, Hungary, and East Germany are trying to make their political systems more democratic.

In Hungary, the communist leaders decided to set up a multi-party political system. Hungary, as well as Poland, wanted to establish closer ties with the West. And in East Germany, the government responded to a growing demand for democracy by promising free elections and freedom to travel. Now that East Germans were free to move to the West, there was no need for a Berlin Wall. And indeed, the East German government announced that the Wall would be coming down. There was even talk about the possible reunification of Germany. It now seemed to many people in the West that the Iron Curtain was finally starting to lift.

India After World War II

In Chapter 24 you read about India winning its independence from Britain in 1947. At that time, Indian leaders agreed to divide India into two separate nations, India and Pakistan. India fell under the control of the Hindus. And the Moslems controlled Pakistan. A further complication was the division of Pakistan into East and West Pakistan.

India held its first general election in 1951. Jawaharlal Nehru was elected as the first prime minister of the Republic of India. Nehru led India until he died in 1964. In 1966 his daughter, Indira Gandhi, was elected prime minister.

There were food shortages and labor strikes in India during Mrs. Gandhi's years as leader. For a time she lost her position. But she returned to power in 1980. Then in 1984, Indira Gandhi was assassinated.

Over the years, India has had border disputes with its neighbors. This led to fighting between India and China in 1959 and in 1962.

In 1965 India and Pakistan fought a three-week-long war. Both countries claimed the same land, called Kashmir, in northern India.

In 1971 civil war broke out in Pakistan. The people of East Pakistan complained because the center of government was based in West Pakistan. The war led to East Pakistan becoming a separate nation called Bangladesh.

Poverty in India: Homeless people

India's Problems

India has always had to deal with poverty and food shortages. The country has a huge population. And it must struggle to provide enough food for all its people. India is one of the world's larger producers of farm products. But there is never enough food to go around. It is said that almost two-thirds of India's people go to bed hungry every night.

The government has tried to teach farmers new methods to increase production. They have allowed Western businesses to come in and build chemical factories. There was hope that the chemicals would increase crops. In general, India benefited from the chemicals. But in 1984, an accident at one U.S. chemical plant caused the worst industrial disaster in history. There was an explosion at the Union Carbide factory in Bhopal, India. A cloud of highly toxic gas spread into the heavily populated area surrounding the plant. Several thousand people who breathed the poisonous fumes died horrible deaths.

Millions of poor people live on the streets of India's cities. Can you name a rich country that has homeless people?

India is trying to combat its poverty with programs for economic growth. Indian leaders try to build industry. They want to make better use of their country's resources, such as coal and iron ore. And India spends billions of dollars building dams to provide power.

Age-old customs contribute to the food shortages. While India has tried to industrialize, most of its people still cling to old ideas. In 1950 the government tried to improve life by outlawing the "untouchable" category in the Hindu caste system. Until then, people called untouchables had been forced to live in the dirtiest, poorest parts of villages. Their children were not allowed to go into schools. They had to sit on the steps outside and listen. If an untouchable walked through village streets, he was supposed to brush away his footsteps with a broom. Old ideas die hard. And India has had to move beyond some of those ideas to make life better for its people.

China After World War II

In the years after World War II, a power struggle was going on in China between two political parties: the Nationalists and the Communists.

Back in 1927, Chiang Kai-shek and his Nationalist party had come to power. Some members of the Nationalist party believed in communism. The Communists felt that Chiang showed favor to rich landowners and businessmen. So the Communists broke away from the Nationalists. And in 1927 they took over the city of Shanghai.

Chiang expelled the Communists from the Nationalist party. A struggle began between Chinese Nationalists and Chinese Communists. Stalin and the Soviet Union supported the Communists. Stalin encouraged them to win support of China's factory workers.

But China's strength did not lie in the city workers. It lay in the farm peasants. A man named Mao Tse-tung, born a peasant, turned to the peasants for Communist strength.

Chiang was the most powerful man in China for more than 20 years.

During World War II the Communists helped defend the peasants of northern China against the Japanese. Mao and the Communists won the peasants' loyalty.

After the war the Communists and Nationalists continued their struggle for China. There were four years of civil war. The Nationalists had better supplies and a larger army. But they no longer had the support of the people. Many Nationalist leaders were **corrupt**. They wanted to become rich themselves while the Chinese people went hungry. The Communists divided land and food fairly among the people. So they received the peasants' support.

By 1948 the war had turned in favor of the Communists. Chiang Kai-shek and the Nationalists decided it was time to get out. They left mainland China to live in Taiwan. In 1949 China was taken over by Mao Tse-tung and the Communists. They called their nation the People's Republic of China.

Mao Tse-tung

The Soviet Union was quick to **recognize** the new government. And so were many other nations. But the United States refused to recognize the Communist government.

The United States recognized the Nationalist government in Taiwan and supported it. Taiwan, calling itself the Republic of China, kept its seat in the United Nations. Until 1971 the United States kept the People's Republic of China out of the United Nations. In 1972 U.S. president Richard Nixon made an eight-day visit to the People's Republic. At the end of the visit, Nixon and the Chinese leaders issued a statement. They promised that both powers would work to bring about normal relations between the countries. In 1979 U.S. president Jimmy Carter finally recognized the People's Republic of China.

Why do you think it took so long for the United States to recognize the People's Republic of China?

Communism in China

One-fifth of the population of the world lives in China! Producing enough food to feed more than one billion people is no simple matter. The Communists knew they had to solve that problem. So they took land away from rich farmers. They set up huge farm **communes.** The peasants had to work on these communes. Sometimes as many as 10,000 people worked on a single commune. The government also took over industries, built new factories, and trained workers.

The Communists insisted on the support and loyalty of all the people. Workers had to attend meetings where they read aloud from Mao Tse-tung's writings. They talked about how Mao's ideas could make them better citizens of a better China.

Wall posters present the official government point of view to the citizens of Beijing.

The Cultural Revolution

Mao and the Communists worried that people might prefer the Old China to the New China. They held their communist meetings to teach people to think the communist way. Enemies of communism were punished. They were **brainwashed**, or forced to accept the communist way of thought.

For a while Mao's harsh policies worked. But from 1965 to 1968 there was a decline in China's economy. During this period, Mao called his policies a "Cultural Revolution." The Cultural Revolution was supposed to build loyalty for the Communists. Young students, called "Red Guards," became soldiers for communism. They helped Mao enforce his policies.

Farm production fell. China closed its doors to visitors from the rest of the world. The Chinese leaders wanted to make sure that no anticommunist ideas could filter in.

Some people say that Americans are "brainwashed" by TV commercials—they are told what to buy and what to wear.

Chinese leaders were
quick to change Mao's
policies after he died.

After Mao's death in 1976, trade relations between China and the rest of the world improved. Under Deng Xiaoping and other leaders, China has been trying to modernize.

But although Deng was willing to give the Chinese more economic freedom, he was not willing to grant political freedom. In the spring of 1989 hundreds of thousands of students gathered in Tiananmen Square in Beijing to demand more democracy. The demonstration was crushed by the army, as tanks rolled through the square. Many students were killed. Relations between China and the West took a turn for the worse, once again.

Conflict in Korea

Korea, with its northern border on China, became a hot spot in the world in 1950. Korea had been controlled by the Japanese from 1910 to 1945. In 1945 the country was divided into two parts. North Korea had the support of Soviet Communists. South Korea had American support.

In 1950 North Korea suddenly attacked South Korea. The Communists threatened to take the whole country.

South Korea turned to the United Nations for help. A U.N. army made up mostly of American soldiers came to South Korea's aid. The U.N. troops and South Koreans pushed the Communists back, almost to the Chinese border. The Chinese began to worry. Then the Chinese Communists sent 780,000 soldiers to help North Korea.

The U.S.-South Korean troops fought the Chinese-North Korean troops for three years. In 1953 a truce was finally declared. The division between North and South Korea stayed exactly as it had been before the conflict began.

Japan After World War II

The explosion of the atomic bomb left Japan reeling. Japan surrendered and World War II was over. Then the Allied forces occupied Japan. U.S. general Douglas MacArthur was the Supreme Commander. His job was to build a democracy in Japan.

A new democratic constitution was written in 1946. The constitution gave power to an elected prime minister. And it gave women the right to vote. Japan would be allowed to keep its emperor. But he would have no power. He would serve only as a symbol of the Japanese spirit. In 1951 the government was put back into the hands of the Japanese. The Allied occupation had ended.

The new Japanese constitution stated that Japan would not maintain a strong military. So the Japanese turned from a policy of war to one of industrial and economic growth.

Today Japan has become a world leader in industry. Japan is one of the world's largest steel producers. It is the second largest manufacturer of automobiles and electronics equipment. And it is a leading shipbuilder. This is quite an accomplishment since Japan has few natural resources of its own. The country's industrial success depends on trade, the import of raw materials, and the export of finished products.

Japan is now one of the richest countries in the world.

Japan is a small, crowded country. There is little room to grow food. Again Japan depends on imports, bringing in at least 30 percent of its food. And Japan has had to combat problems caused by overcrowding, such as **pollution** and housing shortages. But Japan has made amazing progress. World War II had left Japan in ruins. But in less than 50 years, Japan has become a great economic and industrial power.

Southeast Asia After World War II

Japan took over much of Southeast Asia during World War II. Before the war all of the area, except Thailand, was colonized by European nations. After the war anticolonial feelings were strong. The nations of Southeast Asia wanted to be free.

Some countries gained independence easily. Others had to struggle. When nations such as the Philippines, Burma, Indonesia, Malaysia, and Singapore became independent, they all faced problems. In many of them there were bitter civil wars.

Conflict in Vietnam

In the1800s France took over an area of Southeast Asia called Indochina. Indochina was made up of the countries of Vietnam, Laos, and Cambodia (now called Kampuchea). During World War II, Japan took Indochina from the French. Then France regained Indochina after the war.

But Indochina was not anxious to return to French rule. Nationalists and Communists had gained a foothold there.

In 1946 the fighting began. The Vietnamese Communists wanted to force the French out of the country. The French set up a government in the South. The Communists, under their leader, Ho Chi Minh, set up a government in the North. The Communists defeated the French in 1954. Then a conference in Geneva, Switzerland, decided what would happen next.

Representatives from France, the Vietnamese Communists, Cambodia, Laos, China, Britain, and the United States all came to that conference. They made their decision. Vietnam was divided into two zones. Ho Chi Minh and the Communists would continue to rule the North. South Vietnam was supposed to hold an election to choose its own form of government.

But a free election never took place. Ngo Dinh Diem took leadership and refused to hold elections. Meanwhile, North Vietnam grew stronger with the support of Communist China and the Soviet Union. The political situation in South Vietnam remained unsettled.

The Vietcong, communist **guerilla** fighters, began an attempt to take over South Vietnam in 1957. In 1963 South Vietnam's leader, Diem, was assassinated. The country's problems increased. The government changed hands nine times in three years.

The United States Sends Help

The Soviet Union and China continued aid to North Vietnam. In the 1960s the U.S. government sent aid to South Vietnam because it believed in the **domino** theory. If dominoes are stood in a line together, the fall of one domino will knock down the others. The domino theory was the idea that if one country became communistic, neighbors would fall to the Communists, too.

At first the United States sent money and supplies. Then in 1965, U.S. president Lyndon B. Johnson sent more than 3,500 U.S. marines to Da Nang, South Vietnam. They were the first United States combat troops to join the fight. Thousands more would follow. By 1969 there were more than 543,000 U.S. troops in Vietnam.

Americans Protest U.S. Involvement

Many Americans didn't want the United States to get into the war in Southeast Asia. When American soldiers began dying in Vietnamese jungles, the protests grew stronger. Hundreds of thousands of people marched against the war, in cities all across America. "Bring home our troops!" they shouted.

Antiwar protesters felt that the war in Vietnam was a matter that should be fought and decided by the Vietnamese themselves.

U.S. marines and wounded Vietnamese civilians in a village in South Vietnam

By March of 1969 only 30 percent of Americans were still in favor of the war.

But the war went on. More and more Americans were killed or wounded. The Vietcong remained strong. There didn't seem to be any light at the end of the tunnel.

By the end of the decade, the United States was a nation in turmoil. The growing antiwar movement had helped to touch off a general youth protest movement. The middle-class youth of America were questioning and protesting against all the values of their parents.

Also during the 1960s, there had been a series of assassinations that had shocked the nation. President John F. Kennedy, in 1963, and his brother Robert F. Kennedy, in 1968, had been shot to death. So had black leaders Malcolm X, in 1965, and Martin Luther King, Jr., in 1968. This was the last straw for many African Americans. They were becoming angry and frustrated at not being able to share in the prosperity of white America. Now feeling that they had nothing to lose, they took their cause to the streets. Rioting occurred in many American cities.

In 1973 the United States decided to take its troops out of Vietnam. About 58,000 Americans had been killed. About 365,000 had been wounded. And the war had not been won.

In general, the 1970s in the United States was a quieter time than the 1960s. However, one more great shock was in store for Americans. In 1972 a team of burglars had broken into Democratic headquarters in a building called the Watergate. They were caught. There was a long investigation. And the burglars proved to have been working for people in the White House. The White House attempted a cover-up. When the cover-up failed, President Richard Nixon had to resign from office in August 1974.

Nixon was the only president in U.S. history to be forced out of office.

National Guard on duty during riot in Detroit's black ghetto

Refugees from Communism: The Boat People

In 1975, Saigon, the capital of South Vietnam, fell to the Vietcong. The name of the city was changed to "Ho Chi Minh City." Vietnam was united as a communist country in 1976. Then the "dominoes" fell. Communists took power in Laos and Cambodia.

The communist rulers of Cambodia, called the *Khmer Rouge*, murdered millions of Cambodians. The situation in Cambodia became very unstable. In 1978 Vietnam invaded Cambodia. For the next ten years, Vietnam had control of the country. In 1989, Vietnam withdrew from Cambodia, giving in to pressure from the Soviet Union. Different groups of Cambodians tried to form a new government.

Many people in Vietnam, Laos, and Cambodia did not want to live under communist rule. They fled their homelands. Many **refugees** escaped by boat. They became known as "boat people"—people who no longer had a home. A large number came to the United States. Some died making their escapes. All suffered hardships along their way.

As the Communists closed in on Saigon, the remaining Americans were forced to flee the city.

Vietnamese refugees

Africa After World War II

During the nineteenth century, Africa had been divided into European-ruled colonies. In 1945, at the end of World War II, most of Africa remained under European rule. Exceptions were the countries of South Africa, Ethiopia, Liberia, and Egypt. Many Africans had joined the armies of their European motherlands during the war. When they returned to Africa, they wanted independence.

The years after 1945 saw European colonies in Africa gain freedom, one by one. Some won their independence peacefully. For other nations such as Algeria, freedom came only through struggle and revolt.

Several colonies were ruled by the British. Most of these gained independence during the 1950s. Sudan, the largest nation in Africa, won freedom from Britain in 1956. And some of the free nations changed their names. When the Gold Coast won its freedom in 1957, it became Ghana.

Kenya was an African nation that had to struggle for independence from Britain. A rebellion by a group known as the *Mau Mau* lasted from 1952 until 1956. A man named Jomo Kenyatta was the leader of the Mau Mau. He was thrown in jail in 1953. Britain granted independence to Kenya in 1963. And Kenyatta became the leader of the new, free nation. He ruled Kenya until his death in 1978.

Freedom Brings New Problems

Freedom did not always mean an end to problems and unrest. The new nations had troubles of their own. In 1966 the eastern part of Nigeria separated and became a country called Biafra. This led to civil war. And with the war came starvation, disease, and death for nearly two million people.

Problems plagued Uganda when General Idi Amin took over the independent government in 1971. Amin saw to it that thousands of Ugandans were killed. Anyone against Amin died! Finally the people revolted. And in 1979 they forced Amin from power. Civil wars have also taken place in Angola and Ethiopia.

Rhodesia Wins Black Majority Rule

Independence did not bring an end to racial prejudice in some new African nations. Sometimes those nations had more problems with the new governments than with the European rulers. When Rhodesia gained independence from Britain in 1965, black Africans had no voice in government. A white **minority** ruled for 15 years.

Britain wanted blacks to have rights. But the new white rulers said no. Britain asked the United Nations to place **sanctions** on Rhodesia. Black revolutionaries began a guerilla war.

In 1980 Rhodesia's first black **majority** government finally came to power through a general election. The new government officially changed the nation's name. Rhodesia became Zimbabwe, an ancient African name for that part of the continent.

White Minority Still Rules South Africa

Of all the independent countries in Africa, only South Africa has a white minority still in complete power. The country is ruled by *Afrikaners*. These are the descendants of Dutch colonists who began settling in South Africa as early as 1652. The Afrikaners feel that the country belongs to them. They helped win South Africa's independence from Britain in 1910.

The Afrikaners wanted to keep white people in control. So in 1948, they set up their policy of **apartheid**, or separation of races. They passed laws to separate people according to race. By law, people of certain races can live, own property, or run businesses only in certain zones.

Do you think the policy of apartheid is fair? Does anyone benefit from such a policy?

Black South African taking a chance by sitting on "Europeans only" bench

Curfews regulate the time black people must be off the streets of South Africa. Separate trains, beaches, schools, and other facilities are provided for blacks and whites. Laws do nothing to stop whites from getting the best facilities and blacks the worst.

Many people in South Africa and around the world are strongly against apartheid. But many South Africans who protest are arrested, and apartheid continues. A white minority still rules in South Africa.

South Africa has been involved in a struggle with its neighbor, Namibia, since 1915. In that year, South Africa took Namibia away from Germany. Ever since then, South Africa has tried to rule there. The United Nations has declared South Africa's rule of Namibia to be illegal. And black nationalists continue fighting to rule their own country.

A country cannot be at peace when people are **oppressed**. South Africa is still a nation of unrest.

African nations become independent

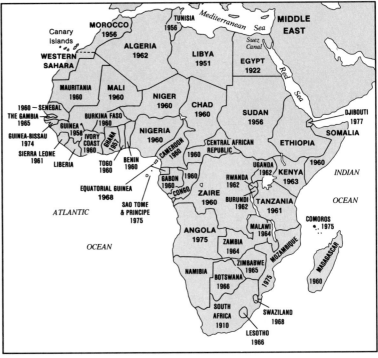

Map Skills

Name two countries that became independent in 1960. Name two countries that became independent in 1962.

Africa, the Great Continent

Africa has been slow to develop economically, politically, and industrially. But it is a continent of free nations now. So Africa is taking a place of greater importance in the world. It is the second largest continent on Earth. Africa alone is as large as the United States, Europe, and China put together.

Fewer than 100 years ago, Africa was called the "Dark Continent," an unexplored land of mystery. Later it became a land to be owned, and it was divided up among stronger countries. Then World War II ended the days of European-ruled colonies in Africa. Today free African nations are growing stronger.

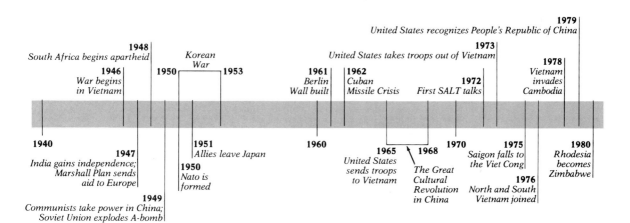

Chapter Review

Chapter Summary

- The Marshall Plan gave aid to war-torn Europe.

- After World War II, Germany was divided into a democratic West Germany and a communist-controlled East Germany.

- The United States and the Soviet Union were allies during the world wars. But after World War II, a cold war began between them.

- The Soviet Union has communist satellites in Eastern Europe, and it encouraged the spread of communism throughout the world.

- The two superpowers hold peace talks to try to limit the buildup of nuclear arms.

- India gained its independence from Britain in 1947 and was divided into India and Pakistan. Both nations face overcrowding and food shortages.

- In 1949 the Communists took over China, forming the People's Republic of China. Nationalist Chinese set up their own government in Taiwan.

- The Allies occupied Japan after World War II. They helped set up a new, nonmilitaristic government there.

- The United States tried to help fight communism in Korea and in Vietnam. In Vietnam, the effort failed, and Vietnam became a communist-run country.

- African nations have gained independence from European imperialism since World War II.

Chapter Quiz

A. Checking Your Facts

Choose the correct word or words to make each sentence a true statement. Rewrite the sentences on a separate sheet of paper.

1. East Germany is called the (Federal Republic of Germany/German Democratic Republic).

2. In 1954 (Italy/West Germany) became a member of NATO.

3. The Soviet Union set up the (Warsaw/Eastern) Pact in 1955.

4. Mikhail Gorbachev and Ronald Reagan signed the (SALT/INF) treaty.

5. Gorbachev's policy of (*Perestroika/Glasnost*) means "openness" or more freedom of speech for Soviet citizens.

B. Think About It!

Write answers to the following questions on a separate sheet of paper.

1. Some people think the United States should do whatever it can to help make Gorbachev's policy of *Perestroika* a success. They believe this will lead to better relations between the two superpowers. Other people are afraid that if Gorbachev is successful, tensions may increase. The Soviet Union could become an even stronger enemy. Who do you think is right? If you were president of the United States, what policy would you follow in dealing with the Soviet Union?

2. If you had to choose between India and China, in which country would you prefer to live? Give two reasons for your answer.

Chapter 31

The Middle East

U.S. president Jimmy Carter applauded when Anwar Sadat and Menachem Begin signed the Camp David Accords. Why was this important?

Chapter Learning Objectives

- Tell why Jews considered Palestine their homeland.
- Tell why Arabs thought that Palestine should be theirs.
- Explain why Palestinians ended up in refugee camps.
- Describe the results of Anwar Sadat's visit to Israel in 1977.
- List the conflicts that continue in the Middle East today.

Words to Know

hostages   people held prisoner by an enemy until certain demands are met

hostile   unfriendly, showing hate or dislike

terrorist   a fighter who hopes to achieve certain goals by using force and random violence to frighten people

traitor   one who betrays a cause, a friend, or a nation

Zionism   the movement to set up a Jewish nation in Palestine

Nationalism in the Middle East

People of the Middle East were often ruled by other lands. For hundreds of years, the Middle East had been part of the Ottoman Empire. After World War I, most of the Middle East fell under British control. Egypt, however, gained its independence from Britain in 1922. Meanwhile, France took control of Syria and Lebanon.

World War II weakened the European countries. This left the door open for Arab nationalists to gain independence for their countries. Most importantly, Arabs took control of their own oil fields. Oil deposits had been discovered in Iraq in 1927 and in Saudi Arabia in 1938. More huge oil fields were later found along the Persian Gulf. European and American oil companies had moved in to control the oil fields. The Middle Eastern nations saw little of their own oil wealth. But after World War II, many Arab nations gained tremendous riches and power because of their oil.

The Middle East includes the area from Libya to Iran.

The Middle East today

Map Skills
Name the country that borders the Red Sea and the Persian Gulf. Turkey borders which two seas?

A Jewish Homeland in Palestine

In ancient days the Jews considered Palestine their homeland. They called it a land promised to them by God. They built a temple in Jerusalem, the holy city.

But almost 2,000 years ago, the Romans drove the Jews out of Jerusalem. Some Jews settled in an area of Palestine called Galilee. But most of the Jews fled from Palestine. They scattered around the world.

This scattering of the Jews is called the *diaspora*.

Many Jews never gave up their dream of the promised homeland. In the late 1800s, Jews in Eastern Europe were persecuted. Some Jews started a movement called **Zionism**. Their goal was to make Palestine an independent Jewish nation. Jews from Europe began to settle in Palestine, which at that time was ruled by the Ottoman Turks.

By 1914 about 85,000 Jews had returned there. After World War I, Britain promised to create a Jewish homeland in Palestine. Meanwhile, the Arab population of Palestine had been increasing, too. And the Arabs living there did not like the strangers in their land.

After World War II, Zionism became more popular. Jews who had felt Hitler's persecution were ready for a homeland of their own. Many came to Palestine.

The State of Israel

In 1947 the United Nations voted to end British rule over Palestine. The United Nations knew there was a conflict between Arabs and Jews in Palestine. Arabs said that the land had been theirs for 2,000 years. Jews said that it had been theirs even before the Arabs had settled there. So the United Nations divided Palestine into two parts. One part was for Jews and the other for Arabs. The Jews agreed to the U.N. plan. But the Arabs were angry. They wanted all of Palestine to be an Arab state.

On May 14, 1948, David Ben-Gurion, the Zionist leader in Palestine, read a declaration of independence. He declared that the Jewish part of Palestine was the new state of Israel.

Israel was recognized immediately by the United States and then by the Soviet Union. The Arabs, however, declared war on Israel. On May 15, 1948, Israel was invaded by armies from the Arab nations of Syria, Egypt, Lebanon, Iraq, and Jordan.

Do you think the U.N. was wise to divide Palestine into two parts?

Refugees of War

The Israelis were greatly outnumbered. And they had a shortage of weapons. But Israel won the war by the end of 1948. The state of Israel was firmly established. The lands left to the Arabs became part of Jordan.

About 700,000 Arabs fled Israel, becoming refugees. The homeless Palestinian Arabs lived in crowded refugee camps outside of Israel. Many live there still. These Palestinian refugees believed that their homes were stolen. Some of them formed a group of fighters called the Palestine Liberation Organization (PLO). Their goal is to win back their land.

After the war in 1948, about 700,000 Jews living in Arab nations were forced to leave. Jews left Iraq, Libya, and other countries. Most went to live in Israel.

Israel had won the 1948 war. But the problems of the Middle East were far from settled.

Middle East Tensions

Soon the superpowers became involved in the Israeli-Arab conflict. In 1955 the Soviets offered to sell arms to Egypt. This was followed by a conflict over the Suez Canal.

In 1956 Egypt took over the canal from Britain and France. Britain, France, and Israel then attacked Egypt. The United Nations arranged a cease-fire. The Suez Canal was held by Egypt. But the Arabs became even more **hostile** toward Israel.

In June of 1967, another war began. Israel fought the Arab nations of Egypt, Jordan, and Syria. In the first few minutes of the war, Israeli planes attacked the Arab airfields. Almost all of the Arab airplanes were destroyed on the ground. Then the Israeli army pushed through the Sinai Peninsula all the way to the Suez Canal. The war was over in six days! Israel occupied all of the Sinai Peninsula, Gaza Strip, and the West Bank. The West Bank was the section of Palestine that had become part of Jordan. And Israel also took control of East Jerusalem.

Arab nations grew angrier. In 1973 Egypt, Syria, Jordan, and Iraq launched a surprise attack on Israel. It was called the *Yom Kippur War*. This was because the Arabs attacked on the Jewish holy day called *Yom Kippur*. This time, the Arabs almost won. Israel managed to defend itself. But it paid a high price in the number of lives lost.

What do you think would have happened to Israel if it had lost any of its wars?

Israeli soldiers searching a Palestinian youth in the Gaza Strip

History Practice

Write answers to the following questions on a separate sheet of paper.

1. Why did the Jews consider Palestine their homeland?

2. Why did the Arabs think Palestine belonged to them?

3. Why was the war in 1973 called the Yom Kippur War?

GREAT NAMES IN HISTORY: Anwar Sadat

In 1977 Egypt's president Anwar el-Sadat visited Israel. His visit surprised the world. It was the first move toward peace with Israel that any Arab leader had ever made. Then U.S. president Jimmy Carter invited Sadat and Israel's prime minister Menachem Begin to the United States. There the three leaders held discussions on how to end the Israeli-Arab conflict. These meetings led to the signing of the Camp David Accords in 1979. Israel promised to return all of the Sinai Peninsula to Egypt in exchange for peace. Israel also promised to allow the Palestinians in Gaza and on the West Bank to govern themselves. This part of the treaty has yet to be put into practice.

Israel had completely withdrawn from the Sinai Peninsula by 1982.

Much of the world praised Sadat. In 1978 Sadat and Begin shared the Nobel Peace Prize. But many Arab nationalists were angry. They said that Sadat was a **traitor** to the Arab cause. In 1981 Sadat was assassinated by Moslem fanatics.

Middle East Conflicts Today

The fighting in the Middle East is not over. The Palestine Liberation Organization (PLO) still seeks a home for Palestinians. In 1970 the PLO was forced out of Jordan. In 1975 it became involved in a civil war in Lebanon.

Do you think that anyone ever has the right to carry out terrorist actions?

From bases in Lebanon, the PLO carried out **terrorist** attacks into Israel. Palestinian terrorists over the years have also been active in other parts of the world.

In 1982 Israel invaded Lebanon in order to destroy PLO bases. The PLO was forced to leave Lebanon. But once the Israeli army withdrew from Lebanon, the PLO came back.

Israel and its neighbors

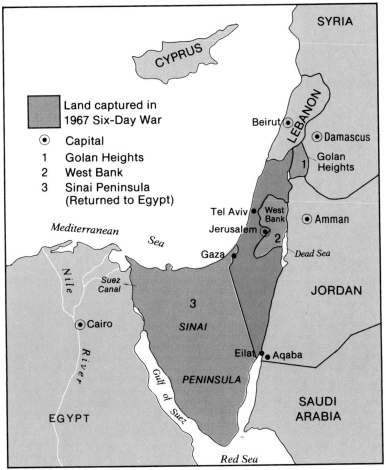

Map Skills
Name the lands captured by Israel in the 1967 Six-Day War.
Which land did Israel return to Egypt?

In December 1987 violent protests by Palestinians broke out in the West Bank and Gaza. The uprising, known as the *intifada*, has continued. The Palestinians want an independent state. They are especially angry that Israel has allowed Jewish settlers to take away some of their land. Most Palestinians regard Yasser Arafat, the head of the PLO, as their leader.

Arafat has agreed to stop acts of terrorism, and he seeks to negotiate with Israel. Israelis have a difficult choice to make. They can give up the occupied lands, and hope that this will bring about a lasting peace. Or they can continue to try to put down the Palestinian uprising by force.

Lebanon's civil war is still going on. It is partly based on religion. Moslems battle Christians for power. And different Moslem groups battle each other. In 1983 the United States became involved in the war. U.S. troops entered Lebanon as peace-

Iraqi soldiers in Iranian territory

keepers. The troops were taken out of Lebanon only after many U.S. marines were killed by Moslem terrorists. Syria also sent troops into Lebanon, and they have become involved in the fighting.

The civil war has all but destroyed Lebanon, leaving its cities in shambles. Beirut, the capital of Lebanon, had been known as the "Paris" of the Middle East. Now much of it lies in ruins.

The country of Iran has seen conflict, too. Iranians were unhappy with their leader, the Shah. The Shah had a vicious secret police who made sure that he kept power.

In 1979, a 76-year-old Moslem leader, the Ayatollah Khomeini, returned to Iran from exile in France. Khomeini led a successful revolution against the Shah. He then set up a Moslem republic following strict Islamic rules. Khomeini's followers wanted the Shah to stand trial for crimes they said he had committed. But the Shah had fled the country. Then in November 1979, Iranians captured the American embassy in Teheran, Iran's capital. They took American **hostages**, and they demanded the Shah's return.

Much of the world was angered by the Iranian action. But Iran would not give up the hostages. The Shah died in Egypt in July 1980. And in January 1981 the American hostages were finally freed.

Meanwhile, in 1980, Iran was attacked by its neighbor, Iraq. There had been bitter disputes over territory. Iraq hoped to win a quick victory over Iran. Saddam Hussein, leader of Iraq, thought that Iran had been weakened by the Islamic revolution. But neither Moslem nation could beat the other. The war dragged on for many years.

There were huge land battles. Then both sides began firing missiles at each other's cities. And each country began to attack oil tankers in the Persian Gulf. In 1987 the U.S. sent its navy to the Gulf to protect the flow of oil.

Finally, in 1988, the United Nations was able to arrange a cease-fire between Iran and Iraq. Both countries had suffered such huge losses that they were willing to begin talking about ending the war.

Oil Power

Much of the Middle East has oil. All nations need oil, and world supplies are limited. Their oil fields give the Arab countries power.

An organizaton called OPEC (Organization of Petroleum Exporting Countries) manages that power. OPEC members include the oil-producing nations of the Middle East and the South American country of Venezuela.

OPEC sets the price of oil. OPEC can force up oil prices or withhold oil from certain countries. This gives OPEC tremendous power. During the Israeli-Arab wars of 1967 and 1973, the Arabs used their oil as a weapon. They cut off the flow of oil to the West. In 1973 this resulted in a severe oil shortage in the United States. Drivers were forced to wait in long lines at the gas pumps. And they had to pay a much higher price for each gallon they bought.

Do you think it is good for the United States to be so dependent on Middle East oil?

Some people in the Middle East are very, very wealthy because of oil. But the oil wealth remains in the hands of a few. Much of the profits from oil sales goes toward building a strong Arab military.

Most Middle East oil comes from Saudi Arabia. Another important oil producer is Libya. In 1969, Muammar al-Qaddafi came to power after he and his followers overthrew the king of Libya. Qaddafi has shown great interest in expanding his country's borders. He tried to seize territory from Chad, the country that borders Libya on the south.

The world's richest oil fields lie beneath the sands of the Middle East.

Qaddafi has spent much of Libya's oil profits on new weapons and a stronger army. He has also supported terrorist actions against Americans and Israelis.

In April of 1986, a disco in West Berlin that was popular with American servicemen was bombed. Two people were killed and 200 were injured. The United States learned that Libya was responsible for this act. In retaliation, U.S. warplanes struck targets in Tripoli and Benghazi, Libya.

Life in the Middle East

The Middle East is, without a doubt, a land of war and conflict. It faces serious problems that will have to be dealt with. Still, the Middle East has fine, modern cities, well-educated people, fertile farmlands, and productive industries.

One of the most industrialized and advanced nations of the Middle East is Israel. About 85 percent of Israel's people live and work in modern cities. Israel's farms are a source of pride. Most of Israel's land is poor. Some of the land is too rocky or steep for farming. Other areas get little rainfall. Only through hard work and agricultural know-how could those lands be productive. Still, Israel produces most of its own food.

Huge irrigation systems pump in water through underground pipelines. Scientists experiment with turning salt water from the Mediterranean and Red seas into fresh water to soak their fields.

The Israelis have not won the perfect land. But they have worked hard to build their nation.

Long before the birth of Christ, the first civilizations were forming along the Tigris and Euphrates rivers and along the Nile River. Those early people concerned themselves with producing food and irrigating dry land. They battled invaders who would take their lands. They argued over how they would worship their gods. In some ways, those people had much in common with today's Middle Eastern people.

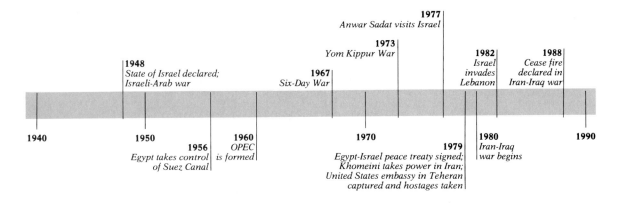

WHICH CAME FIRST?

Use the time line to choose the event, year, or period of time that came first. Write your answers on a separate sheet of paper.

1. Six-Day War *or* OPEC is formed?
2. Khomeini takes power in Iran *or* Iran-Iraq war begins?
3. 1977 *or* 1967?
4. Yom Kippur War *or* Israel invades Lebanon?
5. Egypt takes control of Suez Canal *or* Egypt-Israel peace treaty signed?

Chapter Review

Chapter Summary

- Most Middle Eastern nations gained independence from Britain and France after World War II.

- Zionists wanted to set up a Jewish state in Palestine.

- The United Nations divided Palestine between Arabs and Jews.

- In 1948 the Jews set up the state of Israel. The remaining lands of Palestine became part of the Arab state of Jordan.

- Since 1948 Arabs and Israelis have fought wars for control of those lands.

- Many Palestinians who had fled from Israel were left homeless. They were forced to live in crowded refugee camps. They formed the PLO and demanded their lands back.

- Many Arab nations have wealth and power because there is oil on their lands.

- The constant threat of war is a major problem in the Middle East today.

Chapter Quiz

A. Checking Your Facts

Choose the correct word or words to make each sentence a true statement. Rewrite the sentences on a separate sheet of paper.

1. After World War I, most of the Middle East fell under (French/ British) control.

2. Almost 2,000 years ago, the (Arabs/Romans) drove the Jews out of Jerusalem.

3. Anwar Sadat signed a peace treaty with (Menachem Begin/ David Ben-Gurion).

4. The Palestinian uprising on the West Bank is called the (*diaspora/ intifada*).

5. (Ayatollah Khomeini/Yasser Arafat) led a successful revolution against the Shah of Iran.

B. Think About It!

Write answers to the following questions on a separate sheet of paper.

1. Both young men and young women are drafted into Israel's military. Why do you think this is done?

2. Israel returned all of the Sinai Peninsula to Egypt, as agreed to in the Camp David Accords of 1979. Israel gave up the land in exchange for peace. Since then, relations between Israel and Egypt have been peaceful. If you were an Israeli, would you now be willing to turn over the West Bank and Gaza Strip to the Palestinians in exchange for peace? Explain why.

Chapter 32

The World Today

Skyscrapers fill the skyline of New York City. In what ways is today's New York different from ancient cities such as Ur and Babylon?

Chapter Learning Objectives

- Name two uses of nuclear power.
- Explain why the late twentieth century is sometimes called the Space Age.
- Explain how advances in communication and transportation make the world seem smaller.
- Tell what is meant by a "third world" nation.
- Tell what is meant by a "developed" nation.

Words to Know

astronaut   a person trained to make space flights

cosmonaut   Russian word meaning *astronaut*

nonrenewable   not replaceable once it's used up

radioactive fallout   deadly particles given off by a nuclear explosion

satellites   objects put into orbit around the Earth

technology   science put to use in practical work

People call these times the "Nuclear Age" or the "Space Age" or the "Computer Age." Today's world is full of brand new inventions and discoveries. There are things now that Alexander the Great, Julius Caesar, Napoleon Bonaparte, or even dreamers like Leonardo da Vinci could never imagine. Yet in spite of all the progress, people today still have much in common with their ancestors.

How are people today the same as their ancestors? How are they different?

The Nuclear Age

The last half of the twentieth century is sometimes called the Nuclear Age. Actually, the idea of nuclear power began about 1905, with Albert Einstein. Einstein suggested that energy was contained in every atom. The first actual use of that energy came in 1945 when the United States exploded two atomic bombs over Japan. Those explosions ended World War II and began an age of development for atomic energy.

The explosion of the first atomic bomb started the nations of the world on a race. It was a deadly race to build bigger weapons. Countries tried to outdo each other in the number and size of the bombs they built.

You read about U.S.-
Soviet treaties in
Chapter 30.

Now many nations have a weapon so destructive
that the results of another world war are impossible to
imagine. So, nations try to avoid that war. They meet
and talk about peace. They discuss ways to limit the
buildup of nuclear arms. The United States and the
Soviet Union have held talks and signed treaties. And
they hope to reach further agreements—perhaps even
to get rid of nuclear weapons altogether. As yet,
however, no complete agreement has been reached.
Nuclear weapons still threaten the safety of the whole
world. It is a reality that today's people must live with.

Peaceful Uses of Nuclear Energy

Although it was first used in a bomb, nuclear power
has peacetime uses, too. The most important use is as
a source of energy.

All nations use oil, coal, and natural gas for energy.
These are all **nonrenewable** energy sources. Once
they are used up, they are gone. As the population
grows, the demand for energy also grows. People
worry that we will run out of those traditional sources
of energy.

The energy created in the nucleus of the atom can
be used to run factories, to heat homes, and to light
cities. Today this energy is produced in nuclear power
plants around the world. Nuclear power is expensive.
But it can provide unlimited energy for thousands of
years. The question is: Is it safe?

Nuclear power plants must have strict safety
regulations. A nuclear accident could mean tragedy. If
something goes wrong, millions of people could be
exposed to **radioactive fallout.**

Accidents happen. One serious nuclear accident
happened in the United States in 1979. At the Three-
Mile Island nuclear power plant in Pennsylvania,

The Three-Mile Island nuclear power plant, Harrisburg, Pennsylvania

failing equipment and human mistakes caused a near meltdown. There were no tragic results, but the public was frightened. People became aware that a disaster could happen. Stricter safety rules were set up. But some people still wondered about the future of nuclear power. They worred that the risk was too great.

In 1986 the Soviet Union faced a more serious nuclear accident. This disaster happened in a power plant in Chernobyl. Twenty-three people died, and the town of Chernobyl was evacuated. A radiation cloud moved from Chernobyl across several European nations. Traces of radiation were found in animals, in milk, and in plant life far from the actual accident site. No one is sure just what the long-range effects of such radiation might be.

Many people protest the building of nuclear power plants. They say that no amount of energy is worth the risk of nuclear disaster. Others maintain that nuclear power is a safe answer to the world's energy crisis. They point out that many people have died in coal mine accidents over the years. Compared to this, only a few have died in accidents related to nuclear power plants.

In a meltdown, the cooling system fails and the core of the nuclear reactor actually melts.

Those in favor of nuclear power also point out that it is clean. It causes much less pollution than coal or oil. But those against nuclear power have one very solid argument for their point of view. No safe method has yet been discovered for disposing of nuclear waste.

History Practice

Write answers to the following questions on a separate sheet of paper.

1. Why is the last half of the twentieth century sometimes called the "Nuclear Age"?

2. Name three nonrenewable energy sources.

3. Why do some people think that nuclear energy is very dangerous?

The Space Age

Sputnik I weighed 184 pounds and was only 23 inches wide. It looked like a shooting star as it moved across the sky.

Sometimes the last half of the twentieth century is called the Space Age. The Space Age began in 1957. That's when the Soviet Union launched the first man-made **satellite** into orbit around the Earth. The satellite was called *Sputnik I*. Soon after, the United States launched its first satellite, *Explorer I*. The space race had begun.

In 1961 the Russians put the first human being into space. He was **cosmonaut** Yuri Gagarin. Then in 1969, U.S. **astronaut** Neil Armstrong became the first person to walk on the moon. Six hundred million people around the world watched this event on TV.

The first woman went into space in 1963. She was the Soviet cosmonaut Valentina V. Tereshkova. In 1983 the United States sent its first woman astronaut, Sally Ride, into space aboard the shuttle *Challenger*.

The exploration of space is exciting. But it is also difficult, expensive, and dangerous. In January 1986, the space shuttle *Challenger* exploded shortly after takeoff. All the people on board were killed. And there have been other accidents in which people have died. But many people feel that the rewards from space exploration are worth the risks.

The space shuttle *Challenger*

Space has been an area where the United States and the Soviet Union race to be the best. But space can also be an arena for peace. In July 1975, three American astronauts and two Russian cosmonauts met in space. As planned, their two spaceships hooked up. Then the Americans and Russians shook hands, shared a meal, and held a news conference for the world to see. They also conducted joint scientific experiments for two days.

The Space Age has only begun. Many people expect that before too long, we will have colonies on the moon. And people from Earth may someday live on Mars and on other planets. Unmanned spaceships have already landed on Mars and Venus and sent back pictures. Other ships have flown close to Jupiter, Saturn, Uranus, and Neptune. Perhaps someday, we may even go to the stars!

LEARN MORE ABOUT IT: The Computer Age

Computers are electronic machines. They solve problems and answer questions. They store information. Computers are used around the world to help people make better use of their time.

Computers have been improved steadily since World War II. At first they were very large, very expensive, and difficult to run. Now they are much smaller and are used by millions of people. A computer that once filled an entire room now fits into a package the size of a breadbox!

At first people worried that computers would replace humans in many jobs. And in some cases this has happened. But computers have created many more new jobs. Computers give people the time and freedom to get more work done.

An office worker using a word processor, a specialized type of computer

The Shrinking World

Developments in transportation and communication have made the world seem smaller. People in one part of the world now know what is happening elsewhere.

Television has changed twentieth-century life as much as any other one invention. So many Americans protested involvement in the Vietnam War because television cameras brought the action to them. They saw for themselves the suffering of American soldiers and Vietnamese villagers.

Television news takes the Israeli-Arab conflict into millions of homes. People of the world see the injustices of apartheid in South Africa and hunger in Ethiopia with their own eyes.

War protest marches were shown on television. The government couldn't deny the power of the peace movement.

Also, hundreds of communications satellites circle the Earth. They beam radio, television, telephone, and computer signals around the world. Satellites in space can take weather pictures to make forecasts anywhere in the world.

New methods of travel have also made a difference. First the railroad, then automobiles, and then airplanes made the world seem smaller. With modern jet planes, a trip across oceans is an easy matter.

As the world seems to grow smaller, nations have a greater influence on each other. Trade has long affected cultures and civilizations. Ideas have always mingled as trade increased. Now it is routine for nations to trade their goods and their ideas worldwide.

Developed Nations and Third World Nations

Some nations in the world are called "developed" nations. They have many industries. They import and export products. Most people who live in developed nations have a fairly high standard of living. They can read and write. They benefit from the advances of modern science and **technology**. The United States, the Soviet Union, Canada, France, Great Britain, Japan, and West Germany are just some of the developed nations.

Many countries are less developed. They are sometimes called "developing" or "third world" nations. The name "third world" comes from the idea that the West developed first, and the East developed second. And now the third world is developing.

Many people in these developing nations are poor. Large numbers live by farming the land. But their methods of agriculture are often outdated. There are fewer industries in developing nations. Their standard of living is lower, and a large number of the population cannot read or write.

India, Afghanistan, and Mexico are examples of developing countries. Many South American and African nations are developing countries. Some of these nations, like Nigeria and Venezuela, have rich oil deposits.

The third world countries are more dependent on other nations. Their economies can be easily upset by weather, by a year of bad farm crops, or by a war. Sometimes the more developed countries help the third world nations by lending them money or sending supplies. The United States has sent thousands of Peace Corps volunteers to third world countries all over the world. There the volunteers teach modern farming methods, health care, and engineering.

The third world includes about 120 countries and more than half of the world's people.

Just Imagine . . . A Trip Forward in Time

Picture the days of ancient Greece. Imagine a Greek athlete running an Olympic race. It is 700 B.C. The young man pulls ahead of the other racers on a dusty road. He gasps the warm air. His lungs ache with the effort. As he crosses the finish line, he closes his eyes and raises his arms over his head in victory.

When he opens his eyes again, he expects to find himself surrounded by cheering Greeks. He can almost feel the crown of olive leaves about to be placed on his head.

Instead . . . the racer finds himself in a crowded, modern stadium. It is A.D. 1984, Los Angeles, California, the 23rd Summer Olympics. People are cheering, but they are not all Greeks. They are people from around the whole world. And no olive leaves await the racer. Instead he is awarded a shiny, gold medal. Somehow our racer has been jolted forward in time more than 2,000 years to the 1980s.

What will he find? What undreamed-of wonders will our racer discover?

He will find a whole new world of medicine. Doctors can actually replace worn-out or diseased body parts. Sometimes those replacements come from people who have died. Other times the parts are man made. The young Greek time-traveler can hardly believe it. These modern doctors can even replace a person's heart!

People treat each other in a different way now. The Greek racer is surprised to find himself surrounded by women athletes. Women, he will discover, have a whole new role in society. In many places they are treated as equals with men. They work side by side with men in all kinds of jobs. Women have become leaders in science, in space travel, in medicine, and in business.

And where are the slaves? At last, most societies realize that all people deserve the same respect and the same chances. They deserve an education, job opportunities, and a fair chance at making a good life. People move more easily from one social class to another now.

Spaceships to the moon, automobiles that speed people to their destinations, airplanes, television, telephones . . . the list of new wonders is endless.

Has anything remained the same? Most people still live in family groups, although many of those groups are smaller. People still have the same basic needs for food and shelter. And people still have trouble getting along. There are still those who want to be conquerors and who seek power at all costs. There are still those who must struggle to hold on to their cultures and their homes. People from different backgrounds still do not know and understand each other well enough. And people still fear what they do not understand.

Human beings are still curious, too. They still need to learn, to explore, and to discover. There will always be some questions to answer: What lies beyond the sun? Are there worlds and peoples other than our own? And can the inhabitants of this world ever live together completely at peace?

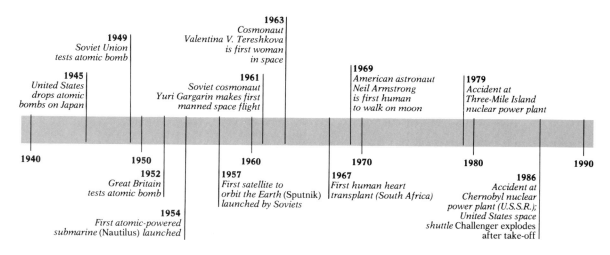

WHICH CAME FIRST?

Use the time line to choose the event, year, or period of time that came first. Write your answer on a separate sheet of paper.

1. Great Britain tests atomic bomb *or* Soviet Union tests atomic bomb?

2. Accident at Chernobyl nuclear power plant *or* accident at Three-Mile Island nuclear power plant?

3. 1957 *or* 1945?

4. First human heart transplant *or* First satellite to orbit the Earth (*Sputnik*) launched?

5. First atomic-powered submarine (*Nautilus*) launched *or* United States drops atomic bombs on Japan?

Chapter Review

Chapter Summary

- Nuclear power is used for weapons and as a source of energy in peacetime.

- People worry about the dangers of an accident in a nuclear power plant and about the safe disposal of nuclear waste.

- Television makes people more aware and concerned about what is going on around the world.

- Developed nations have advanced technology, a higher standard of living, and strong trade programs.

- Third world nations are less developed, poorer, and more dependent on other countries.

- There is more opportunity for movement between social classes in today's world.

- Many things have changed, but people still have to deal with problems of ignorance, prejudice, persecution, and war.

Chapter Quiz

A. Checking Your Facts

Choose the correct word or words to make each sentence a true statement. Rewrite the sentences on a separate sheet of paper.

1. In 1986 a nuclear disaster occurred at (Three-Mile Island/ Chernobyl) in the Soviet Union.

2. In 1961 (Neil Armstrong/Yuri Gagarin) became the first human being to travel in space.

3. The first woman to go into space was (Valentina V. Tereshkova/Sally Ride).

4. An unmanned spaceship has landed on (Mars/Saturn) and sent back pictures.

5. The United States is a (developing/developed) nation.

B. Think About It!

Write answers to the following questions on a separate sheet of paper.

1. Recent developments in communications and transportation have made the world seem smaller. Give two reasons why you agree or disagree with this statement.

2. Explain the difference between a developed nation and a developing or third world nation. Give two examples of each.

3. What are two similarities between ancient peoples and people of today?

Unit Ten Review

Write answers to the following questions on a separate sheet of paper.

1. List three changes in the Soviet Union for which Mikhail Gorbachev is responsible.

2. What happened to the countries of Eastern Europe after World War II?

3. Relations today between the United States and the Soviet Union are improving. Give two reasons why you agree or disagree with this statement.

4. What efforts have been made to protect the world against a nuclear war?

5. What led to war in Korea?

6. What happened back in the United States after the U.S. sent troops to Vietnam?

7. Once a colony becomes an independent nation, what problems is it likely to face?

8. Name two conflicts that continue in the Middle East today.

9. What is apartheid?

10. Name two great challenges that today's world has to face.

Appendix

Glossary

Index

Glossary

A.D. (Anno Domini)   dating from the year Jesus Christ was born

acupuncture   treating pain or illness by putting needles into certain parts of the body

addicted   having a strong habit that is hard to give up

agents   people who have the authority to act for some other person or company

agriculture   the use of land for growing crops and raising animals; farming

alliances   nations joined together for some purpose

ambition   the drive to become powerful, successful, or famous

amphitheater   a circular or oval area with sloping sides and seats rising in rows around a central open space

ancestors   people from whom one is descended

annul   to cancel; to make something no longer binding under law

anthem   the official song of a country

anti-Semitism   prejudice against Jews

apartheid   the separation of races based mainly on skin color

apprentices   people who learn a trade under a master

aqueducts   man-made channels that carry flowing water over a long distance

archeologist   a scientist who studies cultures of the past by digging up and examining the remains of ancient towns and cities

armistice   an agreement to stop fighting; a truce before a formal peace treaty

arsenal   a place where guns and ammunition are stored

artifact   a simple handmade object, such as a tool or weapon

assassinate   to murder a leader or other important person

astronaut   a person trained to make space flights

astronomy   the study of stars, planets, and other heavenly bodies

athlete   a person trained to take part in competitive sports. The ancient Greek word athlete means "one who tries to win a prize in a contest."

B.C. (Before Christ)   dating from before the year Jesus Christ was born

barbarians uncivilized primitive people; people living outside Greece or Rome in the days of the Roman Empire

bartered traded goods or services without using money

betraying giving help to the enemy; being unfaithful to; for example, betraying one's own country

bishops high-ranking church officials; from the Latin word that means "overseer." A bishop oversees the churches in his district.

brainwashed trained to have a whole new set of ideas and beliefs

burros small donkeys, usually used as pack animals

campaign a series of battles all aimed at one military end

canal a man-made waterway

capital a city or town where the government of a nation or state is located

capitalist having business and industry privately owned and operated for profit

caravans groups of people traveling together, often through a desert

cartridge a small metal or cardboard tube that holds gunpowder and a bullet

castes the social classes into which the people of India are divided

casualties soldiers who have been killed, wounded, captured, or are missing

censor to examine communications before they are released and to remove any parts that are objected to

chancellor the head of government, or prime minister, in some European countries

chariot an open two-wheeled cart, pulled by horses

citizen a person who has certain rights and duties because he or she lives in a particular city or town

city-state an independent city and the surrounding land it controls

civil disobedience the refusal to obey rules, orders, or laws

civil wars wars among people who live in the same country

civilization the society and culture of a particular people, place, or period

classes groupings of people according to social rank

clergy people trained or ordained for religious work

collective run by a group; a collective farm

colonial having settlements in far-off lands; for example, Great Britain was a colonial power because it ruled colonies in many parts of the world

colonies groups of people who settle in a far-off land but are still under the rule of the land they came from

commandment a law or order, most often a religious law, as in the Ten Commandments in the Bible

commonwealth a nation in which the people hold the ruling power; a republic or democracy

commune a group of people working or living closely together, often sharing property and tasks

communism a political system based on an absence of social class, common ownership of industries and farms, and a sharing of work and of goods produced

concentration camps prison camps for people thought to be dangerous to a ruling group

confederation a group of independent states joined together for a purpose

conference a meeting of people to discuss something

conquer to get control by using force, as in a war

conqueror a person who gains control by winning a war

conquistadors Spanish conquerors

constitution the laws and rules of a government

contract a legal written agreement between two or more people

converted changed from one religion to another

corrupt dishonest, evil, selfish

cosmonaut Russian word meaning astronaut

council a group of people that meet to decide something or to give advice

craft a trade or art that takes special skill with the hands

crescent something shaped like a quarter moon

crucifixion the putting to death of someone by nailing or tying that person to a cross

culture the way of life—religion, ideas, arts, tools—of a certain people in a certain time

cuneiform a wedge-shaped form of writing used in ancient Sumer

curfews times after which certain people cannot be on the streets

declaration a public statement

declines periods of increasing weakness

democracy a government that gives the people the ruling power

depressions periods of low business activity and high unemployment

descendants   people who come from certain ancestors

desert   dry, sandy land with little or no plant life

dialects   forms of a language used only in a certain place or among a certain group

dictator   a ruler who has total power

dike   a wall built along a river or sea to hold back the water from low land

diplomat   a person in government whose job is dealing with other countries

discrimination   treating a person or people unfairly because of their race or religion

divine   of or having to do with God or a god; like a god

dominance   the act of ruling, controlling, being most powerful

dominate   to be most important, most powerful, strongest

domino   a small, rectangular piece of wood or plastic used in a game; one side of the piece is either blank or marked with dots

dungeons   dark, underground rooms used as prisons

dynasty   a series of rulers who belong to the same family

elect   to choose someone for an office by voting

emperor   a person who rules a group of different countries, lands, or peoples

empire   a group of lands all ruled by the same government or ruler

enlightened   knowing the truth

estate   a large piece of land with a large home on it

exiled   forced to live away from home in a foreign land

factories   buildings where goods are made by machinery

fallow   land not used for farming during a season

fascists   dictators and their followers who take away rights of the people and glorify war

fast   to go without food

fertile   able to produce large crops, as in rich soil

feudalism   the political and military system of Europe during the Middle Ages; the system of exchanging lands for services

fleet   a group of warships under one command

forge   to work into shape by heating and hammering

fortress   a building with strong walls for defense against an enemy

forum   a public square in an ancient Roman city; lawmakers met there

fraternity   brotherhood

freemen   people who are free, not slaves, and who have the rights of citizens

frontiers   lands just beyond the border of a country

fronts   the different places where the actual fighting is going on during a war

galleons   large Spanish sailing ships of long ago, having many decks

generals   high military officers

genocide   an attempt to kill all the people of a certain race or religious group

geography   the natural surface features of the Earth, or any part of it

glaciers   large, slow-moving masses of ice and snow

gladiators   men who fought animals or other men in the arenas of ancient Rome

governor   a person chosen to run a province or territory

guerilla   one of a group of fighters who are not part of a regular army, and who usually make surprise raids behind enemy lines

guild   a medieval organization formed to protect the interests of workers in one craft or trade

guillotine   an instrument used for cutting off a person's head; it has two posts crossed by a heavy blade

haciendas   large Spanish-style ranches or country homes

harness   leather straps that fasten a horse to a plow, cart, or wagon

heretics   people who are against the teachings of a church

hermit   one who lives alone, away from others

hieroglyphics   a system of writing using pictures or symbols to represent objects, ideas, or sounds

historian   someone who writes about the past; an expert in history

Holocaust   the killing of millions of Jews by Germany's Nazis

homage   a pledge of loyalty; a promise to serve, made to kings and lords during the Middle Ages

hostages   people held prisoner by an enemy until certain demands are met

hostile   unfriendly, showing hate or dislike

humanism   a concern with the needs and interests of human beings rather than religious ideas

idols   images of a god that are used as objects of worship

imperialism the practice of conquering other lands, forming colonies in other lands, or controlling the government and wealth of weaker lands

imported brought into one country from another

imposed forced one's ideas or wishes on another

impressed affected thoughts and feelings

independence freedom from control by others

indirectly in a roundabout way

industry business and manufacturing

inferior not as good as someone or something else

influence the power to affect other people or things

insurance a guarantee that a person or company will be paid money to cover losses

interest money paid for the use of other people's money

interference meddling in another's affairs without being asked

international having to do with many nations

investments money lent to businesses in order to get even more money back

investors those who expect to make a profit by lending money to a business

irrigate to bring water to dry land by means of canals

isolated set apart from others; alone

journeyman a person who has finished his apprenticeship and receives wages, but who is not yet a master

jousts fights with lances between two knights on horseback

junks flat-bottomed Chinese sailing ships

jury a group of people who listen to the facts and decide if a person on trial is guilty or not guilty

justice fairness according to the principles of right and wrong; what is deserved; the administration of law

knights high-ranking soldiers of the Middle Ages who received their titles from a noble

labor unions groups of workers who join together to protect their wages, working conditions, and job benefits

legislature a group of persons who make the laws of a nation or state

liberator one who frees a group of people

loincloth a small cloth worn about the hips and lower part of the stomach

looms machines for weaving thread or yarn into cloth

loyal faithful and true to one's country or to a person

maize Indian corn

majority a greater number, more than half

manor the lands belonging to a medieval lord, including farmland, a village, and the home of the owner

medieval belonging to the Middle Ages

merchant a person who buys and sells goods for profit; a trader

Middle Ages the period of European history extending from the Fall of Rome in A.D. 476 to about A.D. 1450

migrate to move away from one country or region to settle in another

militarism a national policy of maintaining a powerful army and constant readiness for war

military having to do with soldiers or the armed forces

minority a smaller number, less than half

missionaries people sent by a church to other countries to spread a religion

modern of the present time, up-to-date

monarchs rulers, like kings, queens, or emperors

monk a man who has taken religious vows and usually lives in a monastery

mosaic a design made by putting together small pieces of colored stone, glass, or other material

motto a word or phrase that expresses goals, ideas, or ideals

mummy a dead body kept from rotting by being treated with chemicals and wrapped in cloth

mural a large picture painted on a wall

myths stories, often about gods or goddesses, that are handed down through the years and sometimes used to explain natural events

nationalism love of one's nation; patriotism

natural resources materials that are provided by nature, such as forests, minerals, and water

navigate to plan the course of a ship; to sail or steer

neutral joining neither side in a war

nobles people of high social rank

nomads people who move from place to place looking for food for their animal herds

nonrenewable not replaceable once it's used up

nonviolent without using force, without causing injury

oath a serious promise, often pledged in the name of God

oppressed kept down by harsh rule

pact an agreement

papyrus a writing paper the Egyptians made from water plants of the same name

paradise a place or condition of perfect happiness; heaven

Parliament England's body of lawmakers

patriots people who are loyal to their own country and show a great love for that country

patrons wealthy people who support artists

pendulum a weight hung so that it swings freely back and forth; often used to control a clock's movement

peninsula a long piece of land almost completely surrounded by water (from the Latin word meaning "almost an island")

persecute to treat in a cruel way, to hurt or injure

petition a written request, often with many signatures, to a person or group in authority

pharaoh a king of ancient Egypt

pilgrimages visits to a holy place

piracy the robbing of ships on the ocean

plague a deadly disease that spreads quickly

plowshare the broad blade of a plow

plundered stole, took by force

policies rules, methods of action or conduct

pollution waste materials in the air or water

pope the head of the Roman Catholic Church

population people living in a place, or the total number of those people

prejudice dislike of a people just because they are of a different race or religion, or are from another country

prime minister the chief official of the government in some countries

prophet a religious leader who claims to speak for God; one who tells what will happen in the future

protest to speak out against or act against something

provinces the parts of a country, each with its own local government, much like the states in the United States

Puritans members of a sixteenth- or seventeenth-century English group of Protestants; they wanted to make the Church of England simpler and stricter

pyramid a huge stone structure with a square base and four triangular sides that meet in a point at the top. Egyptian rulers were buried in the pyramids.

racism the idea that one race is better than another

radioactive fallout deadly particles given off by a nuclear explosion

raw materials matter in its natural condition, not changed by some human process

reaper a machine for cutting down and gathering grain crops

recognize to accept the government of a country and deal with it in business and trade

reform to change for the better

refugees those who flee their country or home

reign the rule of a monarch; or to rule as a king, queen, or emperor

reincarnation a belief that living beings are reborn in a new body

Renaissance the revival of art, literature, and learning in Europe in the fourteenth through sixteenth centuries

representation sending one or more people to speak for the rights of others before a body of the government

representatives people who are chosen to act or speak for others

republic a government in which the citizens have the right to elect their representatives to make laws; a democratic government

resistance the act of opposing, working against

revolt to rise up against a government; to refuse to obey the people in charge

revolution a complete change, especially in a way of life or a government

riot a violent disturbance created by a crowd of people

sagas long stories of brave deeds

samurai a class of warriors in the Japanese feudal system

sanctions actions taken by one nation against another for breaking international law; for example, a shipping blockade

satellites (1) countries that depend on and are controlled by a more powerful country; (2) objects put into orbit around the earth

scapegoat a person or group blamed for the mistakes and problems of others

scholars people who have learned much through study

scribe a person whose job it was to write out copies of contracts and other manuscripts. People worked as scribes before the invention of printing.

sculptor a person who makes statues out of wood, stone, marble, or other material

senate a governing or lawmaking body

serfs people legally tied to the land; farm workers who were almost slaves

settlement a small group of homes in an area that hasn't been populated

shareholders people who own one or more parts (shares) of a business

shrine a place of worship believed to be sacred or holy

shuttle a device in weaving that carries thread back and forth between threads stretched up and down

siege the surrounding of a city by soldiers who are trying to capture it so that food, water, and other supplies cannot get in or out

smuggled moved something into or out of a country secretly because it is against the law

sniper a person who shoots from a hidden spot

societies groups of people joined together for a common purpose

sought looked for, searched for

specialize to work in, and know a lot about, one job or field

staff a pole used for support in walking or to hold a flag

stock shares in a business

submarines warships that travel under the water

superiority a feeling of being better than others

surplus more than what is needed

swamp an area of low, wet land

symbol an object that stands for an idea; for example, the dove is a symbol of peace

sympathy feeling sorry for another's suffering

tablet a small, flat piece of clay used for writing

tax money paid to support a government

technology science put to use in practical work

temple a building for the worship of a god or gods

territory the land ruled by a nation or state

terrorist a fighter who hopes to achieve certain goals by using force and random violence to frighten people

textile cloth or fabric made by weaving

theory an explanation of how and why something happens, usually based on scientific study

tomb a grave, usually one that is enclosed in stone or cement

torpedoed attacked with a large, exploding, cigar-shaped missile

traitor one who betrays a cause, a friend, or a nation

transportation the act of carrying from one place to another

trappers people who trap wild animals for their furs

treaty an agreement, usually having to do with peace or trade

trenches long ditches dug in the ground to protect soldiers in battle

tribe a group of people living together under a leader

tribute a payment or gift demanded by rulers of ancient kingdoms

truce a time when enemies agree to stop fighting

turmoil a condition of great confusion

tyrant a ruler who has complete power

uncivilized savage; primitive; without training in arts, science, government

unification bringing together into one whole

upstream in the direction against the flow of the river; at the upper part of a river

Vandal a member of a Germanic tribe that invaded the Roman Empire. A vandal is a person who damages or destroys things.

vassals nobles who received land from a king in return for their loyalty and service

viceroy the governor of a country or province, who rules as the representative of his king

victor the winner of a battle, war, struggle, or contest

vision something seen in the mind or in a dream

volunteers those who offer to do something of their own free will

ziggurat a huge, towerlike temple

Zionism the movement to set up a Jewish nation in Palestine

Index